ACKNOWLEDGMENTS

In the course of writing this book I have had help from so many people that it would be impossible to name them all. But one in particular has been there whenever I needed her. Jill Leuw, together with her husband David, has been unstinting in reading the manuscript, sorting archives and offering her own material for my use. She has truly been my right-hand woman and I cannot thank her enough.

Many archivists, librarians and curators have let me browse among their precious possessions, in particular those at Southampton University, British Library, London Library, Leo Baeck College Library, Westminster Synagogue Library, London Metropolitan Archives and the Wiener Library.

But it is to the men and women involved at some time or other with the West London Synagogue to whom perhaps I owe the greatest debt: Reform Rabbis Julia Neuberger, Thomas Salamon, Jonathan Romain, and Jackie Tabick; as well as Esther Barron, Valerie and Ernest Bello, Neil Benson, Morris Bentata, David Cassell, Claire and Ivor Connick, Michael Cutter, Tina Elliot, Kathryn Forro, Lewis Golden, Jackie Gryn, Sdelka Husserl, David Jacobs, Alex Knapp, Jack Lynes, Geoffrey Marx, Joyce Morton, Simon Myers, the late Mary Ann Southam (née Marks), Darrell van der Zyl, Marie van der Zyl, Nikki van der Zyl, and Wendy Woolf. And also all the staff at West London who have always given me their kind and willing help.

LIST OF ILLUSTRATIONS

PROLOGUE

Before the Beginning

The earliest synagogue to be established in London, after the re-admission of the Jews to England in 1656, consisted of two small rooms in Creechurch Lane in the City. The majority of these Jews were Sephardim, from Spain and Portugal. Some had fled from the Inquisition to find sanctuary in Britain, often as Marranos, New Christians, who had converted to Christianity to save their lives while remaining secret Jews. A few others had stayed on after the expulsion under Edward I in 1290, though officially they had no place here, living and worshipping in secret. Once they could practise their faith openly, they were able to establish an organised community, setting out rules of conduct, choosing leaders and determining how they wanted to govern their lives. Many were from wealthy, educated families – jewellers, dealers in gold and precious stones, even doctors - well able to hold their own in the more aristocratic circles of London society. In 1701 they opened a splendid new purpose-built synagogue in Bevis Marks, very like the synagogue in Amsterdam, from where some of them had come.

However, other Jewish immigrants were arriving in England in considerable numbers. They came from Germany and Holland, and some from Eastern Europe and Russia, poorer families, unskilled labourers, forced to earn their living as best they could as old clothes men or street traders. They lived mostly in the East End, meeting for prayer in their own homes and speaking mainly Yiddish. One or two of the wealthier families from Germany in 1690 were able to finance the building of the Great Synagogue, in Dukes Place, the first true place of worship for Ashkenazi Jews. It was rebuilt in 1722, almost next door to Bevis Marks, and again in 1790, but was totally destroyed by German bombs during World War II. A small community of perhaps one thousand souls at the time of the re-admission had grown in one hundred and fifty years to some 15-20,000 Jews in England, the great majority in London, almost exclusively in the eastern part of the City; about 12% were Sephardim. Both sections of the Jewish community followed the forms of service of their fathers and grandfathers, unable or unwilling to contemplate even the smallest changes. There was considerable disagreement between the two, stretching at times almost to enmity.

The 1776 constitution of the state of Virginia in America had stipulated that equality should exist between all men, whatever their religion, and the Enlightenment movement in Europe, together with the French Revolution, followed suit. The Jewish people began to emerge from the ghetto, seeking their right to play a full part in western society, a right which was, at least to begin with, by no means fully achieved. Enlightenment, as far as the Jews were concerned, meant freedom to explore intellectually, not simply the Talmud and the Bible, but the wider sources of learning that other European peoples could enjoy. It was Israel Jacobson, sometimes known as the father of Reform Judaism, who with others in Germany established the beginnings of change. A wealthy financier, he was a fervent follower of the *Haskalah* movement, the Jewish Enlightenment inspired by Moses Mendelssohn. This amorphous assembly of German Jews sought equal rights in society, dropping their native Yiddish in favour of German, while maintaining their study of Hebrew and Biblical texts. Mendelssohn himself translated the Hebrew Bible into German, but he and his fellow Jews were determined to keep their orthodoxy intact. Rabbinic Judaism insisted not only on the total acceptance of the written law handed down by Moses to the Israelites, but also of the Oral Law, the *Shulchan Aruch*.

Mendelssohn's claim to reforming Judaism lay in his attempt to give Jews an education beyond the narrow confines of the Talmud. In spite of his devotion to the minutiae of Biblical revelation, he ensured that his children's minds were opened to enlightened thought. As a result they abandoned their faith, unable to reconcile their new intellectual reasoning with their father's beliefs and practices.

By 1810, however, when the first Reform synagogue was established by Jacobson in Seesen, in Lower Saxony, many German Jews felt a need for change in synagogue services and in the liturgy itself. They sought an improvement in decorum, the liturgy abbreviated with sermons in the vernacular, and an organ added to choral singing, male only in the early years. This first community was open to Christians as well as Jews (as Jacobson insisted), and called its place of worship a temple rather than a synagogue (as indeed is so in America today), introducing certain prayers in German. But its leader found himself at odds with orthodox Judaism. The new community lasted only three years, until the authorities in Westphalia closed down much of Jewish life. It was in Hamburg in 1818 that the young Reform movement found support for a new synagogue which was to flourish in spite of the disapproval of the local rabbis. As David Philipson put it: 'The introduction of the first reformers really sounded the death knell of the Talmud as the absolute rule for Jewish practice.'[1]

In England the situation was rather different. The Sephardi Jews from the Spanish and Portuguese Synagogue already considered themselves enlightened (apart from their manner of worship). They had never known a ghetto since medieval times. They had access to a broad education (though not yet a university degree) and many were well-established, accepted at court and in the city. They were preoccupied more with achieving emancipation in their political life than in improving their religion. Much the same was true of the Ashkenazi Jews, especially those who had already lived in England long enough to acquire a certain polish, to speak English without an accent and become respected in their working environment.

In the older synagogue, Bevis Marks, the situation regarding the conduct of the service was little short of a disgrace. As early as 1780, an anonymous writer, probably Jewish, wrote a vitriolic account of what went on behind synagogue doors. Calling his book *A Peep into the Synagogue,* this unknown worshipper considered it his duty 'to expose the clouds of bigotry and superstition that have for so long developed and held in darkness the minds of men.'[2] He estimated that only one man in five hundred understood Hebrew, so how could the congregation pay attention to the prayers? Instead they chatted to one another, discussing 'the fluctuation of the markets and the advancement or fall of stocks, and other matters that interested them'.[3] He described the Sanctuary as a sales room where the *shammas* or beadle auctioned the *Mitzvot* ('One penny for opening the doors of the Ark!') and the worshippers as 'cringing servile sycophants'.

He was contemptuous of Jewish women, hardly seen in the synagogue, unable to read or write mainly because to do so would have meant going to school where they might have to associate with Christians. He was particularly virulent about the ministers ('ignorant, illiterate, avaricious characters'), recommending for them a reasonable salary and some degree of education, so that 'they may become decent and respectable members of society'.[4] Most of the changes he suggested were still occupying the minds of the community fifty years later. It seems therefore that *A Peep into the Synagogue* was the first published argument in this country in favour of reform. It claimed that services should be in the vernacular, that the rabbi should be an educated, well paid man and that money offerings during the service should be abolished.

One of the earliest indications that Reform might be on the way was a meeting of the Elders of the Spanish and Portuguese Synagogue in 1803 which was addressed by Isaac Mocatta. Long-time members of Bevis Marks, the Mocatta family was to play an important part in the affairs of Anglo-Jewry for years to come, and especially in the emerging movement for Reform. According to Dr. Moses Gaster (Haham 1887-1918) whose *History of the Ancient Synagogue* was published in 1901, Mocatta 'in scathing terms condemns the spiritual decay of the community and draws a lurid picture of the way in which education has been neglected.'[5] This seems to have heralded an urge for change in the Sephardi community. A new Haham, H.H. Raphael Meldola was appointed who was later succeeded as leader of the community by his son David Meldola, though he never took the title of Haham. The effects of Mocatta's onslaught were minimal, though it did result in the setting up of a committee to make recommendations and the reorganisation of the communal schools.

A few years later it was agreed that minutes of meetings should be in English instead of Portuguese, a language hardly understood by any of the contemporary community. Other members of the Synagogue were beginning to express their dissatisfaction. There were complaints about the lack of decorum in the services and about the behaviour of the younger members of the congregation. Some improvements were put in train; a choir was introduced, a better curriculum, including English, in the schools, and a proposal for a sermon in English. It was also suggested that more members of the *Mahamad* (Council) should attend and stay to the end of the service. This would be helped by cutting the service somewhat (it was at that time about four hours long). The boys should chant instead of singing, and decorum should be improved. Most of this the Elders agreed and in 1829 a meeting was convened to deal with the question of the English sermon. Moses Montefiore (later Sir Moses) described the meeting as 'long and stormy as many members of the congregation were greatly attached to the Spanish tongue.'[6] He made the point that even though their treatment in Spain had been vicious, they still viewed their native land with affection. They were prepared to consider a sermon in English every Sabbath afternoon, as long as they could vet what was to be said beforehand. But the request, perfectly reasonable to later congregants, was refused. One reason was that the majority of ministers spoke very little English, scholarly though they may have been. However, the Chazan, David de Sola, who had married the daughter of the Haham, did give the first sermon in English there in March, 1831. It took twelve months for there to be another.

Attendance at services in Bevis Marks was sparse. This was hardly surprising as many congregants, from there and from the Great Synagogue, had moved westwards. The Rothschilds were in Piccadilly, the Goldsmids in Regents Park, as well as many in the Bloomsbury area and as it was considered quite out of the question to ride on the Sabbath, the devout Jew was left with only two alternatives: either to abstain from attending, or to walk to the City and back. Moses Montefiore and his wife chose to walk from his house in Park Lane to Bevis Marks and back, a total distance of some twelve miles, and did so every Sabbath until he was over eighty years old. Not everyone was so stalwart. An application to found another Sephardi synagogue further to the west was made in 1822 but was adamantly refused, the authorities quoting Ascama No. l, the law which forbade any Sephardi synagogue being founded within six miles of Bevis Marks.

The membership of the Spanish and Portuguese Synagogue began to dissolve into different factions, some joining Abraham Mocatta to form a 'Committee for Promoting Order and Solemnity in the synagogue'. Others sided with David Abarbanel Lindo (a nephew of Benjamin D'Israeli), calling themselves by the clumsy title of 'The Society for supporting and upholding the Jewish Religion as handed down to us by our Reverend Ancestors and for preventing Innovations or Alterations in any of the recognised Forms and Customs, unless sanctioned by properly constituted Religious Authorities'. When Rev. Moses Gaster came to write about Reform it was very clear which side he was on: 'The cry for Reform grew ever louder and louder, and became more reckless when it passed from men of learning to men of ambition, who joined with it a false note of assimilation with their non-Jewish neighbours.'[7] He drew the distinction between the older Anglo-Jewish families in his own community and those Sephardim who had arrived more recently, between those who very strictly obeyed the law and those who opted for change.

In 1836 members of Bevis Marks tried to import some of the reforms carried out by the Hamburg Synagogue, purely in accordance with traditional custom. The Elders, together with the majority of the congregation, refused to listen. The observances insisted on by the leaders of the community had been 'sacred for centuries and are binding on every observant Jew.'[8] This abortive attempt at change, however, did bring about an improvement in the decorum and conduct of the services. There had been continual complaints about the Reader 'gabbling' the prayers, so that the majority of the congregants could not understand what he was saying, and the formation of a choir did exert a measure of control over the youngsters, some of whom were reported to be rushing about during the prayers and even sliding down the banisters.

There was at this time no Jewish press in this country. The *Jewish Chronicle* did not come into being until 1841, preceded by, and for a time running concurrently with, *The Voice of Jacob,* which was founded in 1840. There had been an earlier attempt at some form of news journal for the Jewish community, the *Hebrew Intelligencer,* but it was a simple parochial journal of about four pages, listing communal charities and other unimportant news, rather irreverent in tone. It lasted for only three issues. Information about the state of the community came by word of mouth, but as the majority of the poorer East End Jews were largely illiterate, and many of the wealthier, better educated were related to each other, this was hardly a problem.

The relationship of the principal Jewish families in England during the nineteenth century was complex. The Montefiores, the Mocattas, the Rothschilds, the Goldsmids, together with the Sassoons and the Henriques, formed a group of very wealthy financiers, bankers and entrepreneurs, who while not always very scholarly, were nevertheless well educated and exerted an influence over their fellow Jews beyond their numbers. 'The Cousinhood was not merely a cluster of relatives. In many ways it functioned as an organic unit and even while its own rights were not yet wholly assured it threw in its wealth and influence on behalf of persecuted co-religionists in other parts of the world.'[9] This influence was equally strong on its home territory. Nor was it divided by the rift between Sephardim and Ashkenazim. Moses Montefiore, from a Livorno family with strong ties to Bevis Marks, married Judith Barent Cohen from an Ashkenazi family, and the marriage took place in Bevis Marks, one of the first 'intermarriages' to do so. The Goldsmids, Ashkenazim with German roots, linked themselves commercially with the Mocattas, of ancient Sephardi origin. This refusal to acknowledge any hostility between the two rival groups was to play a vital part in the establishment of a Reform community in London. So bitter did the antagonism in other sections of Anglo-Jewry become that many a family, faced with the possibility of a marriage between two children of opposing factions, had actually sat *shiva* for the renegade son or daughter.

The rumblings of discomfort over the situation in the synagogues of both the Ashkenazi and Sephardi communities were concerned for the most part with practicalities: decorum, the lack of English, the length of services, the state of education. But for those unhappy with the theological aspects of contemporary worship, matters went deeper. A refusal to contemplate any change was met with the insistence of some scholars that change had always been a vital element in Jewish worship. David Philipson writes that 'Reform insists on change where change is necessary for the proper execution of Jewish life in a modern world.'[10] He quotes from the Pentateuch, in which, when some of the Israelites were unable to keep the laws concerning the Passover - for valid reasons - they were permitted to make changes accordingly. 'No ceremonial law can be eternally binding.'[11] The traditions of the Talmud, accepted long after Biblical instructions were received by Moses, were as typical of change as the reforms put forward in Victorian England. The crux of the debate lay, not so much in the amendments to the services, as in the insistence of Rabbinical Judaism as much on the Oral Law (the Talmud) as on that given to Moses, which it did not regard as the be-all and end-all of religious conformity.

There was a clear possibility that had the would-be reformers on both the Ashkenazi and Sephardi sides confined themselves to these relatively innocuous demands, both communities, over a period of years, would have accepted them without too much demur. Bevis Marks was half-way to conceding a 'branch' synagogue being established in the West End, though it insisted that it should be under its control, with exactly the same liturgy and observances as its own. But more radical changes were being promulgated on a national scale. It was the age of emancipation when Jews were fighting for political recognition, and if they were going to be free to enter Parliament, receive university degrees and be called to the Bar, surely they should enjoy the same freedom in their own affairs. But inexperienced in statesmanship and political diplomacy as they were, they had at this time little access to either rabbinical authority or religious leadership. The post of Haham had fallen vacant and the control of the Spanish-Portuguese community was in the hands of their *Beth Din*, a group of ill-educated, inexperienced clergy; and the Ashkenazi Chief Rabbi, Solomon Hirschell, was old and sick. According to Michael Meyer, he never learnt English properly and was satisfied to live out his long tenure quietly among his books, oblivious to religious crisis, and unsympathetic to pressures for change.[12]

An event occurred in 1837 which would have a far greater effect on Britain than any squabble between the two elements of a small minority of her people. The young Queen Victoria came to the throne. Her uncle, William IV, had been very wary of granting too much liberty to his Jewish subjects. During the process of the emancipation, he had told a bishop regarding the latter's vote in Parliament, 'I do not mean to interfere in any way with your vote except on one subject, *The Jews,* and I trust I may depend on your always voting against them.'[13] But the new sovereign had a mind of her own. Those who wished to control her, among them her mother and members of her household, were surprised to be faced with an independence and determination they had not reckoned with. Years before, as a small girl, she had made friends with the family who lived next door to her mother's house at Ramsgate. The large gentleman who welcomed her into his garden and gave her a golden key to let herself in through the gate, was Moses Montefiore. They remained friends throughout both their long lives, as Victoria did with her favourite Prime Minister, Benjamin D'Israeli, who, in spite of having been baptised at the age of eight, never forgot his Jewish roots. Victoria's other uncles, particularly the Dukes of Cambridge and Sussex, had been interested in Jewish life. They were friendly with the Goldsmid family, visiting them in their homes, and were taken to the Dukes Place Synagogue to attend the service, studying Hebrew and learning something of Jewish history. Curiously, their brother the Duke of Kent, father of Queen Victoria, had lived before his marriage in a fine London house, now the home of the Westminster Synagogue.

All attempts to achieve the aims of the would-be reformers seemed to come to nought. Both the Ashkenazi and Sephardi authorities were either adamant that they would never countenance change, or having allowed that change might have to come were so dilatory in moving towards it that the reformers lost patience. They decided to take matters into their own hands.

CHAPTER I

The First Synagogue

On 15th April 1840, a meeting was held at the Bedford Hotel in Southampton Row. Twenty-four gentlemen were present, the majority related to one another. It was inconceivable at this time that any woman might attend. At this gathering, there were nine members of the Mocatta family, among the earliest to return to England after the re-admission. There had been Mocattas among the founders of Bevis Marks and they were to be found in most of the institutions of the Jewish and non-Jewish community of London: at the Stock Exchange (where only twelve Jews were admitted), on the Board of Deputies of British Jews (founded in 1760), in the bullion market, as silver brokers and wherever financial resources were needed. Many were scholars, one a distinguished architect, and almost all were observant and religious Jews. Comprising three generations of sons, uncles and cousins, the Mocatta clan on this momentous day in 1840 included Abraham, Abraham Lindo, Abraham Jnr, Aaron Asher, Jacob, Moses, David, Benjamin, and Daniel.

Another group well represented, and long associated with the Mocattas in business as well as by family, were the Goldsmids. The name varied slightly with their origins, some coming from Germany or Holland but all were Ashkenazi Jews, distinguished members of the Great Synagogue at Dukes Place. They too had settled in England many years earlier, though not as early as the Mocattas. Like the Rothschilds they had been sent from Germany by their father to open branches of the family firm in London, where Aaron Goldsmid had entered into a profitable financial association with Abraham Mocatta. His two sons established their own business but in spite of a very prosperous venture and settled marriages within the community, as well as huge mansions in London, both were subject to deep depression and eventually both took their own lives. However, their children continued to prosper and Aaron Asher, Frederick and Francis Henry were all present at the meeting. Francis and Frederick were the sons of Isaac Lyon Goldsmid (Aaron Asher was his brother), perhaps the most distinguished of the Goldsmids at this time. Isaac Lyon was much involved with the emancipation movement and had been largely responsible for the foundation of University College, the first college of London University and the first in any university to admit Jews. He was made a baronet in 1841. Francis Edward, who inherited his father's title when he died, was the first Jew to take silk (in 1858), and the first professing Jew to be called to the Bar (in 1833). Sir Moses Montefiore, in spite of calling a meeting to discuss improvements at Bevis Marks, was always resolutely opposed to Reform in any important respect. He had no children but his younger brother Horatio, who had married the daughter of Daniel Mocatta, did come to the meeting, together with his two sons, Moses Jnr. and Joseph.

The Cousinhood, the affectionate name bestowed on these interrelated Anglo-Jewish aristocratic families, counted within its distinguished ranks the Henriques, represented at the meeting by three members, David Quixano, Joseph Gutteres and Jacob Quixano (the name Quixano had entered the family by marriage with a lady from a wealthy Spanish family). The Henriques family had come to England from Jamaica where they had been prosperous merchants. The remaining gentlemen present at that first meeting were from both communities: Albert Cohen, Montague Levyssohn, Hanamel de Castro, A. Melhado, Solomon Lazarus and Joseph D'Aguilar Samuda. Daniel Mocatta took the Chair, with Francis Goldsmid as Hon. Secretary. The decisions taken were clear and far-reaching. At the end of the meeting those present signed the following Declaration:

'We the Undersigned, regarding Public Worship as highly conducive to the interests of religion, consider it a matter of deep regret that it is not more frequently attended by members of our Religious Persuasion. We are perfectly sure that this circumstance is not owing to any want of a general conviction of the fundamental Truths of our Religion, but we ascribe it to the distance of the existing Synagogues from the places of our Residence; to the length and imperfections of the order of service, to the inconvenient hours at which it is appointed; to the unimpressive manner in which it is performed and to the absence of religious instruction in our Synagogues. To these evils, we think that a remedy may be applied by the establishment of a Synagogue in the Western part of the Metropolis, where a Revised Service may be performed at hours more suited to our habits, and in a manner more calculated to inspire feelings of Devotion, where Religious Instruction may be afforded by competent persons, and where to effect these purposes, Jews generally may form an United Congregation under the denomination of British Jews.'[2]

The meeting resolved: 'to establish a synagogue in the Western part of the Metropolis under the denomination of the United Congregation of British Jews'.[3] This title was shortly afterwards amended to The West London Synagogue of British Jews. The Hebrew name of the new congregation was *Sha'are Tzedek* – Gates of Righteousness, a phrase from Psalm 118. An important part of the original thinking behind the name of this first reformed congregation was to avoid drawing any distinction between Sephardim and Ashkenazim, a schism which had already caused considerable heartbreak. There was to be 'a revised service in the Hebrew language in conformity with the principles of the Jewish religion in the manner which may appear best calculated to excite feelings of devotion.'[4] There would be religious discourses periodically delivered in English, and a subscription was to be entered into to form a total of £3,000 as a Building Fund for synagogue premises. Thus did the first Reform synagogue in Britain come into being

The expected explosion in the community did not materialise. As Lucien Wolf , the distinguished historian of Anglo-Jewry put it, speaking of the new synagogue, 'There was nothing in its programme to indicate that a schism was at hand.'[5] There was virtually no Jewish press to intrude; all those present at the meeting were of one mind, and another event of international importance had occurred to occupy the minds of the leaders of the community. The 'Damascus affair' revived the old blood libel of Jews killing children to use their blood for baking matzah, and Jews all over the world were outraged by the horror.[6] Less than a week after the meeting at the Bedford Hotel, another group of Jews met at the home of Sir Moses Montefiore in Park Lane to discuss this terrible affair, at which several of the founders of the Reform synagogue were present, as well as other distinguished members of the London Jewish community. A deputation was appointed to confront the Foreign Secretary, Lord Palmerston, who promised that Her Majesty's government would do all it could to address the concern felt by right-minded Englishmen of every persuasion.

Once the problem of the Jews of Damascus had been placed in proper hands (Sir Moses Montefiore was empowered to deal with the situation, and did so with all the tact and diplomacy characteristic of 'The Grand Old Man' of Anglo-Jewry), the reformers could proceed with their plans. They met again, this time at Freemasons Tavern, Great Queen Street, on 11th May, with most of the original 'founders' as they termed themselves, present. Proposals were drawn up making their intentions clear. Services would be held on Sabbaths and Festivals only and these would last for a maximum of two-and-a half hours (except for the Day of Atonement, of course). A selection of prayers to suit the shorter service would be read, not chanted. The Psalms would be sung by a male choir.

This small nucleus of a congregation had already collected £1,700 towards their target of £3,000 for a Building Fund, and it was anticipated that the rest would be found by August. Donations were coming in thick and fast, one of £200 from 'A Friend of Reform', and others for anything from £5 to several hundred. The Hon. Treasurers were Horatio and Jacob Montefiore, and a Trust Fund was set up to deal with the finances, the Trustees to be Horatio and Jacob Montefiore and Aaron Asher Goldsmid. Another decision taken at the meeting was the insistence on a sermon and certain prayers in English. This would entail an entirely new Prayer Book for which a special subcommittee was appointed. What was needed most urgently was a man of stature, of scholarship, whose feelings coincided with the reformers, or 'seceders' as the traditionalists called them. Few such candidates existed in the community who could speak perfect English and who would feel at home in the surroundings of the new West London Synagogue, but the search began.

By the summer things were moving quickly. Another Committee was appointed to find a minister, as usual composed of Mocattas, Henriques's, Goldsmids and Montefiores. They put out feelers in the community to find the man they wanted, approaching the distinguished scholar Isaak Marcus Jost of Germany to help in their search. Jost was the first modern historian of the Jewish people, his work being pre-eminent until overtaken by the more comprehensive volumes of Heinrich Graetz. Jost approached the Chief Rabbi of Dresden, Zachariah Frankel, a conservative scholar who tried to steer a course between tradition and reform. He declined to help, believing that 'no sufficient principle of Reform was put forward and that in order to do battle they must have a standard to raise.'[7] But the reformers did not want to 'do battle'; they wanted to get on with their plans with the help of a like-minded minister whom they could work with and respect.

The man they found was David Woolf Marks, at the time an assistant reader and secretary in the Liverpool Synagogue. Marks, only thirty years old when he joined the reformers, was born in London and educated at the Jews Free School (then in Bell Lane in the East End), though he already had a good grounding in Hebrew and the Scriptures from his father. After a short time as pupil-teacher at a Jewish boarding school in Hammersmith, where he continued his own studies after school hours, he was taken on as reader by the Western Synagogue, then occupying premises in St. Albans Place, off the Haymarket. The Western Synagogue (formerly the Westminster Synagogue) was the only independent synagogue in Britain at that time and for many years afterwards. It was founded in 1761, one of the earliest Ashkenazi synagogues and the first outside the city of London, and was to play an important role in the development of the West London Synagogue.[8]

Marks then moved up to Liverpool, an orthodox, though quite progressive-minded, Ashkenazi synagogue. Liverpool had had a synagogue since the eighteenth century, but had erected a splendid new building in Seel Street in 1808. Here the congregation gained something of a reputation for progressive thinking, with the first sermon in English being preached there. The city boasted the biggest Jewish community in Britain after London, and had split into two after disagreements in 1838, not unlike the problems that were facing London synagogues at about the same time. 'Certainly, disenchantment with what were perceived as ultra-conservative ruling cliques, and alienation from forms of divine worship regarded as archaic and off-putting, were common to all three.'[9]

So young Mr. Marks found the Liverpool congregation more to his taste than the orthodox London communities, even though he was prepared to take his modern theology a stage further. The Appointment Committee's members warmed to this scholarly but forward-looking young man, and he liked them. He agreed to come to London (he was not a Rabbi or even a qualified theological leader) to discuss the position of Reader and Lecturer with the West London Synagogue.

The Council of Founders was now meeting twice a month. There was much to do. It was agreed that £2,000 out of the original £3,000 should be reserved for building or purchasing premises, and procuring a burial ground (the Trustees were instructed to invest the rest in government securities). It was decided that the form of prayers to be used should be either from Scripture or from the forms of service now used by the several congregations of Portuguese and German Jews in London, and that no other should be adopted, but that many of these should be shortened or omitted 'to engage as far as possible the unvaried devotion and attention of the Congregation.'[10] By June they had made good progress in the arrangements for the Sabbath services. They were to last no more than two-and-a-half hours, starting at 9.30 in summer and 10 in winter, there was to be a properly trained choir, pronunciation of the Hebrew was to be according to the Portuguese Jews, 'care being taken that the Service is invariably read in the synagogue slowly and with perfect distinctness'.[11] There should be only two offerings from any one individual made in the synagogue service, to counteract the interminable *mi-shebarach* memorial offerings which were usual in the orthodox synagogues, one of the most common complaints which had led to attempts at reform.

The meeting with David Marks went very well; he was found to be 'extremely eligible' and was engaged for three years at a salary of 200 guineas per year as Secretary, Reader and Lecturer, his appointment to commence in six months' time so that he could give due notice to Liverpool. A message was sent to the Liverpool congregation for the 'kind and liberal manner in which, by releasing Mr. Marks from a part of his engagement with them, they have facilitated his new appointment in London'.[12] Consideration was to be given to appointing an assistant to help with the preparation of the new Prayer Book. This was a matter of some urgency, as by now the Founders were starting to look around for a suitable building to use as a synagogue, and it was essential that the Prayer Book be in print by the time they were ready to proceed with a service of consecration. By the end of 1840 the compilation of the new Prayer Book was well under way. The form it was to take and the prayers to be included were agreed by the Committee and the sum of 50 guineas was set aside for Mr. Marks to obtain an English translation of the *Mishna*. He was also asked to find and purchase a suitable *Sefer Torah*. Offerings would be expected from the congregation on Passover, Pentecost and Tabernacles.

The new congregation obeyed almost all the Jewish laws as far as their behaviour outside the synagogue was concerned. They were, after all, orthodox Jews, always walking to the services on the Sabbath, and keeping strictly to the dietary laws. In fact, they set up in Burton Crescent, just round the corner from the synagogue, a kosher butcher, the Beadle of the congregation acting as *shochet*. This gentleman was the personal *shochet* to Sir Isaac Lyon

Goldsmid. Sir Isaac was as yet not a member of the West London Synagogue, and the *shochet* had a clause in his licence restricting him entirely to working for his patron and for no-one else. The Chief Rabbi closed down the shop. Some years later a court case arose concerning another English butcher who employed a Dutch *shochet*. The butcher maintained that his man's licence was international but both sides sought Counsel's opinion and the expert witness in the case was Rev. David Marks, who found for the Chief Rabbi, surely not the expected outcome.[13]

As far as premises were concerned, this was not proving so easy. As well as a suitable building for worship, it was essential to find a burial ground. The problem came to a head when Horatio Montefiore's first wife, Sarah, the daughter of Daniel Mocatta, died in childbirth. The family, long-time members of Bevis Marks, requested that she should be buried in the Spanish and Portuguese cemetery in Stepney. But this was refused, an unnecessarily spiteful response to the seceders. It was the Western Synagogue, now in Maiden Lane, that came to the rescue. They agreed to allow the burial to take place at their cemetery in Bancroft Road, after which the West London Synagogue agreed to pay them a sum of fifty guineas a year for burial rights until their own ground should be found. Benjamin Elkin, a devoted member of West London, had expressed a wish to be buried beside his wife in the cemetery in the East End belonging to the Great Synagogue. When he died in 1843 Solomon Waley, his brother-in-law, approached the Chief Rabbi, Nathan Adler, who agreed on the condition that no minister, only the beadle, should carry out the ceremony. Elkin had stipulated that no conditions of the kind should be imposed and he was duly buried at West London's own burial ground at Balls Pond Road.

Several possibilities were suggested as sites for the new synagogue. One in Albany Street, north of the Euston Road, had the advantage of a plot beside it that might have suited as a burial ground. Another in Charles Street in Mayfair seemed suitable, and David Mocatta, a Founder Member and an eminent architect, gave his opinion that the premises could be converted for use as a synagogue for about £1,000. He was instructed to proceed with the purchase. The prayer book was ready to go to the printer. Mr. Marks had purchased a scroll for the sum of £28.8s. and he was asked to start making arrangements for a confirmation service at the age of thirteen for both boys and girls, something of an innovation at the time. It is interesting to note that all the internal contemporary records reporting the formation of the West London Synagogue use the English form for Jewish festivals and ceremonies, appropriate for its pride in its English roots.

In the wider world of Anglo-Jewry the question of the acceptance of Reform was becoming critical. Probably at the suggestion of Mr. Marks, West London decided to abolish the second day of the Festivals, a daring and provocative move, which arouses controversy to this day.[14] This left one day for New Year, first and seventh day for Passover, one day for Pentecost and first and eighth days for Tabernacles. The anti-reformers accused West London of refusing to admit that the Oral Law was the Word of God and should be obeyed to the letter. This was manifestly not the case; where West London differed from the traditionalists was in the view that as the Oral Law had not been handed by God to Moses, as had the *Torah*, it did not have the same definitive bearing on the conduct and beliefs of the Jews of the present day. In ancient times the Karaites had held similar views. An austere sect, speaking Arabic, they too had concentrated more on the written than the oral law, but attached much importance to ceremonial, unlike the modern reformers.

Little progress was being made in regard to premises in Charles Street when Sir Isaac Goldsmid proposed a new idea. He was not a founder member of the new congregation, but was sympathetic towards its plans, and was particularly anxious to heal the rift between Ashkenazi and Sephardi Jews. He was a life-long member of the Great Synagogue, but he changed his will, leaving a considerable sum, not to the Great, as originally planned, but to the West London Synagogue. He was something of an admirer of Robert Owen, the philanthropist and social reformer who had founded the mill at New Lanark which became an early experiment in philanthropic management, and who was considered by many to be the father of English socialism. Owen's socialist chapel in Burton Street, Bloomsbury, Sir Isaac thought, might prove the ideal answer to the new congregation's search for a place of worship. David Mocatta investigated the premises and was of the opinion that for the sum of about £500 it would suit the purpose very well. It was big enough to seat ninety, with another sixty or so in the gallery. The present tenant of the building had a lease until 1843, two years to run, but the Council decided to offer him the sum of £200 to leave before his tenancy was up. He accepted and the building was taken on a seven year lease for £100 p.a. The only alternative, other than Charles Street, was a room at University College, now used as a lecture room, but the unanimous decision was to take Burton Street where the community could be entirely independent and might make any alterations to the premises that suited them. Mr. Marks was asked to take a house nearby, towards which the congregation would pay £25 pa, on condition that it could use a room for meetings and have its correspondence sent there.

However, the apparent tranquillity in Anglo-Jewry at this time was merely the calm before the storm. The new Prayer Book and the appointment of David Marks as Reader, together with the renting of the premises as a House of Prayer, were becoming a matter of public knowledge. The lay leadership of the Anglo-Jewish community was represented by the Board of Deputies of British Jews. Founded in 1760, the Board considered itself the mouthpiece of all the Jews in England, whereas in fact it had no provincial representation and of course no link with the new Reform movement, which did not consider itself subject to the jurisdiction of the Chief Rabbi or the Haham.

The President of the Board was Sir Moses Montefiore, who had always been vehemently opposed to any deviation from orthodoxy. In May 1841 a letter was received by the Board, sent jointly by Solomon Hirschell, the Chief Rabbi, and David Meldola, the Dayan of the Spanish and Portuguese *Beth Din*. It began ominously, 'Schism has introduced its baneful influence among us,' and went on to maintain that no alteration of the laws or practices of the Sephardi or Ashkenazi communities could ever be entertained. 'The whole of our laws form an entirety – we cannot understand or obey one part without the other.' Moses Mocatta turned down an offer to meet with the Elders of Bevis Marks, and both sides awaited developments.

They were not long in coming. The leaders of both orthodox communities met at the Chief Rabbi's house (Rabbi Hirschell was too ill to be able to go out) to issue a Declaration. 'Information having reached me, from which it appears that certain persons calling themselves British Jews, publicly and in their book of prayers, reject the Oral Law, I deem it my duty to declare that, according to the laws and statutes held sacred by the whole House of Israel, any person or persons declaring that he or they reject and do not believe in the authority of the Oral Law, cannot be permitted to have any communion with us Israelites in any religious rite or sacred act.' It went on to caution all those Jews, 'especially parents', to attend to the declaration and 'be not induced to depart from our Holy Laws.' It was signed by Hirschell and Meldola, though apparently with some reluctance, and although it was meant to be read publicly in all synagogues in Britain, it was in fact held back for a while to see if the implied threat of excommunication had any effect on the seceders. The point at issue remained the authority of the Oral Law, which the reformers did not repudiate altogether.

Meanwhile the Founders of the West London Synagogue went ahead with their plans for the consecration of the Burton Street Synagogue. The work on the building was going according to plan, with extra gas lights in the gallery where the women were to sit, and applications for seats were beginning to come in. The seats were offered at £7 or less according to the position in the synagogue and for the more costly seats the head of the family was entitled to seats of a corresponding kind for members of his family resident with him. The Founders were to have £7 seats. The Forms of Prayer for the consecration service, to be held on Thursday 27th January 1842, were drawn up, and the choir was already practising under the command of Mr. Alexander, with the musical help of Mr. Maintzer. Rev. Marks was asked to purchase a cloak and hat for the occasion. A Beadle, Mr. Alexander Cohen, was appointed at a salary of £35 and a noticeboard was erected at the entrance to the synagogue requesting all persons to enter before worship commenced so that silence might be observed during the service. A Royal Prayer was to be included in the service, reading 'We pray for Queen Victoria, His Royal Highness Prince Albert, the Prince and Princess of Wales, and all the royal family'.

The new Prayer Book attracted a great deal of vilification from the orthodox community because of its variation from the old familiar text, all in Hebrew of course. It carried a long introduction written by Rev. Marks, in which he set out his views on change in the Jewish community, and especially in the forms of prayer it used. 'Nothing can be more incorrect,' he wrote, 'than the current notion that the whole of the Prayer Book, as we now possess it ... has as fixed and immutable a character as the Sacred Code itself. Nothing, we repeat, is more fallacious than such a notion; and the mere existence of considerable differences between the rituals now in use is alone sufficient to establish its inaccuracy.' He explained the thinking behind the changes that the new synagogue was making, 'that the prayer should be perfectly intelligible to the mind of the humblest supplicant and that the sentiments which it expresses should be of a pure and elevating character.' He spoke of the decision to shorten the Sabbath morning service which 'should be confined within such a period of time as to afford ground for the expectation that, from the beginning to the end it may be able to command the constant, unwearied and devout attention of the congregation.'

By the end of 1841 preparations were almost complete. The building was insured for £800 and the contents for £500; Mr. Marks's housekeeper was granted a gratuity for providing refreshments for committee meetings, and the choir were given new hats for the occasion. (There were three choristers who were paid £12 each and three who received £3.) The Wardens were to be Abraham Mocatta, Jacob Montefiore and Francis H. Goldsmid. Two ushers, Solomon Lazarus and Emanuel Mocatta were to show the gentlemen to their seats and David Henriques and David Mocatta would do the same for the ladies (the men and women were seated separately). It was arranged for charitable donations to be made on the day of the consecration.

Before the service was due to commence, a small celebration was arranged in the Committee Room when Rev. Marks was invested with his cloak. The senior member of the Council, Moses Mocatta, made a short speech constituting him the 'Official Minister' of the West London Synagogue of British Jews. He warned him of the difficulties which might ensue when he took up his post. 'All eyes will be upon our minister,' he said, 'and therefore unremitting circumspection will be indispensable on your part, for on the least deviation, unqualified censure will be heaped upon us, and the self-styled Orthodox of our Co-Religionists will gladly seize on the minutest point to vilify our minister and cast obloquy upon our Congregation.'[15] He wished him every happiness in his domestic life (he was engaged to be married) and a long and profitable career.

However, a heavy cloud was hanging over what should have been a momentous and indeed joyous occasion. Five days before the consecration was due to take place, on the preceding Sabbath, the Declaration was formally made a *cherem*, an excommunication, to be read in synagogues throughout the nation. Not all communities obeyed. The Western Synagogue, already friendly towards the reformers and not formally allied to either Ashkenazi or Sephardi Judaism, was the only one in London to refuse. Outside London, Liverpool, the former home of Mr. Marks, did not obey and one or two others also refused. The validity of the *cherem* has been called into doubt. The *Jewish Encyclopaedia* describes it as 'the highest ecclesiastical censure, the exclusion of a person from the religious community which among Jews meant a practical prohibition of all intercourse with society'. Although it had been pronounced by the leading Rabbis of the English Jewish community, it was maintained by one eminent scholar of the time, Tobias Theodores[16], that rabbis are only teachers, Jews like any other, and have no more authority over their fellow Jews than other men, unlike, say, Catholic priests. The authority is the Talmudical Law, and a *cherem* was a medieval form of Jewish excommunication which should have been accompanied by the sound of horns and trumpets. If the *cherem* was unlawful there was no need for repentance by the sinners. It seems that the authorities of Bevis Marks were themselves doubtful about the legality of the pronouncement, because a year or two later, in connection with the possibility of marriage between a member of the Spanish-Portuguese congregation and the Reform community, they passed a resolution that such a marriage would have no objections and that they 'had never sanctioned nor does it desire to sanction the enforcement of this penalty.'[17] Although the West London Synagogue was determined to go ahead with its plans, it did go so far as to put aside £30 for a 'paper' to be composed as a reply to the 'Declaration of the German and Portuguese *Beth Din*', and set aside the following Sunday to consider it.

The day of the consecration was bitterly cold. It had been snowing earlier in the week, and although the snow had turned to rain the temperature was still near freezing. However, about midday the rain ceased and all seemed set for a fine start.[18] In accordance with the new arrangements for a Reform synagogue the service started on time, with everyone in his place. A few special guests, such as Mr. Maintzer (who had arranged much of the music) and his wife, were in good positions. Another distinguished guest (not at the consecration but at the first Sabbath service) was Isaac d'Israeli, frail and almost blind, whose conflict with Bevis Marks resulted in his resignation from that congregation and later in the baptism of all his children, including Benjamin, the future Prime Minister, then aged eight. He said to Rev. Marks afterwards that had such a synagogue been in existence some years earlier, he and all his family would have continued to profess Judaism. English history would no doubt have followed a different path.

The sermon by Mr. Marks had been eagerly awaited. This was, after all, the first public intimation of the aims and objects of the Reform movement. He did not let his congregants down. He took as his text the twenty-second chapter of the Book of Joshua, where God permits the children of Israel to change their ways in order to better worship Him. 'And the thing pleased the children of Israel.' 'We must not confound the law with the substance', he said, 'nor regard an infinity of ceremonials as the final aim of religion.'[19] He explained to a rapt congregation that it was not a desire for innovation, nor a want of respect but a 'paramount obligation, a deep sense of right, a conviction, that impels us to those measures we consider the only means of arousing our brethren from that indifference to spiritual matters into which they have unhappily sunk.'[20] He spoke of the Oral Law, the cornerstone of the disagreement between the reformers and the orthodox. 'It is not our intention to vilify the character of the traditional records. We recognise in them a valuable aid for the elucidation of many passages in Scripture. But we must deny that a belief in the divinity of the *Mishna* and the Talmud is equal to the divinity of the Law of Moses. It is of human composition … there is one immutable Law, the Scriptures.'[21]

He went on to innumerate the differences that the new synagogue wished to introduce, explaining that it was due to eastern custom and the over-fondness for the opinions of bygone times that services were so degraded. In particular he stressed the position in which Jewish women found themselves. This was an unheard of subject for a public synagogue service. 'Woman,' he said, 'is a helpmeet for man and in every way his equal, to participate in the full discharge of every moral and religious obligation.' She had become degraded below her proper station. He spoke, too, of the use of Chaldaic instead of Hebrew, of the double festivals (not commanded by God), of levity during reading, the sale and distribution of *mitzvot* and a want of instruction from the pulpit. He finished with a prayer for the congregation and for himself. 'Show me the way I should go and the way I should lead this congregation.'[22]

No Jewish newspaper reporter was present at the opening; the *Jewish Chronicle* and the *Voice of Jacob* did make mention of the event but obtained their material from either *The Times* or *The Morning Chronicle. The Times* edition of 1st February carried a small but friendly paragraph: 'OPENING OF NEW SYNAGOGUE. This ceremony took place on Thursday, 27th January in Burton Street. By three o'clock most of the leading members of the new congregation were present, among whom we observed Mr. H. Montefiore, Mr. F. Goldsmid, Mr. A. Mocatta, Mr. D. Henriques and a great many more of the Goldsmid, Mocatta and Montefiore families which constitute the most respectable among the Jews. The ceremony commenced with the chanting of Psalms by the Minister of the new congregation, the Rev. D.W. Marks and a small but well-trained choir. The rolls of the Mosaic law were then placed in the Ark, which is of a most simple but neat construction.'[23] The first Reform synagogue in Great Britain had been born.

✡

A remarkable series of letters from a young man of fourteen to his mother were preserved and extracts published in the *West London Synagogue Magazine* nearly ninety years later, which gave a delightful view of services at the new synagogue. Henry Michael Behrend, of Liverpool, while at college in London, was staying at the home of the Rev. David Marks and duly wrote home to describe his weekly visit to the Burton Street Synagogue. On March 21st 1842, two months after the consecration, he wrote, ' It was much more like a church, the quiet was so universal ... the choir sang most beautifully a *mizmor l'david* – it was a very pretty air and well adapted for divine service.'[24] He goes on to describe the atmosphere in the synagogue. 'Throughout the utmost silence prevailed, not a word was spoken but by those in office; I never thought the Hebrew service could have been so silently conducted. There were not half-a-dozen ladies' seats unoccupied.' He hopes his parents will come to London and join the synagogue. 'I am sure, whether I return a better scholar or no, I shall return a better Jew.' He came back for the next Saturday morning service, which again he found to his liking. 'Then came the most affecting part; the family of the late Mr. Montefiore, together with his wife's father and brother, all came to the Ark and said a prayer composed on the occasion of his death by Mr. Marks.' He closed his letter with a request for another coloured waistcoat.

The following week Master Behrend wrote again, assuring his mother that he longed for the *Shabbat* to come round. 'It is quite as if we went into a village at a quarter to ten. I see them all going in, family after family; not a Christian to be seen, we are all quite retired; no noise of carts, horses or children playing outside.' This observant young gentleman described some of his fellow congregants: Sir Isaac Lyon Goldsmid was 'a little, fine looking gentleman – his wife's hair is silvery white.' He was introduced to the family, intrigued that Lady Goldsmid 'has not been to any synagogue for eighteen years ... she was so much pleased that she intends to sleep in Tavistock Square on Friday nights so as to be able to attend regularly.' He is hugely delighted that as Rev. Marks commenced the Prayers for Rain, 'there came such a pelting shower of hail, although the day had been beautiful before and was beautiful afterwards.' He continued his correspondence to his parents and to his brother George, regaling them with accounts of the synagogue services, together with as much gossip as he could glean, clearly enjoying his visits. He told his brother of Mr. Marks's wedding, 'Marks marries at his own Shule in London; they wouldn't marry him here (Liverpool) nor would he be married by 'em. Of course I shan't go up for the wedding, tho' I shall be invited.'

Another letter described a Christian lady who came every Saturday to synagogue. She apparently then went every Sunday to church 'to erase the impression made upon her the day before.' Rev. Marks refused to convert her. But young Behrend had a mind of his own when it came to obeying the rules he had been brought up in. 'I don't care a rap about living "cosher", he told his mother. 'I wouldn't eat anything forbidden, but I don't care how my meat is cooked. At home (Rev. Marks's house) we eat meat and butter together, as all that humbug is exploded. As for ham, that I never touched, tho' I don't know if I'd have any invincible scruples so to do: the fact is, it has never come my way.' Henry Michael Behrend went on to a brilliant academic career, studying at University College (founded by Sir Isaac Goldsmid), becoming a surgeon and eventually President of the Jews' Hospital and Orphan Asylum at Norwood. Among his many publications was one on the defence of *Shechita*.

CHAPTER II

Margaret Street

A rrangements for the West London Synagogue's own burial ground were proceeding. A large plot of land at Balls Pond Road, Dalston, had been found, and the Council ordered the cemetery to be walled and a small chapel built; a gardener was taken on to keep the grounds in good order. Mr. David Angel was appointed as keeper. He had a house on the premises, and his duties were clearly laid out. He was expected to keep the little house clean and tidy, with fires in the hall, to attend all interments in a 'decent suit of mourning', to see that the grounds were fit and orderly, keep an eye on the state of the tombs, and to report to the Wardens. He was to have no lodgers in his dwelling, or to carry on any business there. He was not to be absent after sunset without permission, and was to supervise personally the watch (the guard over the grounds) and to make sure that all gates were locked. He had to keep a book with the names of the watchmen attending each night and any 'irregularities' committed by the watchmen were to be reported. He also had to keep a register of all burials, with the names in English and Hebrew, with details of the deceased and the precise location of the grave. The graves had to conform exactly to the dimensions laid down by the Council.

Other matters essential for the yearly organisation of a Jewish house of prayer were also in hand: prayer books for the Festivals, a *Haggadah* for Passover and a *Ner Tamid* to hang above the Ark, as well as the necessities for other occasions such as *Lulavim* and *Etrogim* for *Shavuot*, a *menorah* for *Hanucah*, and white covers for the scrolls on the High Holydays. Here the ladies of the congregation came into their own. They had formed themselves into a Ladies Committee, for 'distributing relief among the poor', as well as many other little jobs, and were generous in their gifts to the synagogue.

The congregation grew rapidly, and it was very soon realised that Rev. Marks could not cope alone with the full responsibility of leading it. The synagogue was fortunate to find in Albert Lowy an Assistant Minister who held similar views to its members and was happy to make his home in London. Lowy was born in Moravia and went to university in Vienna. Here he founded an association for the welfare of the Jews, *Die Einheit,* and came to London to seek support. His English was good but not perfect, and he soon found in West London a community with whom he could work in concord. His scholarship and knowledge of Hebrew was of particular help when he cooperated with David Marks in writing the new Prayer Book and he stayed with West London until 1892. He was instrumental in founding the Anglo-Jewish Association.

One outstanding and very important matter remained to be dealt with, the question of marriage registration. Until 1836 the marriage of two persons of the Jewish faith could be solemnised by a recognised marriage secretary and registered accordingly. But in that year a new Marriage Act insisted on the registration of such a secretary only through the offices of the Board of Deputies. Thus the newly created Reform synagogue was at the mercy of the Board, whose President was Sir Moses Montefiore. As soon as the consecration of the Burton Street Synagogue was over the Council wrote to the board, asking for the Rev. Marks to be granted recognition as a marriage secretary, but Sir Moses, never willing to be helpful to the new community, refused to recognise the West London Synagogue as a Jewish congregation unless the Chief Rabbi agreed. His answer was a clear refusal, as he did not recognise 'the place of worship in Burton Street to be a synagogue.' The matter was somewhat urgent as a member of the choir, a Mr. Davis, had asked to be married in the synagogue.

A copy of the correspondence was forwarded to the Superintendent Registrar, pointing out that before the Marriage Act no such certificate was required from the Board of Deputies, and that Jewish marriages should continue to be solemnized as before. The letter continued, 'It would be impossible to satisfy a Court of Law that a body of men, declaring themselves Jews, who obey the law of Moses and adopt the Jewish creed (the *Yigdal*), is not a Jewish synagogue.'[1] The Board of Deputies consulted the Solicitor General and an eminent barrister. However, the Burton Street community did not wish to bring the matter to the view of the general public nor to contend with the Board in legal proceedings. They therefore decided on a compromise. Those wishing to marry should have their ceremony solemnised before a Registrar, after which, on the same day, they would be married in the synagogue according to Jewish rites, with the full details of bride, bridegroom, minister and witnesses entered into the synagogue books. It took another ten years before a Marriage Registrar could be appointed for the West London Synagogue, which was then authorised to grant similar certification to secretaries of other Reform synagogues. This is still the case today; any Reform synagogue wishing to appoint a Marriage Secretary must first get permission from the Council of the West London Synagogue. Reviewing the West London marriage certification one hundred years later, Edward Henriques (then synagogue treasurer) commented that toleration and fair play were exhibited in public by a Christian Legislature in order to remedy a wrong perpetrated by Jews upon their fellow Jews.

The marriage ceremony itself at the Margaret Street synagogue was somewhat different from those carried out at other synagogues. A guest at a wedding at the West London Synagogue in 1853 noticed in particular that the men and women sat together, unlike at orthodox weddings he had attended.

When the bride and groom came into the synagogue they turned first into an ante-room where the necessary civil ceremony was performed. Then the Rev. Marks took his place by the *Chuppah* in front of the Ark (where the *Sifre Torah* were dressed in white satin). The bridegroom entered with his friends from the left and the bride with her bridesmaids from the right, while the choir sang. The bridegroom spoke his promise in English as did the bride. The Minister joined their hands and the bridegroom placed the ring on his bride's finger. The bridegroom stamped on the glass, while the choir sang the 150th Psalm. No *Ketuba* (marriage certificate) was read out under the *Chuppah*, the custom in orthodox synagogues, as this had happened in front of witnesses before the ceremony. The guest was very pleased at this. He felt that the whole form of the *Ketuba* was a gross absurdity, and that 'it would not be tolerated if the document were to be translated into English.' Apparently several of the guests were very critical of the fact that the civil ceremony had to take place first because of the intransigence of the Board of Deputies.

Once the marriage problems had been dealt with, the Council decided they should also regularise births and deaths certification. A child should be named according to Jewish rites and registered in the books of the synagogue after a civil certificate of registration had been obtained. A death certificate had to be shown before a funeral could take place and all certificates and registrations should be kept by the synagogue. It was not until a new Marriage Act in 1856, known as the Religious Opinions Relief Bill, was passed, that the West London Synagogue, specifically mentioned in the Act along with dissenting chapels, could certify its own marriages.

One specification that the reformers had paid particular attention to when discussions about changes had first been mooted, was that they wished to continue to donate to charities, even after they had struck out on their own. Moneys were given to many deserving causes, usually suggested by the ministers when approached by those in need. The Rev. Marks was especially interested in helping in the education of the poorer children in the community, who had little access to schooling of any kind. The Education Act of 1870, granting education to all children whether they could pay or not, was still some way off. Some of the poorest children would be prevented from attending a West London school (either they were already apprenticed to a trade or they lived too far away).

Towards the end of 1844 the Council discussed at some length the matter of founding a synagogue school. A sub-committee was set up under Mr. Marks' guidance (he was appointed Goldsmith Professor of Hebrew at University College in this year), and reported that it was thought that about twelve children might become pupils (boys only at this stage) and there was no reason why the school should be confined to one congregation. It was felt that many others might want to be associated with it so the numbers might reach fifteen to twenty. The possibility of taking girls was discussed but as this would mean another schoolroom and a second teacher, it was decided to put this off to a later date. Funds were limited so the Council felt it might be possible to find a room in the house of a congregant. A good English teacher would be required for four to five hours a day, five days a week. The Ministers would be happy to attend in the afternoons for an hour for Jewish instruction, free of payment. The rent of a room (£25 pa), the teacher's salary (£40 pa) and books, sundry expenses, etc, might total about £85 in all. The Ladies Committee agreed to contribute £10 and £20-30 would come from the Council, leaving the rest to be taken from annual subscriptions.

The West Metropolitan Jewish School opened on 7th April 1845, having advertised in the Jewish press for a teacher 'qualified to give a sound English education', and another to teach Hebrew 'grammatically and according to the Portuguese pronunciation.' The number of pupils grew rapidly (instead of the envisaged number of around twenty, some sixty children enrolled before the opening day) and the question of a girls' school soon came before the Council. It was agreed to take girls in the same building as that which had been taken over for the boys in Little Queen Street, Lincoln's Inn Fields and the school was well supported financially, not only by the members of West London but also by the parents of pupils coming from the city synagogues. The *Jewish Chronicle* published a report from the Committee which congratulated the school on an excellent attendance record and on its progress in 'Grammar, Mental Arithmetic and in the knowledge of natural objects'. A Miss Topham was taken on as mistress of the girls, most of whom apparently entered the school 'unable to spell or read and knowing little more than the letters of the alphabet'. Not only were the children's academic needs catered for but they were also taken on outings, once to the Theatre Royal in Drury Lane, once to Beulah Spa, Norwood 'in covered vans' where they enjoyed 'a roast beef dinner and a plentiful supply of tea and plum cake in the evening'. There was a yearly outing to the seaside, often paid for by the children themselves, who were taught how to save by the opening of a school savings bank to which they could contribute or withdraw their savings as they wished. In 1853 the school moved to Red Lion Square, and an infants' class was added (there was then no Jewish kindergarten in western London).

In order to finance the much larger premises in Red Lion Square a dinner was held at Willis's Rooms, St. James's, attended by many of London's Jewish elite, together with several members of Parliament, city dignitaries (including David Salomons the future first Jewish Lord Mayor) and several distinguished non-Jewish guests, and over £1,000 was raised for the welfare of the school. It was now accepting non-Jewish pupils, at the wish of the Headmaster, Mr. Brooke, and had formed a friendly and useful relationship with other Jewish schools in London. The standard of teaching was high and the results excellent, the instruction following modern educational methods such as the Pestalozzi and Birkbeck systems and including adult education classes for men and women. No corporal punishment was permitted (unusual for schools in those days). A contemporary non-Jewish visitor was very impressed with the school and the pupils, describing the girls as 'little Hebrew maidens with oriental faces'. He was struck 'with a certain air of respectability and uprightness among these little creatures, as they sit there, so self-possessed, keen-eyed and well-mannered'.

The 1870 Education Act brought many changes to the school. In order to be able to claim the annual government grant the school had to submit to national regulation which did not always coincide with the wishes of the governors, so they withdrew it from national control, forfeiting the grant. Gradually more and more pupils were drawn from orthodox families, with fewer coming from working class families, and the school became in 1878 the Jewish Middle Class School and offered the possibility of girls training as teachers after obtaining Oxford or Cambridge Examinations. The boys' classes, meanwhile, had declined in numbers and when the lease of Red Lion Square came to an end, they closed altogether. The girls moved to a new building off Bedford Square, funded by Miss Isabel Goldsmid, the daughter of F.D. Goldsmid, with the Chief Rabbi, Dr. Hermann Adler, on the committee. The original founders, the West London Synagogue, were almost forgotten. The school became the Jewish High School for Girls, and as numbers declined it had eventually to close altogether in 1897. One of the very reasons that the West London Synagogue had come into being in the first place – the movement of Jews from the City westwards – lay behind the closure of the school it had founded, namely the movement even further to the west where local schools were becoming available.[2]

Chief Rabbi Hirschell died in 1842. He has been recognised as the first Chief Rabbi of this country, having been Minister of the Great Synagogue in Dukes Place, the home of the Ashkenazi Jews in London. 'As a single-minded, inflexible rabbi of the old Eastern European type, he could not accommodate demands for change and found himself out of his depth.'[3] He was succeeded by Nathan Marcus Adler, born in Hanover, who was of a more modern frame of mind, though no less stringent in his views on Jewish law. University educated, and an internationally known scholar, he took over from Rabbi Hirschell at Dukes Place and proceeded to assess the state of Jewry in Britain. Together with Sir Moses Montefiore, he set about publishing the *Laws and Regulations for All the Synagogues in the United Kingdom*, but this was something of a misnomer as he had no control over the Sephardi Jews of Britain nor, of course, over the Reformers. He wished particularly to improve the poor standard of Jewish education in the country, founding Jews College in 1855 and was largely responsible for the establishment in 1870 of the United Synagogue. He was almost as adamantly opposed to Reform as his predecessor had been, but he did allow the foundation of a second Reform synagogue in Manchester in 1856.

Adler's interpretation of the validity of Reform Judaism was questioned in the case of Jane Angel's marriage. Jane was the daughter of David Angel, the West London Synagogue's keeper of the cemetery at Balls Pond Road, and she was engaged to marry Morris Hyman, an Ashkenazi Jew. She naturally wished to be married under the auspices of the West London Synagogue, her father being a valued member of its staff, but she was faced with an adamant and very stern Chief Rabbi. He condemned Hyman for wishing to marry into a Reform family and refused even to meet Jane's father. She was informed that unless she agreed (and signed a note confirming her agreement) never again to set foot inside a Reform synagogue, no marriage could take place. This she eventually agreed to do - Hyman had said he would not marry her unless she did - and the marriage duly took place. Nathan Adler, however, did himself later perform the marriage of Sarah Henriques, sister of an eminent member of West London, to an Ashkenazi Jew, though the marriage was not solemnized in a synagogue but in Sarah's home.

Another proposed marriage which caused problems and again involved the Chief Rabbi was that of Mr. Lambert Ellis. He wished to marry a Miss Levy at West London, but an intricate situation faced the Council. Mr. Ellis's father had married the widow of his brother and there were two children of that marriage. The marriage took place in Holland, but was regarded as incestuous both in Jewish law (Leviticus xviii, 16 and xx, 21) and the law of the land. The offspring were regarded as *mamzers* (illegitimate) and not permitted to marry as Jews. So Mr. Ellis had been denied a licence to marry in an orthodox synagogue. Mr. Ellis's brother had in fact married in such a synagogue, without revealing all the facts. The Rev. Adler wrote to Rev. Marks, 'I must express the hope that your synagogue will not authorise the union.' He also severely rebuked the minister who had married the brother, for not investigating the background more fully. Rev. Lowy queried whether the law of the land was right. If so, then the religious question did not arise. He suggested that West London should seek the opinions of the Chief Rabbis of France and Belgium, and of Dr. Jellinek of Vienna and Dr. Lazarus of Breslau, eminent scholars in Jewish law. There is no indication of any such marriage taking place in this country.

By 1846 a new problem faced the Council. The lease of the Burton Street premises was drawing to an end and the strength of the congregation seemed to indicate that a larger and more suitable building might have to be found. The Wardens were asked to put their minds to the possibility of constructing a purpose-built synagogue. There was a sum of £5,000 already in hand, and it was estimated that another £5,000 would need to be raised either to build a completely new synagogue or to adapt a suitable site as a house of prayer. Before the end of the meeting called to discuss the situation, the sum of £2,000 was already promised. It was decided to call an Extraordinary General Meeting to place the matter before the members.

Together with the synagogue's architect, David Mocatta, the Wardens began their search. David Mocatta was the son of Moses Mocatta, one of the founding fathers of the West London Synagogue, who had apprenticed his son to the eminent architect Sir John Soane. His articles stated that he would remain with Soane for six years, in return for a premium of one hundred and fifty guineas, working from nine until eight, except for 'Hebrew Festivals and the Sabbath'. His time with Soane stood him in good stead, for while he was there Soane designed, among other buildings, Trinity Church Marylebone, the Committee Rooms at the House of Lords, and the New Grand Masonic Hall in Great Queen Street.

West London wanted to stay, as far as possible, in the Bloomsbury area where so many of the congregants lived, and found two possibilities: one in Mortimer Street and the other in Cirencester Place (where William Blake had once lived). It is now Great Titchfield Street. This seemed suitable particularly as it had a small house attached, but as the investigations went on, the premises were found to be in too bad a condition to be worth extensive repair. Other possibilities were some land in Margaret Street, off Cavendish Square, and another site in Oxford Street. In the meantime the Council renewed the lease on Burton Street for another six months to give it more time to find the right answer. No. 50 Margaret Street seemed the most likely spot. It was on the estate of the Duke of Portman and was then occupied by a John Donaldson, a coachmaker, so David Mocatta was instructed to obtain the best terms he could. After considerable difficulty (and 'some trifling outlay'), the Duke's agent obtained the consent of the neighbouring occupiers for a synagogue to be built, and it was estimated that a sum of £5,500 would be needed. The Trustees of the building were appointed: J.L. Elkin, Francis Goldsmid and Frederick Goldsmid. It was unanimously agreed to ask Baron de Goldsmid to lay the first stone. He graciously accepted, 'being much flattered by the polite manner in which you have made the application .' Sir Isaac Lyon Goldsmid had been created Baron de Palmeira, a Portuguese title, and was the first Jewish baronet. He was always friendly and encouraging to the Reform movement, though he was perhaps better known for his commitment to the political emancipation of the Jews in England.

Early in 1848 it seemed that difficulties were arising in getting the previous tenants out so that building could begin, even though they were in arrears with rent. The Duke was approached to help and eventually the site was cleared for building to go ahead. Five tenders were obtained and the work was awarded to the firm of Grimsdall's, who had already been employed on the Burton Street building. The Baron donated £300 towards the cost of the building and applied for a seat in the new synagogue. He was unanimously elected to the Council.

Meanwhile the day-to-day running of the West London Synagogue in Burton Street was proceeding as usual, with all the problems experienced by every synagogue, particularly concerning births, marriages and deaths. An application for membership was received from Solomon Kello, but there appeared to be some question of whether he was really Jewish. A letter from the Mohel, Mr. Dyte, confirmed that indeed he was!

The Foundation Stone of the new synagogue was laid on 5th June 1848, and the following day the *Morning Chronicle* reported the event in full. Some two hundred people were present and a preview of the plans was announced. There were to be (as well as the synagogue itself) two houses adjoining for the ministers and between the two an archway leading from the street to the synagogue building. The brief service was led by Rev. Marks who read prayers 'in the Hebrew tongue', and the architect, David Mocatta, handed the silver trowel to Moses Mocatta, the senior Founder, who passed it to Baron de Palmeira. Rev. Marks gave a short address, explaining that the object was 'to stamp with permanence and efficiency, by the establishment of the new synagogue, those excellent improvements and modifications in the arrangement and conduct of their ancient religion which they had long, but at length successfully, struggled to accomplish.' Then the Baron laid the first stone and deposited within a glass case a parchment which read: On this day, 4th Sivan A.M. 5608 (June 5th 1848), in the 11th year of the reign of Her Most Gracious Majesty Queen Victoria, the first stone of this synagogue, called the West London Synagogue of British Jews, was laid by Sir Isaac Lyon Goldsmid, Baron de Goldsmid and de Palmeira; David Mocatta, architect. Also in the case were some coins of the present year. The Baron spoke with great emotion, explaining the background and looking forward to the promotion of 'a common bond of union among all classes and sects of Judaism.' Rev Marks then read several prayers and 'wound up the solemn proceedings of the day'.

A progress report on the Margaret Street building from David Mocatta was given to the Council at the beginning of 1849. By now the work was almost complete, to the architect's 'entire satisfaction'. The 'warm air apparatus' was working well, gas pipes had been introduced and the seats, reading-desk and pulpit had been installed. The party wall of No. 51 was found to be in a dangerous state and needed replacing (the Duke of Portman graciously agreed to the remission of half a year's rent), and it seemed likely that the new synagogue might open after the Pentecost holidays. The Form of Service was prepared and the Council discussed the possibility of introducing instrumental music for the day of consecration. On 17th June it met for the first time in the Committee Room of No. 50 Margaret Street. The ladies offered to provide new covers for the *Torah* scrolls, the pulpit and the reading-desk and other gifts, including a handsome candelabrum, were warmly received. The next door house at No. 48 was now ready for Mr. Marks, and Dr. Lowy, too, was comfortably installed within the precincts of the building. All seemed set for the West London Synagogue to move into its new home.

The *Jewish Chronicle* devoted two pages to a description of the splendid new building on the occasion of the consecration on 29th June, 1849. The synagogue, square in form, was approached by a long and well-lit passage. The architecture was of sixteenth-century Palladian style, with Ionic octagonal columns supporting the gallery, and from here rose smaller ornamental columns. Above these were semi-circular arches, surmounted by 'a bold cornice with enriched spandrels and trusses forming the key-stones to the arches.'[4] Those pillars facing the entrance formed part of the structure of the Holy Ark. The Ark was approached by wide semi-circular steps of marble leading up to a platform from which rose three further columns on each side, arranged as wings, the third recessed behind the other two. Between the two wings were the richly ornamented doors of the sanctuary. Above the doors was a Hebrew inscription 'surmounted by an ornate and gilded entablature which supports the niche-head that forms the receptacle for the tablets of the law, which are embedded in palm-leaves that overshadow them.'[5] Before the Ark were seats for the ministers and the wardens, and a raised platform for the choir. The acoustics were good, the newspaper reported, and so was the ventilation, which was 'severely tested on the day (a sultry one) of the inauguration, without any inconvenience arising in the synagogue from the heat in its crowded state.'[6] The house was full, holding 250 worshippers downstairs and another 150 in the gallery.

The service was described in detail: the opening prayers, the bringing in of the Scrolls which were duly placed in the Ark, the singing of the Psalms, the Royal Prayer and Professor Marks's sermon. He reviewed the history of the congregation and the motives of the founders. He spoke of the principles on which they were to conduct their new synagogue. The years of infancy were over, he explained, and they were now moving into the virile state, an epoch of existence during which the preservation of life itself was subordinate to the preservation of honour, and to the acquisition of a good repute for wisdom and beneficence. The consecration programme called the sermon an address, as distinct from a religious discourse, but the *Jewish Chronicle* could not forbear to query whether this would not have been the moment for a 'religious exhortation, instead of an account of the contentions and disputes of the past.'[7] It left it to its readers to decide. It did, however, compliment the community on the 'elegance and taste' of its new synagogue and the decorum of the service. A dinner was held in the evening at The Thatched House Tavern to which the Founders and their friends were invited. 'The company did not separate until midnight.'

The membership of the fine new synagogue was steadily increasing, and the attendance for the average Sabbath morning service was estimated at about 140 worshippers. In the Census of Worship taken in 1851, in which ministers of religion were requested to complete a form declaring membership and attendance figures, the Rev. Marks stated that West London was the only synagogue 'where an English sermon is preached on every Sabbath and Festival', which was felt to be one reason for its popularity.[8] The actual membership numbers do not appear on the form. But with the growing congregation the old concerns about decorum returned. The *Jewish Chronicle* may have praised the behaviour of the congregation when comparing it with the habits of the more orthodox communities, but within West London itself it was felt that standards were slipping. So the committee asked the beadle to prepare some printed cards to be handed to late-comers requesting them in future to present themselves before the start of the service. However, members were not slow to complain if they felt themselves to have been unfairly treated. One congregant was stopped by a policeman when he arrived on a Sabbath morning at noon. He was told that he might not enter. He asked permission to wait in the vestibule until the sermon was finished, was refused and told to wait in the street, in spite of the 'appearance of rain'. He did not hesitate to address a strong letter to the chairman.

Some congregants felt that that the Council should take into consideration the means of 'avoiding the impropriety of introducing unsuitable music' into the service, so Mr. Hart, the choirmaster, met the Council and it was agreed that all new compositions should be heard and approved by the Wardens. Other problems arose, as they might with any growing organisation of the kind: there were difficulties with the undertaker (one member refused on his deathbed to be buried by the current holder of the post) and changes had to be made. One member married under the auspices of the Church of England and was found – according to the Minutes of the Wardens - to have virtually separated himself from the congregation and therefore could no longer be considered a seat-renter (i.e. a member – all members were termed seat-renters, no-one who did not pay for a seat could be a member). Those non-members who applied to be married in the synagogue were tactfully informed that it was customary to make an offering to the funds of the synagogue.

In 1851 the Rev. Lowy informed the Council that he was proposing to be married to Miss Gertrude Lindenthal. She was the daughter of the Secretary and Assistant Rabbi at the New Synagogue in Great St. Helens and he asked if the Council would permit his future father-in-law to marry the couple. The Wardens of the New Synagogue had consented to allow this unusual task for an orthodox Rabbi (who told the bridegroom that he was 'always agreeable to compromise') and as West London also gave their permission, the wedding went ahead at the Margaret Street synagogue. Rev. Lowy also explained that he would like to extend and improve his home within the synagogue buildings. So Mr.Cohen, the Beadle, was told he would have to 'remove from his rooms' and find alternative accommodation. He was compensated with an additional £25 p.a. for 'lodging and coals' and the Rev. Lowy and his new wife moved in. He was presented by the Council with a 'purse' of £176.2d. to which were added six guineas from the members, and he expressed his 'deep sense of thankfulness for the liberality evinced by the Congregation'. However before very long he found himself fallen on hard times (they had eventually nine children) and had to ask for an increase in salary to avoid 'difficulties that are adverse to the position of a Minister of the West London Synagogue.'[9]

Relations with the wider Jewish community were still not on an entirely friendly footing. The Hon. Secretary of the newly founded Jews College wrote asking for a list of the names and addresses of West London members so that they might be circulated with news of the College (presumably to ask for funds). The Council replied in a rather starchy tone that as they had not been invited to the meeting at which the plan for the College was decided, they 'would be going beyond the limit of their function' in allowing such a list to be forwarded.

The Board of Deputies was already under some criticism for the autocratic way in which it ran its affairs. Elections were secret, the President (Sir Moses Montefiore) had a final vote and the Deputies were without exception from an elite class of wealthy Londoners. Only two represented provincial synagogues and they both lived in London. In the triennial elections of 1853, four deputies were elected to represent the provinces and they not only lived in London but were also members of West London Synagogue. The Secretary of the Board, Henry Harris, wrote an irate letter to the Synagogue Council, protesting that West London should not have allowed any of its members to stand for election as deputies for provincial synagogues, as by so doing they infringed the Board's decision not to recognise Margaret Street as a Jewish synagogue. The fact that the four also belonged to an orthodox synagogue did not recompense them for belonging to a Reform one as well. When the results of the election were known (three of the four were present) the meeting ended in uproar and the police had to be called. A special meeting was arranged to deal with the matter; the West London members, asked to withdraw whilst their eligibility to stand was queried, firmly refused. West London felt that its integrity as a synagogue and as a part of the London Jewish community was being challenged. The problem lay in the extent to which the religious authorities could control the Board. 'Was the Board a religious assembly or was it a secular one and only under the guidance of its ecclesiastical authorities when it was dealing with religious matters?'[10] The motion put before the Board to exclude the four Reform deputies resulted in a tie and Sir Moses gave his casting vote against them. Some deputies resigned and the numbers fell considerably three years later when elections were held again. It took another twenty years and the end of Sir Moses's presidency before West London was allowed to be represented and to hold marriage certification, and even then its own Council was unwilling to be a party to a religious authority with which it could not agree.

In 1858 Professor Marks wrote to the Council to raise the possibility of an organ being installed at Margaret Street. There had not been room for one at Burton Street, though it is possible that a small harmonium had been in use there in its days as a socialist chapel and it may have been played during the early services there. But now the splendid new synagogue would, it was felt, benefit from such an instrument to 'increase the impressiveness of the service.'[11] A separate account was set up to handle the expenditure involved in the purchase of the organ and the necessary alterations which would be needed to the building. A sum of £750 was estimated to cover the cost. A committee of five members was set up. Among them were John Simon and

Charles Kensington Salaman. John Simon (later Sir John) had been involved with the Reform movement in this country since its inception. Born in Jamaica, Simon was sent to England to study law, arriving in Liverpool as a young student. He was taken under the wing of David Marks, whose ideas he found congenial and whom he followed to the West London Synagogue as soon as it was established. Simon went on to study for the bar and was only the second Jew to be called (Francis Goldsmid was the first). He was much involved in the fight for Jewish emancipation and worked all his life for the betterment of Jews wherever in the world they met oppression. He had married Rachel Salaman, sister of Charles (who married Simon's sister Frances). After that of the Rev. Marks (he had married Cecelia Woolf in 1842), Simon's wedding was the first to be celebrated at the West London Synagogue – after the necessary certificate had been obtained in a civil ceremony.

Charles Salaman, who had become a member of West London in the Burton Street days, was a distinguished pianist and composer. He had trained under Charles Neate, a close friend of Beethoven, and was elected to the Royal Academy of Music at the age of ten. He set many poems – written in English, Latin, Italian and Hebrew - to music, and spent some time in Rome, conducting the first performance of a Beethoven symphony there; he was present in 1847 at the removal of the gates of the old ghetto. He founded the Musical Society of London and the first amateur choral society in England. At West London – he had always been interested in the Reform movement – he composed a setting of the 84th Psalm for the Margaret Street consecration service and several of his musical settings are used in synagogue services to this day, his setting of Psalm 100 being particularly popular at weddings. He was also the author of *Jews As They Are,* published in 1885, an interesting account of Jewish life in England.

In order to accommodate an organ, part of the ladies' gallery had to be altered, and as some repairs on the synagogue were needed anyway, it was decided to undertake the whole work at the same time. The organ was ordered from Gray and Davison, a long-established firm of organ builders. They had installed magnificent pipe-organs in churches and cathedrals all over the country, including Eton Chapel, St. Giles Church in London and the drawing room of Buckingham Palace. After the alterations were finished and the organ was working well the synagogue was reconsecrated in September 1859, but the next difficulty lay in finding an organist. The very fact that this was the first synagogue in Britain to have an organ, meant that no Jewish musician had any experience in playing an organ for use in Jewish services. The organ committee reported to the Council that in spite of advertising in the *Jewish Chronicle* and in the foreign Jewish press, no Jewish organist could be found. However, in Charles Verrinder (not a Jew) the West London Synagogue was fortunate enough to find an organist of the highest calibre, and the committee 'was very satisfied with his talents as well as with his exemplary conduct in the synagogue'.[12] After a trial period of six months on a salary of £50 p.a.,

Verrinder was given a permanent appointment at £80 p.a. He was given 'the entire and undivided control of the choir which must submit to his direction and attend rehearsals at his discretion.'[13] Verrinder always tried to find music that counted as Jewish, even if composed by a non-Jew. He often played music derived from Biblical themes, such as those by Mendelssohn, Handel or Meyerbeer.

Charles Verrinder was a remarkable man and a distinguished organist and composer. The West London Synagogue still uses many of the melodies he composed for the services. He gained his Doctorate of Music at Cambridge and went on to become organist at several important churches, became head of the Hebrew Choral Association, having taught himself Hebrew in order to become familiar with the services, and played the organ at West London for forty-five years. Among his most loved settings to the prayers were *aneh ani* on the Day of Atonement, *barechi nafshi* (Psalm 103) and *esah enai* (Psalm 121); one particular melody is still known as the Verrinder *adon olam*.

The choir wore gowns, hats and white bands for services and had to take their place a quarter of an hour before the service started. It was also felt appropriate to install a railing between the choir and the ladies' gallery. Additional singers joined the choir for the festival services, but it was not always easy to find adequate male voices. So three ladies joined the choir, but 'their attendance left much to be desired.'[14] Charles Salaman was asked to have the scores conveniently bound and the music was kept in the charge of the organist. One further problem was to find a man to blow the organ pipes. This was solved by installing a hydraulic engine for working the bellows. It was agreed that the West London Synagogue should have free use of all of Charles Kensington Salaman's compositions and of his musical adaptations, but that he should retain the copyright. A complete collection of the music for the synagogue was published in four volumes by Novello and Co. in about 1892, '*The Ancient Melodies Harmonised and the whole Arranged with Obbligato Organ Accompaniment.*'[15]

The Margaret Street organ was the first to be installed in any synagogue in this country, although some Reform synagogues in Germany were starting to use one. In 1836 at a meeting at Bevis Marks when Moses Mocatta had made proposals for change not unlike those adopted by West London, he had suggested the installation of an organ to aid improvements in decorum, but the authorities refused to consider it. There has been much debate about the use of the organ in Jewish religious services. It is known that in ancient times the organ was a part of Jewish musical life. A form of the instrument had been used in the Temple but its use on the Sabbath in later times was felt to contravene the laws on Sabbath behaviour (the playing of an instrument) and the traditional mourning for the destruction of the temple. Many orthodox communities viewed it as being too close to Christian forms of worship, while some Christians felt it was too pagan (or even too Jewish!) for their use. In some synagogues a harmonium was permitted for use at weddings and special occasions, but the English Reform movement was trying to turn away from the ghetto ambience of their forefathers and introduce a more culturally enlightened quality to their worship. In his article on Organs and Organ Music in *Christianity and Judaism*, Walter Hillsman maintains that Reform leaders seized on Western art music as a means of 'introducing an atmosphere of Western-style decorum into Sabbath and festival services, and thus of appealing to sophisticated contemporary Jews.'[16] Professor Marks himself, in his sermon when the Margaret Street organ was consecrated, had referred to the frequent mention of musical instruments in the Psalms in connection with prayer. The Margaret Street organ was used to play opening and closing voluntaries and the music sung by the choir. The congregation did not join in until much later in its development.

Another interesting part of synagogue life at Margaret Street was the Bar Mitzvah ceremony. It was always referred to as 'confirmation' (in accordance with the preferred use of English rather than Hebrew for ceremonies, festivals and Jewish events – Sabbath for *Shabbat*, Pentecost for *Shavuot*, New Year for *Rosh Hashanah*, etc.) and it was the first such ceremony in this country available for girls as well as boys. The *Jewish Chronicle*, by now fully accepting the arrival of the Reform synagogue, whether or not it agreed with its practices, described the day in full. There were ten children involved, six boys and four girls, and the occasion took place in October, 1860, New Year's Day. 'This interesting ceremony took place after the reading of the Law, with the young people ranged around the semi-circular steps of the Ark. Having been examined in the leading tenets of their faith, to which they responded admirably well, they united in an appropriate prayer invoking the blessing and protection of their Almighty Father. The address on the occasion by the Rev. Professor Marks, was even more than usually impressive and affecting, in consequence no doubt of the fact that two of his own children were among the confirmands. This was followed by the harmony of a well-trained choir and the solemn tones of the organ.'[17] It is interesting that no mention is made of the children reading from the *Sefer Torah* or taking any part of the service, as is in common use today. It was quite usual for such ceremonies to take place on the Festivals, though not of course on *Yom Kippur*. The occasion to mark the formal welcome of a young person into Jewish life was to trouble West London on many occasions in the future. However, one visitor to a confirmation service was most impressed. He wrote to the *Jewish Chronicle* to say so. 'This synagogue is the only one in London in which the stranger is at all times readily, freely and courteously admitted, who feels a yearning to go to the house of worship, to commune with his God, and pour forth his heartfelt prayer on the sacred spot.'[18]

CHAPTER III

Upper Berkeley Street

The synagogue in Margaret Street had been in use for only about twelve years when the first suggestions were put forward that the congregation was outgrowing its space. Although there was no indication that the Council was seriously thinking of another move, it did divert £600 into an Accumulating Fund for 'the enlargement of the synagogue or for the erection of a new synagogue.'[1] The idea was that when the debt incurred for the building of Margaret Street was extinguished all surplus income should go into this Fund. It would seem that either the founding fathers of the new and expensive synagogue were very short-sighted when planning the move away from Burton Street, or the increase in membership had taken them by surprise. Twelve years is a very short time for a place of public worship, purpose-built for a wealthy community, to endure before a change becomes necessary. When the congregation did move to Upper Berkeley Street in 1870, it did not make the same mistake again.

Another important move made by the Council of the West London Synagogue was to inaugurate a scheme for training young men for the ministry. Professor Marks's health was giving some cause for anxiety and he was advised by his doctors to take a three months' break. Although Rev. Lowy was more than capable of leading the community in his absence, it was felt that there were no young rabbis coming along to help out and perhaps eventually to take over the reins. The newly founded Jews College was firmly entrenched in the orthodox side of Anglo-Jewry and would probably not have accepted for training any young man whose inclinations were towards Reform. The first student to enrol under the new West London auspices was Philip (later Sir Philip) Magnus. Philip, the son of Jacob and Caroline Magnus, attended University College School, in preparation for entry to University College, London. The school's curriculum offered a wide range of subjects in the humanities and in science, unusual for that time. It was also founded to enable Jewish and Non-Conformist children to be well educated at a reasonable cost. At University College Philip graduated with a first in arts and the following year took another first in science. He frequently attended the West London Synagogue which he found very much to his liking in its attitude to Jewish Reform and its modern approach to Jewish life. With the encouragement, and some financial support, of the Synagogue's Council he studied for the rabbinate in Berlin at the Reform seminary, returning to London from time to time and preaching in the synagogue. He came

back for good in 1866, when he was offered the post of Assistant Rabbi at
Margaret Street.

Philip Magnus stayed with the West London Synagogue for fourteen years,
taking on some private tutoring and lecturing at University College. In 1870
he married Katie Emanuel, writing to the Council, 'I have every reason to
believe that my alliance with that young lady will render me in various ways
more serviceable to the congregation and I therefore trust that it will receive
your sanction and approval.' He asked for a rise in salary. In 1880 he was
appointed director and organising secretary of the new City and Guilds of
London Institute for the Advancement of Technical Education. He published
several works on science and technology and was in the forefront of the
establishment of Imperial College; he was acknowledged to be the leading
authority on technical education, later representing London University as an
MP. He was created a baronet in 1917, and although not a Zionist was very
proud of being a Jew. He helped to see the West London Synagogue through
its early days in its third synagogue, Upper Berkeley Street, later serving as
Warden, and was one of its first representatives on the Board of Deputies when
the congregation finally gained membership. Lady Magnus was a writer and
historian; her *Outlines of Jewish History* is still enjoyed today.

West London, as the first Reform synagogue in Britain, was followed in 1856
by a synagogue in Manchester, calling itself the Manchester Congregation of
British Jews, but apart from a small group in Hull who followed the Reform
ritual, the Reform movement as a whole was slow to spread. When problems
arose regarding ritual or social matters, Margaret Street was approached for
a ruling. Thus, in 1862 when it was learnt that a Manchester congregant's
wife, who was a convert to Judaism, had been refused the services of an
orthodox mohel to circumcise their son, West London wrote to Manchester
regretting the Chief Rabbi's decision to refuse 'as it furnishes a fresh proof of
his determination to persist in a line of conduct, of which the wisdom of the
past might well have induced him to question.'[2] They then sent a mohel from
their own congregation.

Another problem, this time respecting ritual, demanded a Special General
Meeting to decide. Professor Marks had suggested to the Council that evening
prayers after the end of the *Yom Kippur* service should be abolished. Few
congregants stayed to hear these prayers after a long day in the synagogue.
At the meeting several of the 'old guard' who fought zealously for as much
of the former Order of Prayer as they could, refused to agree to the change so
the matter was postponed for a later decision. Other difficulties were arising
with the music in the services. The Music Committee was dissatisfied with the
choir. Attendances were poor, some choristers turned up late or did not turn
up at all for rehearsals. The congregation, which was now asked to join in the
singing, did so reluctantly and Charles Salaman felt that Mr. Hart, who had
been in charge of the choir since Burton Street days, was 'utterly inefficient'.
Rather than being summarily dismissed from his post he was allowed to

work out six months' notice after being asked to leave. Charles Verrinder, the organist, who was all that any committee in charge of the music could desire, agreed to take over the running of the choir and his salary was increased accordingly.

By the beginning of 1863, the planning committee looking into the possibility of new premises was investigating the leases of the adjoining premises to see if the building might be expanded by buying up or renting the surrounding land. The debt on the building was gradually being paid off and it seemed that it might soon be possible to accommodate comfortably a larger congregation on Sabbaths and Festivals. Towards the end of the year the synagogue was approached by the North London Railway Co. to take over a portion of the burial ground at Balls Pond Road. The company was asked to submit plans and measurements. If it were possible to come to some arrangement this might produce a very useful source of income for any new premises that could be found. The synagogue's architect, Mr. Young, together with the advice of David Mocatta, was looking into the possibilities offered by the old barracks building in Portman Street. They were no longer required by the guards regiments which had occupied them and were in a bad state of repair. The architect reported that they could be made available at a rental of £500 a year. He was also looking at a site in Montagu Street but decided the space was too small.

Another reason for thinking ahead was the situation concerning the adjoining property where Rev. Marks and his family lived. He wrote to the Council asking if he might make a move, as he felt the house was becoming 'injurious to his children on account of offensive smells.' The porch was apparently over a cesspool, his doctor's bills were high and he felt he could never have a clean bill of health while he lived there. 'Margaret Street', he added, 'has become a focus of the lowest indecency and vice. In the hottest weather I am forced to have every window in my house closed from nightfall in consequence of the scenes of prostitution that take place, and the revolting language trumpeted forth by the degraded women who come out in companies from the public house at the corner of the street. My daughters who are now growing to womanhood are most sensitive to the annoyance.'[3]

A committee of the three wardens, together with David Mocatta and Jacob Elkin, was asked to take the matter a stage further. In December 1865 Daniel Mocatta, the synagogue's first chairman, died at the age of 92. Daniel, the son of Abraham Lumbrozo de Mattos (the name was changed to Mocatta in the eighteenth century), could trace his family in England back to the time of Oliver Cromwell. Daniel, like many of the Mocattas, had played an important part in the affairs of the Bevis Marks synagogue, and had been Parnas Presidente, the congregation's president. Some years before the schism which led to the foundation of the West London Synagogue, Daniel had tried to persuade his fellow Sephardim to introduce reforms at Bevis Marks, including the introduction of a choir, improved decorum and English sermons, but when his proposals achieved no result, he joined the 'seceders' in establishing the new Reform Synagogue.

At the beginning of 1866 Sir Francis Goldsmid, the new chairman, told the Council rather mysteriously that he had 'obtained information about a new site in an eligible situation,'[4] and that enquiries were being pursued. These enquiries must have been somewhat difficult, because it took nearly three years before the Building Committee was able to present its report. It told the Council that it had found a plot of land consisting of one house in Upper Berkeley Street, near Marble Arch, and four houses in Adam Street West (now Seymour Place) with some ground behind them, available from the Portman Estates at an annual rent of £550 for 99 years from 1872. Negotiations had indeed been difficult 'rendering imperative great perseverance on behalf of your solicitors.'[5] Four designs were obtained for the building and after considerable examination and a report from the synagogue's Consulting Architect, Mr. P. G. Hardwick, the designs of Messrs. Davis & Emanuel were chosen. The announcement of the new scheme appeared in *The Builder* on 13th July 1867 to the effect that a 'select competition' had been held to find the right architect and five firms had applied. As well as David & Emanuel three other firms - Mr. C.R. Cockerell, Mr. H.H. Collins and Mr. Wyatt Papworth - presented a design. The unsuccessful candidates received an honorarium of 50 guineas each, and Mr. P.G. Hardwick acted as Consulting Architect.

Unfortunately this announcement provoked a hurt reply from one of the unsuccessful candidates, Mr. Henry Herbert Collins. On 3rd August, *The Builder* published a letter from him. 'Permit me in justice to myself and other unsuccessful competitors,' he wrote, 'to correct a statement appearing in your journal of three weeks ago.' He claimed that Mr. Hardwick was *not* consulted nor did his opinion guide the committee. 'I competed,' he went on, 'solely under the belief that the inferential obligation as conveyed in the instructions to architects would have been fulfilled by the committee, and that Mr. Hardwick's well known ability and impartial judgment would at least have guided, if not determined, the ultimate solution.'[6] The editor added a footnote to the effect that the statement that Mr. Hardwick had been consulted came from the committee. The successful architects, David & Emanuel, followed this up with their own letter, confirming that Mr. Collins' statement was quite erroneous, that Mr. Hardwick had been away but immediately upon his return they had met and he had given authority to state that he was indeed consulted and had reported his advice to the committee. The architects also had the permission of the committee to state that Mr. Hardwick's report was considered and was mainly instrumental in its ultimate decision. Mr. Collins' letter was also printed in the *Jewish Chronicle*, where he stated that there had been no free competition for the design of the new synagogue and that the selection was made by the judgment of the committee and council only. No reply was printed.

Davis & Emanuel were distinguished architects who had set up an independent practice in the City. Both Henry David Davis and Barrow Emanuel were members of the West London Synagogue, Emanuel being the brother of Katie Magnus, wife of Philip Magnus. So although both men were young (in their twenties) and their experience lay mainly in commercial work, offices, banks and warehouses in the city and the East End, it seemed sensible to keep the designs for the new synagogue 'in the family'. In fact, although the new West London Synagogue was their first commission for a religious building, they later went on to build the East London Synagogue at Stepney Green and the Sephardi synagogue at Lauderdale Road, and the Romanesque chapel at the Jewish cemetery at Hoop Lane, Golders Green, as well as the City of London School.

Lord Portman's surveyor refused to sanction the plans unless the main building was removed to a certain distance from the rear of the houses in Upper Berkeley Street. So the committee was compelled to take a piece of ground to the north at the rear of another house in Adam Street West, with the reversion of that house in 1901, at a further annual sum of £50, making a total rental in all of £600. It was also felt that the entrance should be widened, so another house in Upper Berkeley Street was added to the lease. Lord Portman demanded a £1000 fine for this and yet another £100 was paid for a narrow strip of land, five feet wide (it still exists), to the north to secure exclusive rights within that distance of the main hall.

An estimate from the architects for the approximate cost of the building was obtained, and this proved to be greatly in excess of the sum the Council had envisaged, but they managed to reduce it by postponing the planned entrance elevation. It still amounted to some £17,000, even before precise tenders were available. The sum available in the Building Fund fell short of what was needed by some £9,000, and no account had been taken of the cost of furniture and fittings or the new organ. It was decided to raise the extra sum needed by means of loans from members, whose names would be inscribed in a book. Interest would be 4%. The tender of Messrs G. Myers & Sons was accepted in the sum of £9,532 for the main building which they expected to complete by the summer of 1870. However, such were the difficulties in gaining possession of the houses, some of which had to be demolished, that the Committee anticipated having to extend the time of the opening, though it still hoped to open in time for the High Holydays of that year.

It was clear that the London Jewish community was very interested to know how the new project was coming along, as the *Jewish Chronicle* published in May a progress report, giving its readers a glimpse of the splendid interior of the new synagogue. 'It promises to mark a new era in synagogue architecture,' it wrote, 'if one may judge by what it will be in a few months hence. The vaulted and domed roof, which is just completed and which is very lofty, is carried on shafts of polished red Devon marble, having on the upper part of the shafts clustered colonettes of marble with the capitals richly carved with Byzantine foliage.'[7] The synagogue would be able to seat one thousand worshippers, five hundred downstairs and five hundred in the galleries. There was a large space for the organ chamber at the east end behind the Ark, separated from the body of the synagogue by an ornamental and gilded iron screen. The Ark, reading desk and pulpit were to be of coloured inlaid marble, and the tablets of the Law of gold mosaic.

On 23rd June the Foundation Stone was laid. The Building Committee had decided that it would not be appropriate to hold any sort of elaborate ceremony for this as the construction work was fully under way and the interior resembled a building site, which was exactly what it was. So a private ceremony was held in the presence of the ministers, the Building Committee and the architects to lay the stone in the foundations of the Ark. Under the stone was placed a glass bottle containing a set of new coins of the realm, copies of *The Times*, the *Jewish Chronicle* and the *Jewish Record*, a fragment of the ancient walls of the temple of Jerusalem and a parchment scroll, bearing the words:

> This scroll doth bear record that on Thursday, June 23rd, 1870 (corresponding with Jewish reckoning 24th Day of Sivan 5630), the stone was laid over which is to be erected the Ark of the new synagogue in Upper Berkeley Street, Edgware Road, London. This is the third Temple of Prayer raised by the West London Synagogue of British Jews since the origin of the congregation in January 1842, officers for the time being: Sir F.H. Goldsmid, Bart., M.P., Chairman of the Council of Founders; George Barnet, Esq., Chairman of the Building Committee; Simon W. Waley, Leopold Schloss, David Mocatta, Wardens; Frederick G. Henriques, Jacob Mocatta, Treasurers; Rev. D.W. Marks, Rev. Albert Lowy, Rev. Philip Magnus, Ministers; Jacob L. Elkin, Secretary; Davis & Emanuel, Architects; George Myers & Sons, Contractors.

Professor Marks said that although the Committee had resolved that this was not a religious occasion, he could not refrain from invoking the blessings of Providence on the congregation and on the holy work of the day.

But the Jews of London had long memories. They had not forgotten the hurt caused on both sides by the schism of 1840 and many felt that the occasion of the building of such a splendid new place of worship was a suitable time to forget and forgive. On 22nd July the *Jewish Chronicle* published a letter signed 'Nemo' which the editor prefaced with the heading 'A ROAD TO RECONCILIATION', which suggested that just such an armistice might now be introduced. As it happened most parties to the dispute were now not only on speaking terms with their opponents but were perfectly friendly, socially and religiously, even if they agreed to go their own ways. Many were after all members of the same families and felt that a continued state of enmity had no benefit for anyone. 'Nemo' explained in his letter that he wrote in peace, 'free from malice or extenuation'. He felt that the Jewish community had changed entirely, inaugurating changes 'at which our fathers would have stood perfectly aghast.' Individual enmity between the several congregations, 'shoolism' as he termed it, was in general a thing of the past. The Chief Rabbi (now the Rev. Nathan Adler) had presided over many changes and metropolitan synagogues were not what they were thirty years before. He laid some blame on the reformers who treated their opponents with scorn. Using the word 'conservative' rather than 'orthodox' he asked for both parties to meet half way, and then made a suggestion which in the opinion of both sides was quite impossible, namely, 'Let Margaret Street invite the Chief Rabbi to inaugurate their new synagogue.' He felt that the matter should be decided by the lay leaders not the clergy. 'Now is the time, let us seize it.'

The replies came in thick and fast. One correspondent felt particularly aggrieved at the abolition by the Reform movement of the second day of Festivals. He explained that he was a relative of the editor of the new prayer book, who although a fine Hebrew scholar, had no authority to make such changes. He confessed to a weakness for the organ, but maintained that no one could expect Chief Rabbi Adler to inaugurate the new synagogue, though if the Reformers ceded the argument about the second day, then 'the other points could be yielded by the other side.' The writer of the letter had the courage to sign his own name, H. Guedalla. Haim Guedalla came from an old Sephardi family, a distinguished member of Bevis Marks Synagogue and a cousin of Sir Moses Montefiore. He had tried over the years to act as a mediator in the conflict over the Reform movement, with little success, though he had been largely instrumental in having the *cherem* removed from the West London Synagogue. He was much involved with the Jewish Press in this country.

The arguments in the press rambled on and in the issue of 16th September 'Nemo' replied to his critics. He regretted the loss to the 'conservative' community of men such as the Goldmids, the Mocattas and the Henriques's, insisting that the split that undoubtedly existed was not ignored nor glossed over. One correspondent had suggested that the Reform differences should be treated in the same way as those between the Ashkenazim and the Sephardim, but Nemo felt that although those differences were quite trivial the rift created by the 'seceders' struck at the very foundations of Jewish polity. 'It is a self-adjusted system, adopted at the whim and fancy of men having little or no knowledge of traditional Judaism'. He appreciated the integrity of the Founders of the Reform movement and the 'cruel obstinacy' of those who fought against them, but fulminated against the 'self-constituted authority' that members of the West London Synagogue believed in. His suggestion that the Chief Rabbi should inaugurate the new synagogue had been met with total disapproval on both sides, much to his disappointment. 'The grief is mine,' he wrote, 'the fault must rest with those who possessed the power of promoting Reconciliation and yet stood aside with folded arms.'

Meanwhile preparations for the consecration were going ahead, the Building Committee reporting to the Council at regular intervals on the progress of the construction work. It was still concerned about the ever-increasing costs, but decided not to raise seat rentals, preferring instead to institute a fourth tier of payments at £3 so that more congregants would have a say in the running of the synagogue, and additional members might be encouraged to join. Some of the costs were offset by generous gifts from members; the Ladies Committee presented velvet covers for the scrolls, and other gifts included stained glass windows for the western gallery and curtains for the Ark. The subject of who was to be invited to be present at the consecration was a thorny one. After some debate it was decided to invite the Chief Rabbis of both the German and the Portuguese synagogues (Rev. Nathan Adler and the Rev. Benjamin Artom), and the Ministers and Honorary Officers of all the London synagogues. The Haham was courteous in his reply to the Council but felt 'I cannot avail myself of their kind attention.' Also invited was Sir Moses Montefiore. It was a personal invitation from Simon Waley, the Senior Warden. Sir Moses, much involved with events abroad, replied cautiously. He expressed a sincere and deep anxiety for the unity of the Jews in this country, wishing to see that unity restored before the day of consecration, and that he and his brother (Horatio), with Dr. Adler the Chief Rabbi, might accomplish the object he had at heart. He didn't come.

The consecration of the West London Synagogue in Upper Berkeley Street took place on 23rd September, 1870. The Council must have been a little apprehensive as they had had little chance to try out the new building's acoustics (which proved to be a problem), or to discover whether a large crowd of worshippers would be comfortable and warm, but not too hot, in their new surroundings. The *Jewish Chronicle* gave a very full account of the proceedings, describing the building as 'magnificent – a monument of architectural ability and artistic taste'[8]. The three ministers, Professor Marks, the Rev. Lowy and the Rev. Magnus, all took part, and the choir, by now highly trained and obedient to the high standards set by Mr. Verrinder, contributed in no small measure to the success of the service. There was particular mention in the press report of 'the beauty of the voices of several young ladies, whose melodious strains were blended with – and graced the stronger tones of the less gentle choristers.'[9] The service began at 3 pm, the organ playing as the congregants took their places. The Ministers walked down the aisle, Rev. Marks carrying the *Sefer Torah* in his arms, while the organ played a specially commissioned setting of the 118th Psalm, 'Open unto me the gates of righteousness that I may enter through them and praise the Lord.' They processed three times around the synagogue, the Ark was opened and the scroll deposited within, while the organ continued with Psalm 24. Mr. Verrinder had chosen a setting of this Psalm by Julius Mombach. Mombach, whose arrangements for many traditional Jewish songs and synagogue music are used today, was a German composer who settled in London and became Choir Master of the Great Synagogue. Although he was much involved in the Ashkenazi tradition, and known internationally as a distinguished Chazan, his music is frequently a feature of Sephardi as well as Ashkenazi services. A special prayer for the occasion was read by Rev. Lowy, followed by the prayer for the Royal Family, and then the address.

Professor Marks took as his text the familiar verse from Chronicles 28, 'David said to Solomon, his son, Be firm, have courage, be not afraid for the Lord God, even my God, will be with thee.' It was a public address, rather than a homily, an encouragement to the congregation who had come so far to pursue 'the road which you have chosen.' He went on to remind his listeners of the momentous thirty years since the synagogue came into being, a time which had seen so many changes, 'vital improvements in education, advantages secured for the Jews, prejudices combatted, antipathies subdued, one manner of exclusion after another has bowed down before the advent of the apostle of modern civilisation'.[10] He recalled the cold withering formalism of thirty years before, and congratulated the congregation on the success they had so far attained. Then the choir sang the 84th Psalm to music by Charles Salaman. Many orthodox Jews were present on the occasion, including several of the Rothschild family, Professor Jacob Waley, and Sir David Salamons (London's first Jewish Lord Mayor).

On the day of the consecration more than £1000 was donated to the Building Fund. However, once the High Holyday services were over, shortly after the consecration, this extra money was much appreciated as several problems had arisen, brought to light by these important services, with so many congregants present. The question of the position of the high pulpit was troubling the committee. Those seated on the same side could not hear the preacher, so a model was made and placed in front of the Ark to test if this was better. But the improvement this made to the acoustics was far outweighed by the detriment it caused to the appearance of the Ark. It was also felt that the donor of the Ark would be very upset by such a change. So it was agreed to consult with the architect to see if some improvement could be found. The pulpit is hardly ever used today for preaching. The steps to it are very narrow and it is difficult to hear the speaker clearly. In the early days the *bimah* was in the centre of the synagogue, so that the reader faced the Ark, but in 1897 it was moved towards the Ark, where it is today, giving room for 96 more seats.

After all outgoings had been met (some £24,000 in all) the synagogue had a deficit of about £2,000. To meet this there was still available the value of the remaining lease of the Margaret Street synagogue. The premises were to be put up for auction with a reserve of £3,000. The Council also suggested that an honorarium of 100 guineas should go to the committee's Hon. Secretary Jacob Elkin for all his work over the previous four years, and that the Building Committee should continue to act until the next Annual General Meeting.

A year later the Committee reconvened and asked its architects, David & Emanuel to prepare plans for some additional office space next to the Council Room. They came up with a plan for a wooden structure to be erected over the vestibule, but the Committee felt that this would not be acceptable to the District Surveyor, and that they should try (not for the first time) to negotiate with the tenant of 33 Upper Berkeley Street to acquire the lease. Difficulties were now arising between the Portman Estate and the synagogue's Trustees as to the latters' rights concerning the land around the building. A proposal had been put forward to Lord Portman for a factory to be built on the north side 'without any limit to height, which would interfere with light and affect the quiet enjoyment originally stipulated'.[11] Mr. Hesketh, Lord Portman's surveyor, denied that the Trustees' agreement had rights of access to the back entrance and the coal shoot, and maintained that the plans for the building had never been sanctioned by Mr. Hardwick. Sadly Philip Hardwick had died shortly after the opening of Upper Berkeley Street, his practice being taken over by his son, also Philip, so he could not give evidence. But he had been unwell for some time and his son was fully aware of the circumstances. It was decided to take Counsel's opinion. Henry Cotton, Q.C., later an Appeal Court Judge, gave it as his advice that the plans for the synagogue had been approved, that the Trust had the power to prevent the erection of any buildings on the west side and also of 'any buildings on the north side that would interfere with light and amenities'. He also suggested that litigation should be avoided, no lease being in existence.

David Mocatta was asked to meet Mr. Hesketh, but felt that any such meeting was really a matter for the Trustees. They duly met Lord Portman's surveyor, but he maintained that any buildings on the west side were strictly within Lord Portman's legal rights. He also informed them that a new public road was to be made leading from Edgware Road to Upper George Street by which the side entrance to the synagogue would be kept entirely free and open. He insisted on the Estate's right to build on the north side (up to the five foot strip) but did add that he wished to interfere as little as possible with the light and air. He asked the synagogue's architects to provide plans of that section of the synagogue showing the under part and the full width of the gallery, promising to communicate with the Trustees before any plans were agreed. He also denied that Mr. Hardwick had approved the original plans – there was no indication of his approval on the plans themselves. The Trustees informed him that they reserved the right to take any measures that they thought fit to resolve the problem.

The synagogue offered to put in order the four houses (at present very dilapidated) in Adam Street West and create an entrance from the passage between them. The rental from the four would amount to about £240 p.a., and the cottage at the rear of one of them could be pulled down and the site used for enlarging the Ministers' robing room. Lord Portman's solicitors were informed. The synagogue was finding its relationship with the Estate extremely difficult. Finally Julian Goldsmid took the matter into his own hands and went straight to Lord Portman's son. Julian Goldsmid, later Sir Julian, was the son of Frederick Goldsmid, a founder member of the West London Synagogue, and like other members of his family had been educated at University College. He was called to the Bar but had relinquished his legal career when he was elected to the House of Commons, first as Member for Honiton and later for Rochester. He had been a Warden of the synagogue and was a member of the Council.

William Portman agreed that the Trustees were perfectly correct in their assessment of the situation and that he would instruct Mr. Hesketh accordingly. On further investigation he discovered that Mr. Hesketh had apparently let the piece of ground at the back (for which the congregation had already paid £100) and this too would be sorted out.

In December, 1870, there appeared in the *Jewish Chronicle* an advertisement from Edward and Henry Lumley, Land Agents and Auctioneers, advising that they had been instructed to dispose of an extensive property which might be adapted for manufacturing or trading firms in a large way of business such as brewers, organ builders, carriage makers, billiard table manufacturers, upholsterers and others for showrooms. It would be suitable for a proprietary chapel or for the use of any religious community requiring a suitable property for public worship whose use might include the music of a full-toned organ. 'There is the principal building, a lofty, well-lit and ventilated hall nearly 50 feet square with galleries, suitable approaches, lobbies and appurtenances, fitted with seats to accommodate more than 100 congregants; a sweet-toned powerful organ by Gray and Davison, a choir loft, etc. There are in addition a spacious boardroom and two dwelling houses with a 48ft frontage to Margaret Street, including the attractive portico entrance to the hall.'[12] It seemed likely that the beautiful purpose-built home of the West London Synagogue might become a centre for billiards or beer. In fact the lease was taken by an upholsterer. Because he was an alien and 'the business of an upholsterer is a hazardous one' an undertaking to apply for a licence before insurance could be taken out was insisted upon.

Although it has become an integral part of almost all synagogue services today to include a reading from the prophets, the *Haftarah*, spoken in English in progressive synagogues, this was not always so. Professor Marks put forward to the Council the suggestion that West London might adopt such an amendment after it was omitted in the first Prayer Book. Inevitably another Committee was set up to deal with the matter. The Committee reported that 'having regard to general opinion that it was not desirable to make many changes to the ritual, and to avoid the service being longer, the Committee consulted the Ministers, who while being very anxious that the *Haftarah* should form part, differed as to the method.' It was therefore agreed that readings from the Prophets – according to the Sephardi pronunciation (i.e. in Hebrew) - should be included during the year 1872, but that 'future selections from the Biblical writings be made annually by the Ministers, and having been approved by the Wardens should be printed in the Table specially prepared for the use of the Congregation.'[13]. These changes would relate to the Festivals as well as the Sabbath services.

In the summer of 1871 the Emperor of Brazil, Pedro II, paid a visit to Britain. The last monarch of Brazil, he was a humane and enlightened prince, well-educated and a scholar of Hebrew. He asked specifically if he might visit a synagogue and attended a Sabbath service at the Central Synagogue in Great Portland Street. A week later he arrived unexpectedly at Upper Berkeley Street. The Friday evening service was just ending but he was warmly greeted by Professor Marks, together with the Countess d'Avigdor and George Lousada, one of the wardens. He admired the building and a scroll was unrolled for him, which he read from, a little hesitatingly, apologising for his nervousness by explaining that he was not used to reading unpointed Hebrew. He had a long chat with Professor Marks, discussing matters of Hebrew pronunciation and the history of the Jews. He was invited to return the next day for the Sabbath service, which he did, listening intently to the sermon, which did not refer to the royal guest, except when the Minister mentioned the 'power of men in high authority to confer benefits on their fellows'.[14] He congratulated Rev. Philip Magnus on his reading.

Pedro II had had a fine widespread literary education, and wrote a series of poems in a mixture of Hebrew and Provençal, including a translation of *Had Gadya* (the Passover song) under the title 'The Kid'. The *Jewish Chronicle* reported the occasion very fully, mentioning that 'the presence of a reigning monarch in a synagogue was an absolute novelty' and that no change in the service was made for the occasion and that there was 'no vulgar staring nor frivolous inattention.'[15]

Unlike modern practice the ceremony of confirmation (Bar and Bat Mitzvah) did not take place on a Sabbath morning. One reason was that because congregants could not travel on a Saturday (an ordinance followed by the Reform synagogues as well as the orthodox) the children might, on a bad day, arrive at the synagogue wet or bedraggled. West London Synagogue arranged its confirmation on one day in the year - often a Sunday - when a group of children, boys and girls, aged sixteen, would together be accepted into the Jewish community. The account of one such ceremony, described by the *Jewish Chronicle*, seems not unlike the equivalent Christian rite of first communion, though the children were older. Its reporter mentioned particularly that many Christians were present, clearly overwhelmed by the quality of the music. The day was chosen to give the pupils 'an opportunity of marking the completion of a course of religious instruction and pious training.'[16]

'The confirmands entered, each accompanied by one parent, the girls in white dresses and veiled. The opening prayers were recited in unison. The young people were then addressed by Professor Marks.'[17] Mosaism, he explained, dealt only with general broad and comprehensive principles, and the chief purpose of the instruction had been to enable them to rebut any attempts to violate the sanctuary of their faith. The boys would soon have to choose a profession. It was a religious duty to be industrious. To the girls he pointed out the value of mental culture. He then said a prayer and opened the Ark, followed by the priestly blessing. The choir sang Psalm 150. The question of the age at which boys and girls should be confirmed in the synagogue was to remain a thorny one for many years to come.

Forty years after the 'secession' had led to the establishment of the West London Synagogue, its early obedience to conventional Jewish ways was beginning to wane. The congregation's attention to orthodox practice is described in a note by a descendant of the Montefiore family, Leonard Goldsmid Montefiore, son of Claude, the Founder of the Liberal movement in this country. Related to the Goldsmid and Montefiore families, he looked back on their affiliation in an article in the *Synagogue Review*, the synagogue's own monthly journal. 'I doubt,' he wrote, ' if Sir Francis (Goldsmid) ever laid *tefillin*. I am certain as can be that my father, his nephew, never did, and when for the first time I saw Mr. Joseph Polack wearing them I wondered what on earth he had on. As for the dietary laws they were observed in a modified fashion in the Goldsmid homes... there was no rigid distinction between milk and meat. The Goldsmids all lived in very large houses, and what went on below stairs was nobody's concern and least of all the concern of visitors. If milk was served with the coffee, the orthodox guest could drink his coffee black. In the country (the Montefiores, like many of the aristocratic leaders of the Reform community, had a country home as well as a town house), I can remember biscuits and bread being removed to the gardener's cottage during Passover, but I am doubtful if the same ceremony could have been observed at Portman Square.'[18]

CHAPTER IV

Fifty Years Young

A lthough the West London Synagogue had been in existence for nearly forty years, it was still not recognised by the Board of Deputies of British Jews. Sir Moses Montefiore had been President of the Board since 1835, but when he retired due to ill-health (he was 89 years old) he was succeeded by his nephew, Joseph Mayer Montefiore, also a long-standing and active member of Bevis Marks. At about the time of Sir Moses' retirement the Portsea Synagogue (which was fully entitled to representation) elected as its Deputy Alfred Henriques, a member of the West London Synagogue and son of Joseph Henriques, a founder member. At a meeting of the Board, the question was raised as to the legality of the Portsea election, as no member of a Reform synagogue could sit as deputy. Sir Benjamin Phillips, a former Mayor of London and a distinguished member of the Jewish community, proposed a resolution to admit Henriques. There were two questions for the Board to decide, he stated. Firstly, did the Portsea congregation have a right to a seat, and secondly, did Alfred Henriques have a right to represent it. Sir Benjamin felt that the time had come when this inconsistency should end. Portsea certainly had the right to elect whoever they wished, and the member they chose sat as a private individual and did not represent a synagogue without such a right. If their choice fell on a member of a Reform synagogue, then no other such member could be rejected. The Board unanimously agreed to the resolution.

The question of whether the Board was truly representative of British Jewry did not only revolve around whom it admitted as Deputies. There were by now other organisations - the B'nai B'rith, the English Zionist Federation and the United Synagogue for example - who claimed the right to speak directly to the government of the day. The *Alliance Israelite Universelle* had been formed in 1860 to combat anti-Jewish prejudice across the world, and when it called a meeting in Paris to discuss the Mortara case[1] the Board refused to attend, though it later played a part in pressurising the British government to act. In 1876 the *Alliance* held an International Jewish Conference to discuss the attacks on Jewish communities in Turkey and Serbia. The West London Synagogue was represented at the meeting but the Board again declined the invitation stating that it would 'continue to rely on the government to look after the interests of Jews in foreign lands.'[2]

The establishment of the *Alliance* had led in 1871 to the founding in Britain of the Anglo-Jewish Association. The Franco-Prussian War had made communications with the continent difficult, and fears were expressed as to the fate of the Jews in the countries caught up in the conflict. Even before this Rev. Lowy, Minister at West London and Dr. Abraham Benisch, a fellow student of his in Germany and later editor of the *Jewish Chronicle*, had wanted to form a society in England with similar aims as the *Alliance*. Now that the latter's funds were restricted due to the war they were anxious to prevent its dissolution and established the Association with the help, particularly, of some of the wealthy members of Upper Berkeley Street. Professor Jacob Waley was the first President, with vice-presidents Sir Francis Goldsmid, Sir Julian Goldsmid, Sir George Jessel, solicitor-general, Sir David Salomons (not a member of West London, but sympathetic to the Reform movement), Mr. Reuben Sassoon and Sir John Simon. The fact that the A.J.A. was guided by so many of West London's leading members was partly due to their dissatisfaction with the organisation of the Board of Deputies, not just because it refused to grant them membership, but because it felt that Anglo-Jewish opinion was ill-served by the traditionalism and inward-looking attitudes of its members. The A.J.A. did invite the co-operation of the Board in its affairs but the reply was that 'for over one hundred years it had undertaken the cases of Jews persecuted abroad and intended continuing doing so, and thus saw no reason to cooperate.'[3]

After the retirement of Sir Moses a motion was put to the Board that members of a Reform synagogue should be permitted to become Deputies, and in December 1873 the motion was carried, with only one voice against. But the constitution of the Board, as it stood, precluded West London from representation, for it still insisted on the Chief Rabbi and the Haham being the final arbiters on matters of religion. Some of the members of West London were Deputies representing provincial synagogues. Finally the Board underwent a considerable reorganisation of its constitution though it was not until 1883 that West London was invited to send two Deputies. Under these amendments, committees (divisions) of the Board were formed to deal with specific matters, a vice-president and treasurer were appointed and the Press was admitted to Board meetings (there had been many complaints that the Board was too secretive in its affairs). But the West London Council was still unwilling to join. It felt that as no changes had been made to the circumstances which the synagogue had refused representation (the religious leadership) the proposal was 'inconsistent with the principles upon which this synagogue was founded.'[4]

Sir Julian Goldsmid wrote to Rev. Marks concerning the Board's first rule: that the Board of Deputies shall consist of the representatives of the metropolitan congregations of Jews, and other congregations having secretaries certified under the Marriage Registration Acts. 'Although West London is not certified under these Acts,' he wrote, 'it is included as it comes under the designation of a metropolitan congregation. Do you not think that this is unfair? It is very objectionable for us to agree to send Deputies when our own act is never referred to and consequently the authority under which we have proceeded is ignored.'[5] The sixth rule read: the guidance of the Board on religious matters (including all matters regarding marriages) shall remain as heretofore with the following authorities: The Ecclesiastical Authority of the United Congregations of the British Empire and those of the Sephardi Congregations of London, to whom all matters involving questions regarding religious customs and usages shall apply. Sir Julian continued, 'The proposal to invite the West London Synagogue to participate was made in the interests of peace, but surely this will create dissension, not peace.'

The West London Synagogue was now regarded as the mother congregation of the Reform movement in Britain. Apart from communities in Manchester and Bradford, other groups were considering allying themselves to the movement. Two conflicting congregations at Leeds tried to establish themselves without success and it took until 1944 before a Reform synagogue was successfully founded there. West London received a communication from a small number of Jews in Clapham calling themselves the South London Congregation of British Jews, with a proposed synagogue in Brixton. They requested help from West London in the form of a *Torah* scroll, a sermon from Rev. Marks on their consecration and assistance from other ministers in the Reform movement. The Rev. Joseph Simmons was anxious to lead the embryo congregation, but the group was too small to be viable; they were under-financed and the plans for the synagogue never really got off the ground. Since that time no Reform synagogue was founded in London south of the Thames until that at Wimbledon in 1950.

In May 1878 Sir Francis Goldsmid, M.P. died. The Goldsmid family had been prime movers in the fight for Reform in Britain. The son of Sir Isaac Goldsmid and his cousin Isabel Goldsmid, Francis gave up the legal profession when he inherited his father's title, and married his cousin Louisa. They had no children and the baronetcy passed to his nephew, Julian. Sir Francis had been involved for most of his adult life with the battle for the emancipation of the Jews and was elected M.P. for Reading, a seat he held for the rest of his life. He worked tirelessly to help the poorer members of the Jewish community, at home and abroad, and was recognised in England for his philanthropy, becoming a J.P. and Deputy Lieutenant for Berkshire. His death was a tragic one at the early age of seventy; he was still in good health though his memory was impaired. He slipped on the platform at Waterloo Station and was dragged by the train along the platform, dying of his injuries. The *Jewish Chronicle* in a long obituary spoke of his achievements and noted particularly 'the unobtrusive way in which privately and often anonymously he disposed of a large part of his income.'[6] It carried a long description of the funeral at the Balls Pond Road cemetery. The hearse was drawn by four horses, with forty mourning coaches and another fifty private carriages. Those present included representatives of University College, the Anglo-Jewish Association, the Society of Hebrew Literature (their representative was Hermann Adler, son of the Chief Rabbi), the Brighton Congregation, the Manchester Congregation of British Jews, the United Synagogue, the Board of Deputies, the Jewish Board of Guardians, the President of the Spanish and Portuguese synagogue and the three ministers of the West London Synagogue. There were boys from the Jewish Deaf and Dumb Home and the Jews Hospital and Orphan Asylum, all particular interests of Sir Francis.

At West London, the question of a new Chairman of the congregation proved difficult. The Council was anxious to have Abraham Mocatta, but he would not accept. Their next choice lay between Sir Julian Goldsmid and David Mocatta. The secret ballot resulted in a hung election. Sir Julian, the new Baronet, stood down so David Mocatta was elected. Sir Francis Goldsmid had left the princely sum of £20,000 to the Synagogue, on condition that the sum was invested and only the interest was put to its use. The Trustees were David Mocatta and Simon Waley. The Council decided to commission a portrait of Sir Francis to hang in the committee room. It is still in the new Council Room today. Another portrait destined for wider exhibition was that of the Rev. David Woolf Marks. After being put on view in the Committee Room it was exhibited at the Royal Academy in 1878. Both portraits were painted by Julia Goodman, a member of the congregation. Mrs. Goodman was the daughter of Charles Kensington Salaman, the musician and composer who had done so much to enable West London to acquire its high reputation for synagogue music. She had studied under Robert Falkner, a pupil of Sir Joshua Reynolds. She married Walter Goodman and due to his delicate health had had to support a large family by her painting. She exhibited at the Royal Academy, the British Institution and the Liverpool Institute of Fine Arts, among others, and lived to be over ninety, having painted more than a thousand portraits.

Today, in almost every synagogue in the land, classes are held to give the children of its members, and sometimes of the members of other synagogues, a grounding in Jewish history, knowledge of the Bible and the elements of Hebrew. This was not always so. Most synagogues relied on parents, private teachers or the rabbi to provide enough learning to get the children through their Bar Mitzvah. A *cheder* existed in many of the European communities and some of the small East End congregations, but the Reform movement in Germany felt that the quality of the teaching was inadequate and too geared to a lifetime study of the *Torah*. Where the children attended a religious school they learned little else. In England the majority of children were taught Hebrew privately, with no guarantee of a satisfactory outcome. At Upper Berkeley Street, Philip Magnus, by now Assistant Rabbi and playing a large part in the affairs of the community, suggested to the Council that it was about time that regular classes were instituted to provide the children of the congregation with a reliable system of religious education, under the control of the ministers, with a regular curriculum and a high standard of teaching. Naturally a sub-committee was formed and the attention of members was drawn to the plans. So few members attended the preliminary meeting that it was deemed impossible to proceed, and the idea was abandoned.

Another project, already under way, that had more success, was the Ministers' Training Fund, which had been started some years before. The founding of Jews College was successful in dealing with the training of ministers for the orthodox community, but at West London the very 'Englishness' of the congregation seemed to be at odds with the ideas and methods of the College. The Council felt that such training should follow a university pattern, with a more secular approach to teaching. It therefore placed an advertisement in the Jewish press asking for applications from suitable young men to train as rabbis in the Reform movement. Candidates 'desirous of studying for the Ministry' were invited to send in an application to the Secretary. A set of rules was drawn up which included qualifications (the student had to be over seventeen, having matriculated at a university in Great Britain), and a recommendation as to his moral and religious character. He was to receive a stipend of £100 per annum for three years, and had to attend a British university to get a bachelor's degree while pursuing Hebrew and Religious studies. After this he would go to a Jewish Theological Seminary in Germany or elsewhere to gain instruction in Jewish Theology for two years. He would then be examined by a Minister of the West London Synagogue and be inducted as a Minister of the Jewish Religion. The synagogue would not be bound to accept his services. In case of misconduct or unfitness (physical or otherwise) his stipend could be stopped. Of the eight young men who replied to the advertisement and who were sent the Rules, four were invited to be interviewed by Professor Marks.

The first successful candidate was Benjamin Corré. His application was not very warmly received, and he was warned, 'There are some parts of your letter which do not exhibit that humility which is the first necessity for a student.'[7] Unfortunately Mr. Corré failed his first BA examinations but the Council were assured that he would be likely to succeed next time. He did indeed pass his intermediate examinations at the next attempt, with Honours in French and English, and it was agreed that for his BA at London University he should study mathematics, Greek, French, Hebrew and Latin. Sadly he died later in Germany while studying at the theological college there.

This problem of finding suitable men to enter the Reform ministry was becoming urgent. The Rev. Philip Magnus resigned from his position as Assistant Minister as he had been offered the post of Director and Secretary of the City and Guilds of London Institute for the Advancement of Technical Education. He had some difficulty with the Council, who felt he had given insufficient notice, and Magnus, always a little prickly, returned their letter of acceptance of his resignation with a note protesting that the Secretary had expressed no regret at his resignation nor any thanks for his offer of unpaid future services. The Chairman calmed him down, but his personality was never an easy one to work with. He sent a printed note expressing his thanks for the gifts he had received on leaving but added, 'The career I chose has not given me the opportunity of exercising the influence I had hoped. I had eventually to choose between comparative idleness in my congregational work and full activity in another occupation. Ministers of religion are not always best qualified to render effective assistance to the cause of religion.'[8]

The Rev. Lowy tried to put down some specifications for those who wished to take up the Ministry in a Reform community. 'He should be able to lead the congregation as members of a body who do not follow the guidelines of the Chief Rabbi. He should be not just a sound Hebrew scholar who understands the Hebrew Bible, but when considering the meaning of scriptural passages he should not need to hire a prompter! He must be self-dependent in the answers he has inherited from Jewish authors. He must be conversant with the literature of our predecessors, and the writings of our continental brothers (Zunz, Rapoport, Geiger, Joel etc.) and he must be familiar with the language in which they were written. He should have Hebrew, German and if possible modern languages. The candidates should be asked to translate a few lines at their interview.'[9]

The Council immediately put out feelers for a replacement and three possible candidates came under consideration. The first was Joseph Simmons, who had been linked with the unsuccessful South London Synagogue. His association with the Reform community had limited his opportunities for joining the orthodox rabbinate and he was anxious to obtain some minor position with West London. His application was carefully considered but the Council thought him too lacking in stature to be an efficient leader at Berkeley Street.

A much more charismatic and scholarly figure was the Rev. Joseph Strauss, a German born Rabbi, who had led the Bradford Reform Synagogue since 1873. He was highly regarded as a theologian and orator, and at ease in orthodox and Christian circles, but he retained his strong German accent all his life, and although he might have been a much-valued religious leader at West London, the anglophile Council decided, on the advice of Rev. Marks, that their congregation would be unable to cope with an almost incomprehensible voice from the pulpit. Their choice settled on the Rev. Isidore Harris.

Isidore Harris, the son of the rabbi of the Hambro synagogue in London, was born in Whitechapel in 1853 into an Ashkenazi family. On his mother's side too he came from a line of English rabbinical scholars. He attended firstly the school attached to Jews College and then went on to the College itself where he studied under Hermann Adler, son of Chief Rabbi Nathan Adler, who was to succeed his father. He learned *Chazanut* under the great musician Julius Mombach, though he maintained he was more impressive as a reading *chazan* than a singing one. After matriculation he studied at University

College where he obtained an MA with honours. His particular interest was in Jewish education and he was responsible for framing a curriculum for teaching by correspondence, children at public schools where no religious education was available for Jewish boys. He was also the Editor of the *Jewish Year Book* for many years. The Council at West London was delighted to find an English born scholar whose ideas coincided with the principles under which it had been founded. Mr. Harris was to serve the congregation well for more than forty years. When his appointment was announced the *Jewish Chronicle* wrote, 'Although Mr. Harris had previously been a member of an orthodox synagogue the Council of Berkeley Street has accepted him. We see that a schism which the community could not afford gives good hope of being healed and a desirable tendency is shown to disregard old animosities.'[10]

In reply to the invitation to come to West London as Assistant Minister, Isidore Harris thanked the Council, referring to the position as 'the dream of my youth'. He promised to conform to the ritual, laws and regulations of the synagogue, and that his journalistic work (he was a regular contributor to the Jewish press here and abroad) would be subordinate to his work for the congregation. He did, however, wish to continue his welfare for Jewish inmates of prisons and asylums, and this was gladly agreed. He was appointed Assistant Minister in 1881. The story is told of Mr. Harris taking prayers on the occasion of the death of Lady Simon. The service took place in the Goldsmid Hall, as the synagogue was closed for cleaning. Her son, Oswald, was to say the memorial prayer and slipped to his knees to do so. Mr. Harris asked him to rise, telling him, 'We are Jews, who are forbidden to bend the knee; I will not tolerate the introduction of any non-Jewish practice.' Mr. Simon explained that his late mother had taught him to pray on bended knee, but the minister refused to allow it.

The ministers had been giving much thought to the changes they wished to make to a new edition of the Prayer Book, though Rev. Lowy warned that some of the new suggestions might contravene biblical tradition. The minor changes included the omission of the benedictions before and after the reading of the Prophets during the Sabbath afternoon service, and of the 49th Psalm, which was intended to be read in a house of mourning, and to substitute another 'less enigmatically worded Psalm'. These were agreed with the Council with little disagreement. But the more radical changes involved the reading of part of the service in English, the omission of allusions to the advent of a personal Messiah, the return to Palestine, the rebuilding of the temple in Jerusalem and the restoration of sacrifices. These major changes, it was felt, could only be introduced if the entire liturgy was recast which might lead to 'sectarian isolation'. It was agreed that the compiling of an entirely new Prayer Book should wait until times were more auspicious. All these changes were eventually accepted as a matter of course.

The Prayer Book as at present constituted was apparently considered perfectly acceptable by some congregations. A community in Port Elizabeth,

South Africa, wrote to ask for a copy of the Marriage and Burial Services used by West London. These were duly forwarded and a further letter asked for details of the Daily and Festival Prayer Books. That congregation was so delighted with what they found that they adopted them at once.

✡

The synagogue building, more than ten years after it was erected, was showing signs of disrepair. The beadle, Mr. Lazarus, complained that the lavatories near his flat were smelly, the drains were clearly giving trouble, and most importantly the Council was aware that there was no second exit from the building 'in case of panic'. The drains were promptly dealt with but the second exit was not so easy. The architects were summoned to provide a plan for escape from the synagogue itself, the offices and committee room and the ladies' gallery. They suggested that a door should be inserted in place of the window leading to the roof, with a wooden staircase leading up to it and an iron staircase leading downward on the outside. They added an escape route from the committee room (the old Council Room), and a door leading out of the organ loft. There were in fact no regulations at that time covering fire escape routes, nor were public buildings or places of worship covered by the Factory Acts or other legislation. Another important addition was the installation of electric lighting. The United Electric Light Co. prepared a plan for putting in a complete system of electrical lighting, including large clusters of lights around the dome and along the aisles with additional lamps for the reading desk and the pulpit. An 'otto' gas engine fitted with an extra heavy fly wheel was needed with an Edison machine in the basement, with 'wires of best quality copper.' The estimate for the entire cost, including the building work was £833.

It was not only the structure of the building that caused a certain amount of soul searching in the Council. There were two beadles employed at West London who, while assiduous in carrying out their prescribed duties in the synagogue and attending to funerals, were not always as polite and subservient as the congregation might wish. The title of 'servant of the synagogue' was assumed by some to mean a menial, at the beck and call of their masters. Samuel Abrahams, who had served the synagogue well for some time, seemed to be becoming somewhat intransigent in his attitude to members. After a complaint was made about him, he wrote to the Council to apologise for his 'unfortunate behaviour' during the *Succot* service. He had apparently left home without breakfast that particular day, and after the Service had two or three glasses of ale. 'It got into my head and caused me to forget myself,' he wrote in his letter. He asked them to 'look over it' as it would never happen again. But that was not the end of it. For another congregant wrote 'through a sense of duty' to report the rude and violent conduct of Mr. Abrahams towards the lady's daughters, laughing at the effects of his insolence and not opening the door for them. She herself had come to fetch two footstools and he allowed her to carry them down to the carriage. When she remonstrated he replied, 'I am not here to look after footstools or to wait on such people as you.' No more is heard of Mr. Abrahams, but his junior, Mr. Lazarus seems to have been no better behaved, for a complaint was received that he had refused to shake the snow off a lady's umbrella, saying, 'I am not here to look after umbrellas.'

A much more serious incident took place on the Day of Atonement a year or so later, again in connection with Mr. Lazarus. The facts were fully set out in a letter from a Mr. L. Rosenthal. Apparently it seemed that Mr. Lazarus was owed a small sum of money by Mr. Rosenthal's father, and when the matter was raised the son told the Beadle to approach Mr. Rosenthal Snr. On New Year he was told by Mr. Lazarus 'in a most impertinent manner' that he had played him a nasty trick. 'This was said very loudly and several people turned round from their prayers.' Mr. Rosenthal requested a seat for *Yom Kippur* but was told by the Beadle that none was available. He approached the Secretary and was told he could have an unnumbered seat for a guinea (some friends had been asked for half a guinea) and decided not to go. However, he was offered a friend's seat half way through the service, found it unoccupied and was told by the Beadle, 'You can't sit there'. A violent argument ensued, Mr. Lazarus called Mr. Rosenthal 'a young monkey' who in turn threatened to slap his face. The fight grew physical (prayer books were the weapons) and blood flowed freely. The constable at the door was summoned and managed to quell the disturbance. Needless to say the Beadle's version of events was slightly different. Mr. Rosenthal threatened to sue the synagogue but withdrew at the request of the Council. Mr. Lazarus was given 'a last warning' but kept his job. Never has the Day of Atonement seemed so exciting.

The synagogue's position in the community was now well-established. It still had something of a reputation for being a 'gentleman's club', and although certain values it adopted seemed to put its members on a superior footing to their fellow Jews, the Victorian setting in which it found itself was perfectly usual at the time. For instance, the burial ground at Balls Pond Road adopted a two-tier system for the graves. Class A tombs were available to members and their families who paid a sum of not less than £25 and not more than £50 a year, while all other contributions merited only a Class B grave. This was later altered to £50-£100 for a Class A. The problems of dealing with funeral arrangements constantly caused difficulties for the Council. On one Sabbath morning a hastily convened meeting of its members after the service (there were only five of them present, together with the Ministers), had to make an immediate decision to solve such a problem – 'a matter of pressing importance.' Sir Edward Stern, the Senior Warden, informed them that he had given permission for the burial on the following day of Mr. Camille Roth, a non-member. However, he had just learned that before the burial the body was to be cremated. This was the first instance on which the synagogue had been asked to inter ashes. Although the ministers felt that cremation was not appropriate to Jewish teaching, it was unanimously resolved 'that the cremated remains of Mr. Camille Roth be interred in the Balls Pond Cemetery on the following day.[11] The orthodox view of cremation was that it betrayed tradition, that it was an imitation of non-Jewish custom, even that it was akin to mutilating a corpse. But as progressive Judaism gained a hold on the ideas and practice of Jews in this country, cremation or burial became a matter of choice for the individual or his family. The Reform service is the same for either, including reciting *Kaddish* and sitting *shiva* (though usually for one night only). Many orthodox communities in the United States and some in this country permit the interment of ashes in an orthodox cemetery.

Then the synagogue was approached by a Mr. Johnasson who wanted to transfer the body of his son, buried at Balls Pond Road Cemetery, to Kensal Rise (a non-Jewish burial ground) and also to have the bodies of his mother, sister and brother brought from the Jewish cemetery in Sunderland to the reserved graves he held at Balls Pond Road. This complicated transaction was held to be contrary to Jewish practice, and the Council refused. They informed the Home Office, who had to give permission for disinterments, that it was impossible to sanction the transfer of Jewish remains from a Jewish to a non-Jewish burial ground.

Another difficulty which was always liable to arise in the life of any synagogue was that of marriage. Miss Charlotte Montefiore, the clever daughter of Nathaniel Montefiore and Emma, daughter of Sir Isaac Lyon Goldsmid, and sister of Claude Montefiore, had married out of the faith to Lewis (later Sir Lewis) McIver. Her family on her mother's side had been associated with West London since its inception and she had no wish to abandon her religion. Nor did her husband, who was to have a distinguished career as a Liberal politician, wish to become Jewish. Charlotte approached the Council for permission to take out membership for herself and be granted a seat. The Council refused, stating that mixed marriages were contrary to the principles of Judaism. However, always anxious for compromise, it did allow her to retain the seat she previously held as Miss Charlotte Montefiore! Charlotte's brother, Claude was by now a warden at Berkeley Street, and was to be the prime mover and first leader of the Liberal Jewish movement when he instigated the Jewish Religious Union in 1902. Partly as a result of the decision on Charlotte, the Council, whilst condemning mixed marriages, did not feel able to refuse membership to a Jew or Jewess who had contracted a civil marriage out of the faith. This decision was duly inserted into the Laws of the synagogue. Some years later an application to marry was received from a Cohen who wished to marry a non-Jewish lady who was about to convert. It was impossible for a Cohen to marry a convert within the orthodox fold, but the young man was told that once his fiancée had converted and if he became a member, the marriage could take place.

The thorny question of election to the Board of Deputies arose again. West London had sent its good wishes to Sir Moses Montefiore on the occasion of his one hundredth birthday, and was represented on the committee set up to commemorate the event. This must have stood the synagogue in good stead in its negotiations with the Board. It received a letter enclosing a copy of the revised constitution inviting two Deputies to sit on the Board, and this was put before the Annual General Meeting and was met with general approval. It was largely due to Sir Julian Goldsmid that the constitution had been revised in such a way as to remove the objections which had so far prevented the synagogue's membership. The *Jewish Chronicle* was delighted, reporting that some of the last embers of the conflagration that was lighted forty years ago had thus been finally extinguished.

West London felt strongly about the part it should play in the affairs of the Jewish community at large. It was fortunate to have among its members some of the wealthiest Jews in London. Their philanthropic ideas, which from a modern standpoint seem paternalistic, even feudal, were at the time welcomed and greatly appreciated. They were invited to be represented on the East End Enquiry Commission. The Commission was set up to deal with the difficulties arising from the huge influx of Jews arriving in the East End as a result of the pogroms in Russia and Eastern Europe. Towards the end of the century they flooded into London, mostly poor, unkempt and dirty, speaking only Yiddish but with a great capacity for work, for family ties and for educating their children. The Board of Guardians was established in 1859 to help them but thirty years later it was overwhelmed by the sheer numbers of destitute Jews needing help. Crammed into overcrowded slums in the East End they were desperately short of food, medical help and support for their often large families. After difficulties were experienced with the local welfare board, the Whitechapel District Board of Works, the Board of Guardians set up a new committee under the chairmanship of Baron Rothschild, to take matters into its own hands. It concluded that not only were these foreign Jews to be housed (in tenement blocks with proper sanitation and cooking facilities), given proper schooling for their children and hospital facilities, but that they should be Anglicised. This would take the form of teaching them English, instructing them how to behave in a 'civilised' community and finding them jobs to achieve financial independence. Thus was founded the Four-per-cent Industrial Dwellings Company to provide homes at much reduced rents, while giving the investors a minimum return. The first homes were called the Charlotte de Rothschild Dwellings, known to this day as the Rothschild Buildings, though the whole area was rebuilt after the bombing of the Second World War. Queen Victoria granted to Nathan Mayer Rothschild the first Jewish peerage – he became the first Lord Rothschild of Tring. The Enquiry had been instituted by the United Synagogue, but the Four-per-cent Company was formed at Rothschild's Bank in the city and included on its Board, apart from Lord Rothschild himself, Lionel Cohen, President of the Board of Guardians, and Samuel Montagu (later Lord Swaythling), and two members of the West London Synagogue, F.D.Mocatta (his father was a founder member), and Claude Montefiore. From this time onward Berkeley Street was to play an important part in the alleviation of the hardship of their fellow Jews, including the establishment of a progressive synagogue in the East End after the first World War under the auspices of Sir Basil Henriques, grandson of a founder member.

Another application for help for a new synagogue, which was to have far-reaching effects on Upper Berkeley Street, was the request from a Hampstead community which wished to hold Sabbath afternoon services in the old Town Hall at West Hampstead. This was because those behind the idea did not wish to compete in any way with the possibility of arranging Sabbath morning services for a Hampstead synagogue. Their purposes were to offer a more moderate form of service – they were not a synagogue. The form of service was to be a slightly modified form of the afternoon service, to read the Ten Commandments (all in Hebrew) plus a scriptural lesson, a Psalm, a Prayer and a Hymn in English. There would be a mixed choir, a discourse and instrumental accompaniment. The West London Synagogue had been formed in part as a result of a wish by London Jews for a synagogue further to the west. In the same way, as families moved further out to the suburbs, so Jews were by now wishing to live in the pleasant area of Hampstead and needed a house of prayer. The new congregation was something of a hybrid, part Orthodox, part progressive, using the Ashkenazi forms of prayer, with a largely female membership. The old Chief Rabbi, Nathan Adler, was not very encouraging, but when his son Hermann succeeded, he was more receptive. The new community was led by the Rev. Morris Joseph, who eventually became West London's Senior Minister, and played a momentous part in the affairs of the Anglo-Jewish community as a whole. The Council was pleased to accede to Hampstead's request for a scroll with appurtenances and a cover for the reading-desk.

It was clear that the London Jewish community was becoming more aware that the Reform movement and its forms of prayer had come to stay. But the original Prayer Book that Berkeley Street had by now grown used to, was not entirely suitable for the next generation of largely British-born Jews. They wanted a shorter service and more English in the prayers, so a new committee set about investigating the possibilities. It found that it would be almost impossible to abridge the Sabbath morning service as it stood without altering the Reading of the Law, the most intrinsic part of Jewish prayers. The only answer was either to read the whole of the *Torah* in a cycle of three years instead of one, or to divide the portion into two halves, one read in the morning and one read in the afternoon. If this was done and certain prayers could be omitted and some of the psalms read instead of chanted, about twenty-five minutes in all could be saved. When the Ritual Committee's conclusions were put to the Council they met with a stubborn refusal to agree to any changes in the reading of the *Torah*, the Prophets or the Psalms. With certain amendments some changes to the prayers were permitted.

However, a few months later Claude Montefiore put a motion to the Council suggesting that a) the Ministers should read a portion of the *Torah* instead of the whole, b) that there should be a reading from the Prophets and c) that that reading should be in English. Finally the Council submitted to the *Haftarah* being read in the morning instead of the afternoon (it had already been regretted by the Ministers that attendance at afternoon services was very low indeed), and that it should be read in English from the pulpit (not from the reading-desk). The translation used was to be that of Dr. Friedlander or a new one by the ministers. Dr. Michael Friedlander was a distinguished Hebraist, Principal of Jews College and particularly known for his translation of Maimonides' *Guide to the Perplexed.* To the horror of the Council, the *Jewish Chronicle* published details of the Ritual Committee's findings (marked on all copies 'Strictly Confidential') before they had been put to a General Meeting of members. However, the paper was very complimentary in its view of change, writing, 'Progress has been imperatively necessitated by the vast intellectual and religious changes which have taken place during the last few decades, and which have made their influence felt by the Jews in common with the civilised world in general.'[12]

The saga of West London versus the Board of Deputies seemed endless. No sooner had the Board officially invited Berkeley Street to send two Deputies to represent them (the two chosen were Sir Julian Goldsmid and Sir Philip Magnus),when a letter arrived explaining that its Committee for Law, Parliament and General Purposes had discussed the matter. 'The Board deeply regrets that the circumstances mentioned in the Report renders it impossible to receive them as Deputies in the present session', read the letter, and that for the time being seemed to be that. In fact, at the triennial elections of the Board held a few months later, Sir Julian Goldsmid M.P. and Harry Sylvester Samuel were elected as representatives for West London and duly took their seats.

CHAPTER V

Into A New Century

The synagogue was now very preoccupied with its own affairs, for it was about to celebrate its Golden Jubilee. The anniversary of the first service held at the Burton Street Synagogue in 1842 was commemorated at Upper Berkeley Street fifty years to the day since the beginning. The Council had been discussing arrangements for the ceremony for some time, and it soon became clear that the Jubilee service was attracting a great deal of interest. Invitations were sent out to representatives of almost every synagogue in Britain, to ministers and lay leaders alike, and almost all accepted. Naturally all the seat-holders of West London wanted to come, even if they hardly ever set foot in the synagogue in the normal way. Invitations were sent to the Chief Rabbi, now the Rev. Hermann Adler and to the Haham, Rev. Moses Gaster. Both refused. The *Jewish Chronicle* gave full publicity to the event, previewing the service beforehand, when it gave an account of the music which was to be played. Mr. Verrinder either composed the music for the occasion himself or adapted settings by Mombach, Charles Salaman, Sulzer and Mendelssohn.

However, if any English Jew believed that fifty years was enough time for old quarrels to be laid to rest he was sadly mistaken. The *Jewish Chronicle* printed on May 9th 1890 an open letter to Lord Rothschild, as President of the United Synagogue, signed by F.D. Mocatta, Philip Magnus, Alfred L. Cohen, Samuel Montagu, Herbert Lousada and Alfred Beddington. The letter spoke of a widespread desire for a 'comprehension' of English Jews under the guidance of one presiding Chief Rabbi who should be the Chief Spiritual Adviser of all the Jews residing in the British Empire, with a certain latitude to individual congregations within well-defined limits to vary the present Order of Divine Service in some details. They asked him to invite representatives of the Spanish and Portuguese Synagogue, the Federation of Synagogues, the West London Synagogue, other metropolitan and provincial synagogues and the United Synagogue, to form a committee to discuss the proposition. They admitted the Chief Rabbi as spiritual head, but as far as the Spanish and Portuguese and the West London Synagogues were concerned, in a consultative capacity only, such congregations to retain their autonomy.

In its issue of 8th January, 1892, a week or two before the Jubilee service, the *Jewish Chronicle* contained a long leader headed Reconciliation. It anticipated that at the Jubilee Service there would be a thoroughly representative attendance with the notable exception of the two Chief Rabbis, and suggested that the event 'might have been the occasion for the coming together of all parties in Anglo-Jewry'. However it noted that most of the Hon. Officers of the United Synagogue would be there, with Lord Rothschild at their head. It also printed a sermon by the Rev. Simeon Singer who thought the moment had come for the hand of friendship to be held out and be grasped. Rev. Singer was a distinguished scholar, the Minister of the New West End Synagogue, whose edition of the Daily and Sabbath Prayer is used in the United Synagogue to this day. In view of his close attachment to West London he was later invited to become its Senior Minister when Rev. Marks eventually retired, but felt himself too close to the orthodox mainstream and too attached to his own congregation to make the move.

On the occasion of the Jubilee the *Jewish Chronicle* printed a whole six-page supplement to commemorate the event. It began by recalling in some detail the circumstances in which the West London Synagogue of British Jews had come into being, from the earliest problems faced by those who wished for change and the *cherem* they had been subject to, printing in full the manifesto that the founding fathers had drawn up, stating their case. It included the letters exchanged between the Council of Founders and the Board of Deputies regarding marriages, and the debate over the justification for abolishing the second days of the Festivals. It spoke of the two previous synagogues, in Burton Street and Margaret Street, of the installation of the organ and the high standard of music the congregation enjoyed and ended this long narrative with the conclusion, 'For many years past the closest domestic ties by marriage, and the growth of general enlightenment and forbearance have combined to reunite the two sections of the community into one; one for all practical purposes of communal action and religious sympathy despite the deviations in external forms of public worship.'[1]

The paper went on to give a comprehensive description of the Jubilee Service. Floral decorations and extra lighting gave a 'magnificent appearance' to the synagogue. There were forty-five voices in the choir and additional seats had been installed. Ministers from other synagogues, and there were many, were dressed in their canonicals and most of the congregation wore morning dress and silk hats. The arrangements and the stewards were apparently so efficient that 'the visitors had no difficulty in finding the seats allotted to them.' The stewards wore white satin 'favours' with a silver border and in the centre the commemorative inscription 'W.L.S. 1842-1892'. The *Chronicle* printed the Rev. Marks' address to the congregation in full. He too recalled the early history of the synagogue, feeling that the length of time that had elapsed since the early troubles justified his remarks that in those days 'the clergy looked upon change as synonymous with heresy, and the large majority of the laity had sunk into a state of spiritual torpor.' He mentioned some of the distinguished Jews who had contributed to the synagogue's success: Sir Francis Goldsmid, Abraham Mocatta, Sir John Simon, and the one Founder still alive to see the Jubilee, Mr. Joseph Barrow Montefiore. He spoke of the changes that had been made to the prayer book, of the music of which the synagogue was so proud and of the hopes that the congregation had for their future. 'Our ritual,' he said, 'satisfies our spiritual cravings, inasmuch as it is in harmony with the great Judaic teachings – the common Fatherhood of God and the universal brotherhood of man.'[2]

Rev. Marks did not refrain from referring to two of the main objections of traditional Jews to the Reform service: the discontinuance of praying for the restoration of sacrifice and the abolition of the second day of Festivals. The latter in particular, still a very sore point in the community, he explained as being derived from the medieval view of Judaism rather than from the Bible, which for Reform Jews was the principal source of their belief and practice. He finished by thanking Almighty God 'for having sustained me in my office through a long series of years and having spared me to take part in the celebration of the Jubilee of a congregation it was my privilege to usher into being.'[3] David Woolf Marks was eighty-one years old, and continued to serve the West London Synagogue for several more years.

The rest of the service followed the traditions which Berkeley Street had enjoyed throughout those fifty years, although for the first time in any synagogue the Royal Prayer was said in English. The *Chronicle*'s account of the service finished with a longer appreciation of the music in the service, congratulating Dr. Verrinder on his own compositions, his choice of the music and the training of the choir. The article was clearly written by someone with a deep knowledge and love of music, who was able to 'trace everywhere the influence of a clever musician, experienced in the traditions of English church music.'[4] As the congregation left the synagogue the choir sang Beethoven's Hallelujah Chorus from *The Mount of Olives*.

With all that had been occupying it in recent weeks the Council could not afford to neglect other matters concerning the births, marriages and deaths of its members. Some complaints had been received concerning the state of the Burial Ground so the synagogue architects were asked to have a close look at it and report back. They found that with some fairly minor repairs (rebuilding part of the walls, improving the drainage system etc.) West London could manage for another nine or ten years, but they advised giving consideration to the possibility of purchasing a new burial ground. They also suggested getting in touch with the United Synagogue to see if there might be a possibility of investing mutually in a new cemetery. The U.S. still had considerable space at their large ground at Willesden and it was likely that some arrangement might be arrived at convenient to both. Another possibility was to enter into some sort of cooperation with the Spanish and Portuguese community. Bevis Marks brought the proposals before the Board of Elders, who felt that for the time being they were adequately served by their Mile End Burial Ground where there was a bigger area of ground available if they wanted it. But they were not against buying more land if an opportunity arose for the distant future, if the additional plot at Mile End could not be used.

In the event a plot of land of some fifteen acres became available at Hoop Lane in Golders Green off the Finchley Road which seemed very suitable. The Spanish and Portuguese undertook to recommend to the Elders that two burial grounds could be established on the site, on the understanding that the Bevis Marks portion could be left fallow until it was needed. The question of whether one or two Burial Halls were needed was left in abeyance for the time being. The whole cost to each congregation, including enclosing the land, draining and laying it out would be somewhere about £5-6,000. The West London Council agreed, providing of course that Home Office sanction was granted. However Bevis Marks were not willing to go ahead unless two mortuaries could be provided and the two grounds were entirely separate. There was also the possibility for West London to purchase a smaller site of some ten acres on the other side of Hoop Lane, but the owner of the land was proving difficult in any negotiations. Eventually the Council went back to Bevis Marks and agreed a price for the larger plot on the west side of the road, but the application for permission to go ahead from the Home Secretary was held up by the insistence on an expensive programme of drainage and filtration. Finally all negotiations were completed, and the Spanish and Portuguese, who had asked for a wall between the two cemeteries, were content with a wide gravel path as a divider and retained a further portion of land to the north. Two prayer halls were erected and the Hoop Lane Cemetery was finally opened in 1897. The first burial was that of Frances, wife of Charles Kensington Salaman, the distinguished composer. The ten acre plot across the road was bought by The Crematorium Society of Great Britain and opened as London's first crematorium in 1902.

When the burial ground at Hoop Lane was finally finished a Conjoint Committee of the two synagogues – West London and Bevis Marks – was set up to administer the ground. The total cost was £4,138, excluding the fine iron gates which were presented by F.G. Henriques. Rules were established concerning grave sizes, and if these were obeyed the surveyors reckoned that the land would suffice for another sixty to eighty years. Families were to be responsible for keeping the graves clean and tidy, but for a reasonable sum the synagogue would attend to this. Three members of each synagogue would form a Burial Committee to oversee the arrangements, whose duty it would be to give approval for tombstone designs. The rules which obtained concerning burial at Balls Pond were equally as stringent at Hoop Lane. The three children of a non-member were buried there but it was later found that their mother had not been Jewish. The Council investigated further and afterwards stipulated that providing girls had not been baptised and boys had been circumcised, such burials might go ahead.

✡

The Synagogue's finances, though considered to be in a perfectly healthy state, would not stretch to being depleted by any further big expenditure.

Both Ministers were by now advanced in years and it would not be long before they would be giving way to younger men who might require higher salaries as well as more extensive domestic arrangements, with the inevitable pension arrangements for those who retired.

The two first (and only) ministers of the West London Synagogue were by now 81 and 76 years old respectively, but it was the younger man who first retired from the pulpit. Albert Lowy wrote to the Council suggesting that in view of his advancing years and delicate health he could no longer give his full attention to synagogue matters. The resignation was accepted, the Council regretting 'the loss of an old and valued friend and Minister after so long a period of faithful and assiduous devotion to the best interests of the congregation and of Judaism at large.' It was agreed to appoint a 'delegate Senior Minister' as it was obvious that it would not be long before two ministers would be needed. Rev. Marks would be appointed Honorary Minister (a post not unlike that of today's Rabbi Emeritus). Isidore Harris was formally offered the post of Junior Minister. He accepted, adding that he intended to apply for the post of Senior Minister when it became available. The Council was not pleased. It wrote informing Mr. Harris that it did not intend to recommend him for the post, that in deciding to recommend him for the junior post it was on the understanding that he was willing to accept that post, for which he had made formal application. Mr. Harris withdrew his letter, remaining as Junior Minister.

The post of Senior Minister to the West London Synagogue was an important one in Anglo-Jewry as a whole. Reform Judaism had clearly come to stay; those who had foretold its early downfall were confounded and it had already had considerable influence over the decorum and services of mainstream synagogues throughout Britain. Most now had sermons in English, better-behaved congregations and were more accessible to their members. Many Jewish organisations relied at least in part on Reform Jews for their work and for their finances, and West London had the ear, if not the entire approval, of the Jewish Press. The editor of the *Jewish Chronicle* was at this time Asher Myers, an orthodox but broad-minded man with a cultured background. He included in the paper's pages articles on literature, art and music and was prepared to give a hearing to any part of Anglo-Jewry that merited inclusion.

There were various possibilities for the post of Senior Minister. Rev. Simeon Singer had already turned it down, and the Council was much in favour of finding an Englishman who would fit in with West London's origins and the unique developments within its membership that had evolved over the years. The favourite candidate was the Rev. Morris Joseph, an old friend of David Marks. Like him, Joseph had been educated at the Jews Free School and then Jews College, after which he was appointed minister-Secretary to the North London Synagogue in Barnsbury. He then went to Marks's old synagogue in Liverpool, now at Princes Road. He was a man of considerable intellect and Jewish scholarship, but his precarious health forced him to abandon the rabbinate for a while, return to London and concentrate on writing and a part-time ministry until he recovered. This part-time work was mainly involved in steering the West Hampstead afternoon services, trying 'to combat the growth of religious apathy within the Jewish community, many members of which perceived orthodox Judaism as medieval and the cause of gradual intellectual alienation.'[5] He was much in favour of the use of instrumental music in the service, of English sermons and some prayers, and held a wider, more enlightened view of the way Jewish life should be conducted in modern England. He had published a volume of sermons which had 'received the highest commendation from gentlemen entertaining the most opposing views, and he is anxious to enter on the wider field of usefulness open to a Metropolitan Minister.'[6]

These qualities which so attracted the West London Synagogue Council to Morris Joseph were the very ones which had been his undoing in his previous application to lead a London community. A new synagogue was being established in Hampstead proper, apart from the Saturday afternoon services in West Hampstead, and Morris Joseph seemed the very man to lead it. His health was now good, he was a scholar and a man of integrity. He had, shortly after West London's Jubilee, given a sermon at Hampstead, emphasizing the contrast of fifty years earlier with the present friendly atmosphere that now existed between the two parties in Anglo-Jewry. 'Thank God,' he said, 'that the old deadly strife that had destroyed some of their most precious things – communal amity and domestic peace – was slain in its turn.'[7] So when Hampstead offered him the post of their Minister he was delighted to accept. But that was not the end of the matter. When Chief Rabbi Hermann Adler heard of Joseph's 'call', he stepped in at once, indicating that he 'must hesitate to grant his certificate.' This permission was essential for any minister working with a synagogue affiliated to the United Synagogue. Unwilling to cause any further embarrassment, Joseph released the Committee from their engagement. The *Jewish Chronicle* gave full publicity to the affair, quoting the Chief Rabbi as saying, 'The US has no room for men like Morris Joseph to preach righteousness in the great congregation.'[8]

On 8th June, 1892, Rev. Joseph wrote a long letter to the *Chronicle* explaining his view of the Chief Rabbi's reasons for dealing with what was deemed 'heresy' and seemed to make him unfit for the ministry. These reasons centred round the use of instrumental music, disbelief in the revival of sacrifices and views at variance with traditional Judaism. He said that his 'call' to Hampstead was quite unsought for on his part and it was repeated over several months. He had accepted on condition that he was allowed to preach his own opinions and to teach a form of progressive Judaism which he hoped would soon become a possibility. But his dream, he added, remained unfulfilled. He would not cast a stone at 'the kind and learned man' who passed this sentence of minor excommunication, and promised to carry on his work for the community.

The correspondence in the paper continued. The first protagonist was 'One Who Knows'. This anonymous correspondent wrote to maintain that the narrow issue 'not mentioned by Mr. Joseph' revolved around the position of Reader at the synagogue which had not been offered to him. He pointed out that if on occasion the Reader was not able to be present, then the Minister would act in his place. He would then have to decline to act as he could not read that part of the liturgy in which the problem of sacrifices was mentioned. 'His liberal views are too advanced even for a "reform" pulpit.' He went on to maintain that the 'chilling and hopeless' opinions set forth at the West London Synagogue, were 'received with great disfavour by an influential section of that congregation.'

The Chief Rabbi added fuel to the flames, confirming the 'inhibition' he felt he had to inflict on Mr. Joseph. Another correspondent declared that 'One Who Knows' was 'an officious jackal who follows the official line', and Oswald Simon, son of the late Sir John Simon, and an active member of Upper Berkeley Street, tried to calm things down. He said that 'One Who Knows' was quite wrong in his assertion that many members of West London disagreed with the reforms that had been introduced. 'The future of Judaism,' he wrote, 'is bound up with the changes of thought that no ecclesiastical power can avert.' The splendid new Hampstead synagogue in Dennington Park Road, architect Delissa Joseph (no relation), was finally consecrated on 23rd September 1892 by the Chief Rabbi, together with the Haham, Dr. Gaster. The large congregation was addressed by Rev. Adler and by Professor David Marks, and the service was led by the new minister, Rev. A.A. Green.

A few weeks later, Rev. Morris Joseph was invited to preach at the St. John's Wood synagogue, of which he was a member. He agreed, asking if the Chief Rabbi's opinion had first been obtained. The wardens admitted that they had not thought this necessary, but would do so. Dr. Adler rebuked them sternly for not having consulted him first, and refused his permission. The wardens replied that they 'failed to see any analogy between the appointment of Rev. Joseph to the post of Minister, and his being permitted to give an occasional address (he is a member).'9 The congregation endorsed the wardens' decision, but the Chief Rabbi confirmed that Mr. Joseph's opinions were 'at variance with traditional Judaism' and that if he allowed this to happen 'every congregation in England' would be justified in following its own path. Morris Joseph withdrew.

At a Special General Meeting of seat-holders of the West London Synagogue on 21st July 1893, the Chairman, Sir Julian Goldsmid, announced that the Council had chosen Rev. Morris Joseph as Delegate Senior Minister, with a probationary period of one year. He pointed out that the decision was not unanimous – he himself had been in favour of a two-year 'settling-in' period - but Rev. Marks was not in good health and had not always been well enough to lead the service. He could not expect, he said, that everyone would agree with everything said in Rev. Joseph's sermons, but 'the general principles which Mr. Joseph had laid down were entirely in accord with those of a Reform congregation such as theirs.' He mentioned a circular which had been sent out anonymously to members asking them to oppose the election of Mr. Joseph. This he felt was dishonourable conduct and he hoped it would never occur again. The matter was put to the vote, and Morris Joseph was elected to the post of Minister by 65 votes to 20.

Rev. Joseph gave his inaugural sermon to a crowded synagogue on 9th September 1893. It was printed in full in the *Jewish Chronicle*. He spoke of the duties of a minister to lead his flock, that he needed to be as strong as a lion to do the will of his Father in Heaven. 'I would that this congregation might vie with and excel all others in devotion to the principles of enlightened religion, not only in a courageous proclamation of the right of the intellect, but in fidelity to the ideals that have been consistently cherished by the noblest souls in Israel throughout the ages and in the strenuous quest of the Heavenly life.'[10]

The new Senior Minister had a great deal to do, not just in the day-to-day running of a big and important Metropolitan Synagogue. Rev. Marks had been concerned for some time about attendance at services, telling the Council that if it were not for the women, the place would be half empty; this was partly due to its being a metropolitan rather than a local one. He described it as being no more than 'a burial club for Jews.' There was need for some changes to the ritual. More English was being inserted into the Sabbath prayers, including the Royal Prayer, a hymn after the sermon and a prayer before the Kaddish. Similar amendments were introduced into the Festival Services. At a Special Meeting to confirm the amendments, ladies were for the first time invited to attend (but not to vote).

✡

The congregation sent delegates to a conference concerned with the education of Jewish pupils at metropolitan elementary schools. The conference was attended by delegates from the Spanish and Portuguese Synagogue, the West London Synagogue, the United Synagogue, the Federation of Synagogues and the Association for the Diffusion of Religious Knowledge. They agreed that funds should be made available for the project and administered by a new body to be called the Jewish Religious Education Board, to which only Jews could be elected. At Berkeley Street there were complaints that the children of certain 'strangers' had been refused confirmation. Their parents did not belong to the synagogue nor did they contribute (when they were perfectly able to do so). The Council confirmed the Wardens' view that this was not permissible.

Another perennial problem that had to be faced was the conduct and behaviour of the choir. There had been complaints about decorum and discipline and about the lack of control by the Organist and Choirmaster. So the Council drew up a set of rules, in consultation with Dr. Verrinder, to cover such matters as poor attendance and disregard of 'respectful and decorous attention at service.' The choir had to attend services according to their contract, with no absence without prior permission. They should attend all rehearsals, and submit to the judgment and direction of the choirmaster in all musical matters, obeying his ruling. They should be in their seats ten minutes before services and stay until the conclusion of the voluntary. They should conduct themselves with decorum and reverence during services and rehearsals and keep their places in the choir including reciting of the Law and the sermon. No books or papers were to be brought in and there should be no conversation under any circumstances. The attendance book was to be signed and there would be a roll call before and after services and rehearsals. A fine of five shillings would be levied for missing a service and of two shillings and sixpence for part of a service or a rehearsal, records to be kept by the wardens. Flagrant breaches of the rules would be met with instant dismissal. Each chorister was given a copy of the Rules which had to be signed. Matters improved instantly.

A year or so later, complaints were made about the quality of the music for the services, not this time about the choir but about the organ. Worshippers were finding that the voices of the choir were being drowned by the organ and Dr. Verrinder asked the Council to examine ways of improving the sonority. It was suggested that the grilles dividing the choir stalls from the body of the synagogue should be removed. This would certainly improve decorum, for the choristers would then be in full view of the worshippers, but this was not advised by the architects. They thought about putting a sounding board above the singers' seats, but Dr. Verrinder explained that it was the positioning of the choir vis-à-vis the organ that was the problem. The sound was travelling from the high pipes down the synagogue and back to the choir. They suggested moving the organ, putting in a gallery for the choir away from the organ, or placing them down on the floor of the synagogue, but none of these ideas seemed to provide the answer. Minor improvements helped somewhat, but the problem was never really solved until modern methods of communication came into use in the 20th century.

In early 1896 Sir Julian Goldsmid, M.P. died. He had had a distinguished career both within the Jewish community and outside it. He had been Liberal M.P. for Honiton, then Rochester and finally St. Pancras South. He was created Privy Counsellor and inherited the baronetcy from his uncle, Sir Francis, a founder member of West London. He held many important posts in the community, including Chairman of the Anglo-Jewish Association and the Russo-Jewish Committee, took a great and active interest in the Jews Free School and University College, and was for some years Chairman of Upper Berkeley Street. He died suddenly at the age of 57, and the *Jewish Chronicle* described him as 'shrewd, possessed of sound judgment and strong pungent good sense; a born man of affairs, he was also a man of ideas and ideals.'[11] The Council decided to erect a Memorial Hall in his honour, to be called the Goldsmid Hall. It would be used for religion classes and meetings and the synagogue's architects were asked to draw up plans for the building. Unfortunately the site chosen, within the synagogue buildings, was found to be impractical and could not be satisfactorily fitted into the existing structure. Instead it was decided to redecorate and convert the synagogue vestibule into a suitable hall for such a purpose (provided the drains under the flagstones were repaired), and contributions were invited to cover the cost. As it turned out, no such conversion ever took place, and additional space for the classes had to wait until the whole building was altered and rebuilt in the 1930s.

Jews, with a few notable exceptions, have never been particularly distinguished as military heroes, but one member of West London acquitted himself in the Boer War with great honour. Lieutenant Frederick Raphael was the second son of George and Charlotte Raphael, and decided to make the army his career. He was assigned to the First Battalion, South Lancashire Regiment and went out to South Africa where the Second Boer War was still raging. In charge of a small force of 130 men, and a machine gun, he confronted at Spion Kop, a small hill not far from Ladysmith, a large contingent of the Boer army. His commanding officer having been severely wounded, Lieutenant Raphael tried to repair the damage as the Boers attacked. He was killed almost at once, apparently trying to save a fellow solider. Colonel O'Leary wrote to his father, 'He had been encouraging his men all morning by word and example, and is reported to have shot five of the enemy dead before his own noble death … he lies decently buried on that ill-fated ridge.'[12] Several 'mourning brooches' were made, at least one of which is still in the possession of the family. The Raphael family remained linked to Berkeley Street through the marriage of Frederick's sister Mary to Philip Waley, a later President of the congregation. Both Philip and his son Frank, joined the Raphael firm of stockbrokers. The Waley family name had originally been Levi, but was changed to Waley by Royal Grant, and in 1834 the family was awarded a Grant of Arms by the College of Heralds. The family motto is *Fortiter et Fideliter* (Strongly and Faithfully).

Another difficulty, one which was to prove an almost permanent bone of contention during all the years of Berkeley Street's existence, was the question of confirmation versus Bar Mitzvah. The Founders, English to the core, had made the decision that the confirmation service, for boys and girls, was to be held once a year, when as many young people as wished would stand before the congregation and declare their Jewish affiliation, reciting a prayer and answering the questions put to them by the minister. This ceremony, not unlike the confirmation and catechism usual in Christian places of worship, never met the approval of the more traditionally minded members of the congregation, and many parents preferred to have their sons Bar Mitzvah according to the ancient rites in an orthodox community. The matter was put before the members at a Special General Meeting, but was turned down. Claude Montefiore was asked to form a committee to investigate the matter more fully.

Claude Joseph Montefiore, who was to become one of the founders of Liberal Judaism, was the son of Nathaniel Montefiore (brother of Sir Moses), and Emma Goldsmid (daughter of Sir Isaac Lyon). His roots were thus firmly in the Jewish Reform movement. He married at West London, and had wanted to become a rabbi. However, his wife's death in 1892, made him abandon the idea. He was a warden of Upper Berkeley Street, until in 1902, with Lily Montagu, daughter of Lord Swaythling, he established the Jewish Religious Union which became Liberal Judaism. His dual allegiance to both the Reform and the Liberal wings of progressive Judaism prompted him on one occasion to suggest that when he died his body should be cut in two, half to be buried as a Liberal and half as a Reform Jew. The idea of working on the question of the children's Jewish coming-of-age, however, did not greatly appeal to him. As he himself said, 'I am personally not particularly good with children. To talk to them is not much in my line, and I am not good at speaking without notes or text.' He passed the task on to Mrs. Morris Joseph, who, he felt, 'was good with children and with parents – she has the great gift of talking with children.'[13] Claude did in fact have one child by his first marriage, Leonard, who was also to play an important part in the affairs of the West London Synagogue.

When the Jewish Religious Union came into being at the instigation of Lily Montagu and Claude Montefiore, it invited Morris Joseph to address one of its meetings. The West London Council gave the new organisation its blessing and suggested a joint committee should be set up to devise a scheme whereby it could hold services at Upper Berkeley Street. It offered the use of the synagogue on Sabbath afternoons. The Liberals welcomed the idea but insisted that arrangements should be entirely under the control of the Union. As these arrangements included men and women sitting together, modern English prayers of Jewish authorship, and that Miss Montagu and Mr. Laurie Magnus (son of Sir Philip) be deputed to formulate the Service, the Council was not too happy. They refused to allow Rev. Joseph to be a member of the Union's committee, or to officiate without the Council's permission. Indeed F.D. Mocatta put on record his 'entire dissatisfaction' with the matters discussed. The Union replied to the Council's offer by thanking them but regretting that 'they did not see their way to accepting under the conditions laid down by your members.'[14] They declined the invitation.

Claude Montefiore first set out his ideas on that form of Judaism which came to be known as Liberal Judaism in a short book *Liberal Judaism – an Essay*, published in 1903. It has a strong personal element to his views, 'No authority attaches to this book,' he says.[15] He speaks of God and the Jewish relationship with God, which may differ from one Jew to another. He touches on Rabbinic Judaism from whose all-embracing control Reform Jews firstly and now Liberal Jews, chose to break away, writing forthrightly that 'in the Mishnah "we are told that seven kinds of punishments come into the world for seven important transgressions. If some give their tithes and other do not, a dearth ensues from drought", with other nonsense to the same effect.'[16] The book outlines Montefiore's beliefs and philosophies, most of which struck a sympathetic cord with many of his readers. But he goes on to discuss some of the more practical aspects of this new form of Judaism, the desirability of worshippers being able to understand what they are saying, i.e. English prayers for English worshippers, though he insists on children learning the language of their forefathers. 'The severance of wife from husband and of mother from son in the house of God seems to many of us unnecessary and unnatural',[17] he maintains. So it was that one of the most distinguished members of the West London Synagogue was to lead another breakaway - though not this time such a bitter one – to found another new form of Jewish practice.

CHAPTER VI

War and Revolution

In 1902 Morris Joseph published what has become a seminal work in the canon of progressive Jewish thought. *Judaism as Creed and Life* is a scholarly work aimed at readers from all Jewish opinions, or none. Joseph says in his Preface that 'it lies midway between the orthodoxy which regards the *Shulchan Aruch*, or at least the Talmud, as the final authority in Judaism, and the extreme liberalism which, setting little store by the historic sentiment as a factor of the Jewish consciousness, would lightly cut the religion loose from the bonds of Tradition.'[1] The subjects covered in the book range from Beliefs, through Ceremonial to Moral Duties and the author is not afraid to touch on some of the problems faced by modern Jews of his own time, such as the role of women in society, when he refers to the Biblical use of 'helpmeet' for the creation of man's companion. 'All talk about the superiority of either man or women is idle,' he says, 'they are co-ordinate.'[2] He speaks of the use of the vernacular in divine service. 'The mother-tongue is the language naturally designated as the language of prayer ... it was urged by pious and learned Jews centuries ago.'[3] He quotes from sources as varied as the Midrash and the Bible, to George Eliot's *Daniel Deronda*. Joseph's book, which has been through many editions, was used as a textbook by the United Synagogue for teaching converts. It was reprinted in 1958 with a Preface by another distinguished holder of the post of West London's Senior Minister, Rabbi Harold Reinhart, who took Morris Joseph as his own particular guide and mentor. 'What makes the book most valuable,' he wrote, 'is its deep humanity. God wants the heart: this book goes to the heart. It teaches real religion.'[4] When Reinhart died he was cremated and his ashes, by his own wish, were scattered over Morris Joseph's grave.

In 1904 the West London Synagogue lost an old and much-valued friend when Charles Garland Verrinder died. He had been with the synagogue for forty-five years, and had gained for Berkeley Street a leading position in the world of synagogue music. Organist and choirmaster, he had never in all that time missed a service or even a choir rehearsal. Not a Jew, he had learned Hebrew to familiarise himself with the prayer book in every detail and published, with Charles Kensington Salaman, four volumes of the West London Synagogue music, much of which is still used today. Speaking to the congregation on the first Sabbath after his death, Rev. Joseph referred to the sympathy Mr. Verrinder had always felt for Jewish public worship. He had told his friends that the hours he spent in the synagogue were among the

The Exterior of the Synagogue in Upper Berkeley Street

THE SENIOR MINISTERS OF THE SYNAGOGUE

Professor David Woolf
Marks (1840-1893)

Rev. Morris Joseph
(1893-1930)

Rabbi Harold F.
Reinhart (1929-1957)

Rabbi Dr. Werner van
der Zyl (1958-1968)

Rabbi Hugo Gryn
(1968-1996)

Rabbi Mark Winer
(1998-2010)

Rabbi Julia Neuberger
(2011-)

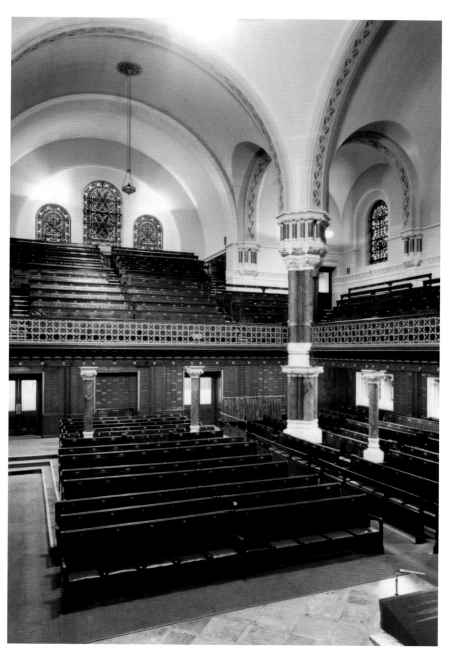

The Interior of the Synagogue from the Ark

The Stained Glass Windows in the Synagogue

happiest of his life. His was a hard act to follow, and the synagogue was lucky to find in Percy Rideout a worthy successor. Rideout was Professor of piano, organ and composition at the London Organ School, and warm testimonials were given on his behalf from the minister of St. Paul's Church, Great Portland Street and the Vicar's Warden at St. Pauls, Wokingham. His knowledge of religious music was comprehensive and he had written many pieces for the organ for use in churches and cathedrals.

After a few years as organist and choirmaster, Rideout, a consummate musician as well as a composer, approached the synagogue Council with a formal complaint about the organ. He found its general condition unsatisfactory, partly from age, partly from neglect and partly from original faults in the construction. 'An organ,' he wrote, 'should be thoroughly cleaned every five years.'[5] Some minor repairs had been carried out but the more serious faults would necessitate the organ being out of commission for some weeks. He explained that organ progress since the Berkeley Street organ was installed in 1870 'has been remarkable as it has been with the battleship, the bicycle and the automobile ... and I have to endure the ordeal of playing it.'[6] The state of the organ was investigated professionally and it was found to need complete reconstruction at a cost of between £1,700-£1,800. The best approach to finding such a sum was to appeal to seat-holders to contribute to the cost.

In 1909 the West London Synagogue's beloved first minister, David Woolf Marks, died at the age of ninety-eight, still bearing the title of Chief Minister. He had seen the congregation through the turbulent years of its early existence, through three buildings and several rabbis, in spite of the unfavourable opinions of the new synagogue that he had had to bear at first. It was said by Leonard Montefiore in an article in the *Synagogue Review* that when the stallholders of Petticoat Lane saw him coming they would shout 'Here comes St. Mark'. It was not only by the Jews that he was loved and respected. He had served for nearly thirty years as a Vestryman (Borough Councillor) for St. Marylebone, retiring at the age of seventy-five, when the Minutes of the Vestry described him as 'able, courteous and enlightened'. Always regarded by the Jewish community, at home and abroad, with respect, even admiration, he never lost his dignity nor his command of the Scriptures and the English language. Letters of condolence were received by the Council from the whole spectrum of Anglo-Jewry. The United Synagogue mentioned 'his earnest desire to bring into close and friendly relations the United Synagogue and the West London Synagogue.'[7] The *Jewish Chronicle* printed a long obituary and included an appreciation of Marks by the Chief Rabbi Dr. Hermann Adler who spoke of him as 'a gifted minister enforced by extraordinary powers of oratory with a remarkable combination of thought, language and delivery which charmed his hearers and riveted their attention.'[8] Another by Rev. Morris Joseph said, 'We always thought of him as a sort of higher tribunal to whose wide knowledge and ripe judgment we could submit our differences in case of need.'[9] The funeral was attended by the Chief Rabbi, the Haham, Dayan Feldman of the London *Beth Din* and most of the eminent members of the Jewish community, including representatives from the United Synagogue, the Spanish and Portuguese congregation, the Board of Deputies, the Anglo-Jewish Association, Jews College and many other organisations, a coming together which in itself was a tribute to the power of Rev. Marks to overcome the divisions that had arisen in Anglo-Jewry.

When the long reign of Queen Victoria came to an end in 1901, the West London Synagogue had changed little from the patriarchal, aristocratic and very English congregation that had come into being sixty years earlier. The Founder families, Henriques's, Mocattas, Montefiores and Goldsmids, were still there, augmented by sons-in-law and grandchildren. Other London Jewish families had joined, often with enthusiasm and young blood, and on the whole the high standards of decorum, musical appreciation and often intellectual achievement were maintained. What these pillars of the community had not yet so far encountered since the old days of schism and excommunication, was any threat to their existence. Anti-Semitism in England hardly affected them at all. Sometimes their children, attending English schools, private and public, were insulted or shouted at, occasionally a lout the worse for wear, might knock off a top hat on a Friday night, but very little concerted animosity troubled their comfortable lives. The appalling treatment of their fellow religionists in Russia and Eastern Europe had little impact. They collected money to improve the lot of the immigrants in the East End, but these 'aliens' were more foreign than Jewish. In fact many London Jews inside and outside the East End were more worried about the lack of control of immigration than about the men, women and children who shared a common ancestry with them and were now beset by troubles beyond their experience.

In 1905 the British Conservative government passed the Aliens Act to restrict immigration into this country. There had been some popular backlash against the apparently endless entry of Jews from the oppressed countries of Europe and the Act was an attempt to control the influx. It permitted the entry to Britain of those whose lives and property were considered to be in danger in their own countries, but it was difficult to administer. Permission to land could be withheld from an undesirable immigrant, who had a right to appeal. However, all immigrants had to prove that they could support themselves and their families, which led to confusion at the ports of entry, for few of those arriving could speak any English. The Act included the 'right to land' for immigrants who could not be refused 'on the ground merely of want of means'[10] if they were truly at risk of persecution . The problems involved in the arrival of so many impoverished Jews in this country were to have two effects on the members of the West London Synagogue. First of all, it led to the immense influence on East End Jews of the social work of Basil (later

Sir Basil) Henriques, son of David Henriques (Treasurer of the West London Synagogue for some years), and to the foundation at the end of the First World War of the Bernhard Baron Settlement. And it was to bring to the fore the often discussed question of Zionism as it affected Upper Berkeley Street, with the immensely important Balfour Declaration being passed in 1917. The first stirrings in this country of a move towards the establishment of a Jewish state are often attributed to Theodor Herzl's visit here in 1896, when he addressed a meeting of East End Jews; the handbill announcing the meeting promised that 'great and illustrious personages from among our English brethren will attend the meeting and some of them will speak.'[11] It was in Yiddish. On this visit he also had a meeting with some of Anglo-Jewry's communal leaders, from the Orthodox and Reform, including Claude Montefiore and Frederick Mocatta, who advised him to stay away from the East End meeting. They were lukewarm in their reception of the idea of a Jewish homeland. 'The idea of a Jewish restoration in Palestine was infinitely more popular in England among upper-class Protestants than among upper-class Jews.'[12] But in fact Moses Montefiore had already paid seven visits to the Holy Land and reported back to the Board of Deputies and to Parliament, though his visits concentrated on improving living conditions for the Palestinian Jews rather than thinking ahead to emancipation and independence. The Zionist Federation was founded in 1897, but the majority of English Jews were either too preoccupied in keeping themselves alive or too concerned with their English roots and their secure Anglo-Jewish synagogues to spend much thought on the land from which their long-ago ancestors had sprung. Apart from Claude Montefiore, already much involved with the Jewish Religious Union and almost virulently anti-Zionist, several distinguished members of Upper Berkeley Street made it clear that they wanted no part in the nationalism of Palestine. Rev. Morris Joseph wrote, 'There are many Jews, and their number is probably increasing, who do not believe in these things (the Return and national revival). They cannot believe in the Restoration of the Jewish state, for they hold that such an event would impede rather than promote the fulfilment of the great purpose for which Israel exists.'[13] They were also nervous, though Joseph did not say so, that their status as English Jews might be diminished if they were to ally themselves with Jewish independence in another land. They were doubtful if it would ever be possible to establish a viable working relationship in that country between religious authority and civil democracy. They were to be proved right.

One member of the West London Synagogue whose anti-Zionist views were publicly stated in *The Times* was Oswald Simon, son of Sir John. He had been at Balliol with Cecil Spring-Rice, Chargé D'Affaires in St. Petersburg in 1903, and tried to enlist the diplomat's help in providing finance for the Jews of Russia, much oppressed by the Tsar's regime. But Spring-Rice refused to become involved, sympathetic though he was. Herzl had thought that if he could raise sufficient capital, he could buy land in Palestine as a sanctuary for the Jews. He had some support from the Rothschilds but the majority of English Jews were very much against any scheme for resettling the Jews in the Promised Land. Young Jews graduating from the universities were often full of Zionist fervour but the majority of support for a Jewish state still came from the poorer and less educated sector of the community. The Chief Rabbi, Hermann Adler, perhaps to his surprise, found himself on the same side as the Reform anti-Zionists, telling a meeting of the Anglo-Jewish Association in 1897, 'I believe that Herzl's idea of establishing a Jewish state there (in Palestine) is absolutely mischievous. It is contrary to Jewish principles, the teaching of the prophets and the tradition of Judaism.'[14]

The debate sometimes veered into the thorny question of Jewish loyalties. The *Jewish Chronicle* published a letter on 9th April 1909 from twenty-five British university graduates insisting that English-born Jews were as English as those born in England who were not Jewish. This was in reply to a published interview with Norman Bentwich, who had suggested that Jews could never completely identify themselves with Englishmen and that 'for them it seems impossible to separate religion from nationality in Judaism.' The signatories to the letter wrote, 'We regard it as dangerous that the rising generation of educated Jews should be encouraged in opinions which must tend to alienate them from other Englishmen.'[15] It was signed by, among others, Philip and Laurie Magnus, Isidore Harris, Joseph Polack, Oswald Simon, J. Felix Waley, Julian Lousada, R.M. Sebag-Montefiore, Claude Montefiore, H.S.Q. Henriques, and H. D'Avigdor Goldsmid, all members of the West London Synagogue. A meeting of the Palestine Committee in 1913 felt that 'the Jew is too intellectual a person to be accepted as a stolid agricultural labourer.'

However, another West London Balliol graduate who did energetically espouse the Zionist cause was Leonard Stein. After a brilliant career at Oxford (he was the first Jew to be elected President of the Union) he was called to the Bar in 1912, served as an officer in World War I and later became a member of the British military administration in Palestine. He devoted much of his career to the situation of the Jews there, serving as Political Director of the World Zionist Organisation and acting as one of Chaim Weizmann's principal aides. He travelled to the States with Weizmann and Albert Einstein to raise support and his book *The Balfour Declaration*, published in 1961, is still regarded as the best account of the event.

One member of the Goldsmid family (though only distantly related to the West London Goldsmids) who was much involved, was Colonel Albert Edward Goldsmid. He, like all the English Goldsmids, was descended from the first Goldsmid brothers to settle in England, but his parents had been baptised. He proudly retained his Jewish heritage, however, and with his wife converted back to Judaism. Born in Poona in India he was a professional soldier and was a firm believer in a return for the Jews to Palestine. He too met Herzl in London, telling him, 'I am Daniel Deronda ... I am an orthodox

Jew. It hasn't harmed me in England.'[16] He was also instrumental in founding the Jewish Lads Brigade.

Nearer to home, Sir Basil Henriques (always known to his 'boys' as the Gaffer) was exploring his own ways of improving the lot of the East End Jews. From a wealthy family, Basil Lucas Quixano Henriques, whose ancestors had come to London from Portugal via Jamaica, had gone to Harrow School and then to Oxford, though he was never a great scholar. He was much influenced by Claude Montefiore in his attitudes to Jewish life, remarking, 'I suppose the world of Judaism is not yet ready or willing to receive a service reformed in bending the knee in prayer, removing the hat in synagogue, praying chiefly in our modern language and retaining the Hebrew for tradition. We want reform, even more violent Reform than your service gives us.'[17] He worked with Montefiore and the Chief Rabbi to establish an academic post in rabbinical studies at Oxford. It was while he was at Oxford that he also met Alec (later Sir Alexander) Paterson, the social and prison reformer, whose work in the East End gave the impetus to Henriques' establishment of the Oxford and St. George's (the East End parish) Settlement in 1914. He stayed for a while at Paterson's Oxford and Bermondsey Mission and, encouraged by his family, concentrated his energies on the poor Jewish element of the neighbourhood, with a view not only to improve their social conditions, but to anglicise their lives in their new land. After a distinguished war record, during which he served with the first established Tank Regiment, he returned to the East End.

Henriques' work – he was by now living nearby – was much lightened by his marriage to Rose Loewe who had formed a girls' club along similar lines. She joined her husband in his life's career and as 'the Missus' was as well-known as he was to the East Enders whom they had come to help. The clubs that the Henriques's founded became models for the improvement of social conditions for young people, and in spite of the difficulties they encountered – most of the boys spoke only Yiddish, were orthodox Jews and very left-wing politically - they met with considerable success. Those who had been associated with the Gaffer remembered him all their lives and were proud to have been a part of his enlightened work. In 1919 the Henriques's founded the St. George's Settlement Synagogue and lived 'above the shop'. The synagogue was the only one to become affiliated to both the Reform and the Liberal movements. The West London Synagogue continued to assist in Basil Henriques' work; when the congregation set up the Junior Membership in the 1930s, many young people went down to the East End to help out, and this continued until long after World War II.

In spite of its interest in such outside events, the congregation's principal concern was of course with its own affairs. All the usual services took place as the seasons turned. At *Succot* the ladies of the synagogue built and decorated a *Succah* on the flat roof. Even the *Jewish Chronicle* came to admire it, describing the roof, 'relieved with bracken in every shade and hanging baskets of flowers, whilst the walls were completely covered with varied foliage, berries, corn, fruit and flowers, and was also ornamented by "Shields of David" outlined in bright-hued flowers and cornucopiae filled with fruit. To complete the beauty of the ensemble, the table from end to end was a mass of exquisite flowers arranged in baskets.'

✡

The situation regarding changes to the Sabbath morning service had been dragging on for years. A Special General Meeting was called in 1909 to approve a resolution that a substantial portion of the service should be in English, that the service should commence at 11 am and last for one and a half hours, and - most contentious of all - that arrangements be made for men and women to sit together. The Council assured the meeting that not only would this probably increase attendances, but that 'such a change is in accord with the wishes of a certain number of members and would involve no infraction of the Mosaic code.'[18] Asked to report on the feasibility of such changes, the Council met shortly afterwards, passed the first two proposals but refused by a substantial majority to agree to the third. After long debate it was recommended that 'ladies desiring to sit near to a relative may be allowed to occupy any seats on the ground floor of the synagogue which are vacant and are not required by the lawful owners thereof.' [19] Not all members agreed but the motion was carried by eleven votes to nine. There were also mutterings that a certain monotony, a coldness, had crept into the services. Perhaps two or three of the silent intervals might be abolished, it was suggested; or that the congregation should recite the *Shema* with the Minister. But as usual there was a disinclination among the members to participate in public worship. Perhaps it was the English reserve that was the problem. Berkeley Street was unwilling to hold a service on the Ninth of Av, because, said the Ministers, the prayers are read to empty benches.

The Bar Mitzvah question again came to the fore. One of the stipulations about re-introducing Bar Mitzvah was that boys should continue their religious training afterwards and subsequently be confirmed. But a sentimental attachment to the old ceremony prevented it from being abandoned. Yet several members of the Council were unsure. Rev. Vivian Simmons (the synagogue's new Assistant Minister), considered the matter at length and reported, 'It is almost impossible to prepare for Bar Mitzvah in the present circumstances (in wartime) ... the amount of religious knowledge attainable by a boy at thirteen is so small that it is obviously exceedingly dangerous for a boy to be allowed to regard his religious education to be complete after he has attained his (falsely called) religious majority. A boy of thirteen is still a child.'[20] He went on to assert the belief in equality of the sexes held by the Reform movement, though Bar Mitzvah gave boys a privilege denied to girls. The Council agreed to allow Bar Mitzvah for boys at the age of fifteen.

Relations with the Liberal Synagogue remained friendly, though each side remained slightly wary of the other. The Liberals approached Upper Berkeley

Street to request burial rights at the Hoop Lane cemetery for their members. The Spanish and Portuguese synagogue had to be consulted, but agreement was reached for twenty-five graves to be allocated with regrets that they could not do more; the Liberals would arrange their own funerals but Berkeley Street was to dig the graves and its regulations concerning tombstones etc. were to be rigidly adhered to.

There was, too, a more friendly atmosphere in the Anglo-Jewish community as a whole. When Rev. J.H. Hertz was installed as Chief Rabbi, West London sent him a warm message of congratulations. His reply was equally cordial: 'Kind messages from congregations and organisations outside my jurisdiction are especially gratifying to me.'[21] However a year or two later Berkeley Street made an attempt to get the United Synagogue to agree to an exchange of pulpits for their respective ministers. The Chief Rabbi seemed sympathetic at a private meeting with Albert Belisha, West London's senior warden, and called on the Editor of the *Jewish Chronicle*, Leopold Greenberg, to print a favourable view of the project. The paper did indeed print an article under the heading of 'Orthodox and Reform' suggesting that the time had come for an exchange of sermons between the two sides, which might even lead to improved attendances at services in both branches of the community. Another meeting with the Chief Rabbi was set up, to include Herbert Lousada, West London's president, Albert Woolf, vice-president of the United Synagogue and Albert Belisha. It was realised that the use of the organ at Berkeley Street on the Sabbath might cause problems for the traditional community, so it was suggested that perhaps the Chief Rabbi might preach there on Hospital Sunday (the yearly service for the Hospital Sunday Fund). But while expressing the greatest regards for the ministers and lay leaders of the Reform synagogue, the idea was considered not acceptable, 'especially as the United Synagogue is likely in the immediate future to be faced with many complex questions in the East End'.[22] What one thing had to do with the other was not made clear.

The Ministers Training Fund had a new recruit. Vivian Simmons had been training for some time under its auspices. He had obtained his BA degree and gone to Germany to the Theological College. Now a new vacancy for an Assistant Minister had arisen and an advertisement for the post was inserted in the Jewish press. The only applicant was Vivian Simmons and he was duly elected. He was the son of Lawrence Simmons, who had been Minister of the Manchester Reform synagogue. He had been as popular in orthodox circles as in reform. His mother was a painter and served as the secretary of the Conference of Jewish Women. The *Jewish Chronicle* welcomed his appointment, anticipating that he would 'maintain the prestige of the congregation, and bid fair to be worthy of his father.'[23]

The First World War claimed many Jewish lives from all quarters of the community. At Upper Berkeley Street, however, the conflict is hardly given a mention in the records of the Council, although individual members clearly found their lives circumscribed by the recent events in Europe. To begin with the Jewish community in England was unsure which side it should be on. Russian Jews were oppressed by the Tsarist regime and many were fleeing to Britain for sanctuary. The Germans were apparently offering their Jews a liberal, assimilated existence where they were able to acquire wealth and safety. The *Jewish Chronicle* made no bones about it. 'For England to fight alongside Russia would be as wicked as for her to fight against the German with whom she has no quarrel whatsoever,' it wrote in July 1914, going on to suggest that it was clearly impossible 'for English Jews, many of whom had family in Germany, to come out in favour of Germany, when such treacherous opinions would bring down on their heads the wrath of patriotic Englishmen, undoing all the years of liberal treatment and happy security.'[24]

The Conjoint Foreign Committee of British Jews, led by Lucien Wolf, was formed as early as 1888 to use the influence of British Jews with HM Government to help Jews abroad. It was formed from the two main organs of Anglo-Jewry, the Board of Deputies and the Anglo-Jewish Association. Almost a microcosm of the West London Synagogue, it relied heavily on the experience and success of the Goldsmids, Montefiores, Cohens and Rothschilds, the aristocracy of British Jewry. It seems obvious now that British Jewry could hardly, even with the support of the Government, have exercised much power over Tsarist anti-Semitic Russia. The two organisations representing it did not always see eye to eye. Both sides were also preoccupied with the Palestine question and concerned that the two problems, the war and Zionism, would become confused in the minds of both the Jews and the government.

Leonard Stein, now a warden at West London, tried to resign his office when he joined the army at the outbreak of the war and rose to the rank of captain, but his resignation was not accepted and whenever he was on home leave he sat in the wardens' box in the synagogue. The Council did take steps to insure the synagogue building and contents against damage 'by aerial craft', and agreed, if asked, to send a minister to France to assist the Chief Chaplain to the Forces, Rev. Michael Adler. They were indeed asked to do so and Rev. Simmons was dispatched to France. He was a popular and hard-working chaplain and he went with the approval of the Chief Rabbi. All accounts spoke of the splendid influence of this young and earnest chaplain on non-Jewish as well as Jewish soldiers. The Council also announced in the *Jewish Chronicle* in June 1915 that they had 'resolved to honour in tangible form the memory of members or sons of members who have fallen in the war.'[25] The form this memorial would take would not be announced until the cessation of hostilities.

British Jews were as quick as any of their fellow countrymen to enrol in the armed forces. A special Jewish Recruiting Office was set up at Camperdown House in the East End, the headquarters of the Jewish Lads Brigade. Many were afraid of conscription after suffering in Russia in the Tsar's armies. Their objections included the possibility of having to eat non-kosher meat, working on the Sabbath, and of Cohens having to look upon dead bodies. Nevertheless many of those whose allegiance was equally to Britain and to Judaism did not hesitate. As the *Jewish Chronicle* put it, 'England has been all she could be to Jews, Jews will be all they can be to England.'[26] Like almost every other organisation in Britain, the West London Synagogue sent its young men to the battlefields, and many failed to come home. Some forty-two members or sons of members of the synagogue lost their lives, and many more were wounded. Their names are read out from the Roll of Honour, together with those who fell in World War II, every year at the Remembrance Day Sabbath service. Philip Waley's son Frank joined the South Lancashire Regiment (the regiment of his mother's brother Frederick, killed in the Boer War) and fought in France. He found himself with a Colonel who had served in the Boer War with 'Uncle Fred', and he used his service pay to buy a second-hand Bugatti. He was wounded in the leg but was awarded the Military Cross for bravery in action.

Frank loved to tell the story of a young rifleman, a fellow Jew, Isaac Rosenberg, in his battalion. As he later scribbled to Leonard Montefiore, on the back of an old envelope, 'Rosenberg was always late on parade, improperly dressed, with his puttees coming down and his cap on crooked – always in trouble and being punished by the NCOs.'[27] His colonel, a humane man who realised that Rosenberg was just a misfit and that punishment would be no good, asked Waley to find him a job. He did so, as an assistant cook. 'He showed me some of his poems, but I had been brought up on Tennyson and Horace and I did not regard R's efforts as anything worthwhile.' He returned to the cookhouse to check on his progress and found the young man scribbling on bits of paper. Sending him back to his duties, he threw the papers into the fire. No-one knows what precious poetry was lost that day.

In April 1916 there were four air raids on the East End, targeting the docks, and causing considerable damage to lives and property. The Germans were now using Gotha planes, long-range bombers with much greater accuracy. A bomb dropped from an enemy aircraft landed in the Balls Pond Road Cemetery on 17th July 1917. There was considerable destruction of tombstones and the chapel was badly damaged. The Government was responsible for repairing damage caused by hostile aircraft, but this did not cover the tombstones themselves. It was necessary for the synagogue Council to contact the individual families of those graves to see what could be done. It subsequently took out insurance to cover such losses both at Balls Pond and at Hoop Lane.

✡

The Anglo-Jewish community now found itself again riven by controversy. Not this time by religious disputation, but by external problems not of its making. In 1917 the events in Russia brought home to the Jews in Britain the question of the participation of the Jews, in Russia and at home, in the Bolshevik revolution. Many thousands of Russian Jews had fled to Britain to escape the pogroms, and had brought with them to the East End of London ideas of equality and freedom which were not always to the liking of their fellow religionists in this country. The *Jewish Chronicle* published an anonymous leader (the author 'Mentor' was the Editor, Leopold Greenberg) which insisted that Bolshevism was 'the hope of humanity', a warning that the old order was changing. He came out strongly in favour of the ideals of social equality and rights for all – 'the first ideals of Judaism' – but questioned its methods. However, when the revolution came the majority of British Jews welcomed it, seeing it as the saviour of the oppressed Russian Jews. The *Chronicle*, under the heading 'Russia Free', greeted the news ecstatically. 'At last the long night for the Russian Jew is ending. Athwart the darkness there has shot a sudden ray of light which will broaden and broaden until the night be gone.'[28] Greenberg, a member of the West London Synagogue, where he had been married (his wife, Florence, was the writer of the best-known book on Jewish cookery), was a fervent Zionist who became a close friend of Theodor Herzl, acting as an intermediary between him and the British Government. He played an important part in the diplomatic negotiations which led to the Balfour Declaration of 1917, when the Foreign Secretary, Arthur Balfour, wrote to Lord Rothschild, 'His Majesty's government view with favour the establishment in Palestine of a national home for the Jewish people, and will use their best endeavours to facilitate the achievement of this object, it being clearly understood that nothing shall be done which may prejudice the civil and religious rights of existing non-Jewish communities in Palestine, or the rights and political status enjoyed by Jews in any other country.'[29]

On 23rd April 1919 the *Morning Post*, a newspaper frequently anti-Semitic in its views, published a letter signed by ten distinguished members of the Jewish community calling attention to the writers' dismay at the attitude of the Jewish press to Bolshevism with which they strongly disagreed. The signatories were Lionel de Rothschild MP, Lord Swaythling, Sir Philip Magnus, Marcus Samuel (later Lord Bearsted), Harry S. Samuel MP, Leonard Cohen, Israel Gollancz, John Monash, Claude Montefiore and Isidore Spielmann. They expressed their pride in their Englishness and desired to dissociate themselves 'absolutely and unreservedly from the mischievous and misleading doctrine which these articles are calculated to disseminate.' This reply from 'the Ten' was intended to counteract the anti-Semitism which the articles in the Jewish press had provoked. But the letter produced something of a backlash. The impoverished Jews of the East End who looked on their Bolshevik fellow Jews as heroes, viewed the West End 'Jewish aristocracy' in much the same light as their 'masters' in their homeland.

These divisions in the Anglo-Jewish community went very deep. They were political rather than religious: Zionists against anti-Zionists, Bolsheviks against anti-Bolsheviks, 'old' Jews against incomers. Members of the West London Synagogue were to be found in the thick of it. In 1917 the anti-Zionists had founded the League of British Jews, who viewed their Judaism in religious rather than nationalistic terms. Small in numbers, the League had a considerable following amongst the more intellectual long-established English families and in 1919 founded its own journal, the *Jewish Guardian*, edited by Laurie Magnus, Sir Philip's son, who saw an opportunity of rivalling the *Jewish Chronicle* and the *Jewish World*. It lasted until 1931 and while the *Jewish Chronicle* concentrated more on parochial news and communal events, the *Guardian* ranged widely over the arts, politics and world events not necessarily within the Jewish community. But the time was coming when internecine rivalries would have to take a back seat. Jewry in England would soon find itself acting as a sanctuary for its fellow-religionists facing the worst oppression their race had ever known.

CHAPTER VII

The Twenties

Once the war was over the West London Synagogue turned its attention to commemorating the dead and offering assistance to the living. A memorial tablet of members and their relatives who had died in the fighting was put up in the Goldsmid Hall, the entrance to the synagogue. The Council suggested giving up the specially composed War Prayers that had been recited every Sabbath, but decided to leave it to the Ministers to make the decision to change this as they felt appropriate. They sent delegates to the Jewish War Memorial Council, with the reservation that they might hold themselves free to oppose any measures that might appear 'inconsistent with the objects for which the West London synagogue was formed.' This organisation, later the Jewish Memorial Council, was set up in 1919 under the chairmanship of Sir Robert Waley Cohen, to establish a permanent memorial to the Jews who had served in the war. The Waley Cohens (Sir Robert was later Lord Mayor of London) remained a separate branch of the Waley family, though interlinked with other cousins. One particular aim, which never came to fruition, was to build and endow a Jewish Theological College at Oxford or Cambridge to which Jews College in London could later be transferred. But the Council was able to provide a better Jewish education for those who desired it and to improve Jewish welfare; it also made better provision for the welfare of the Jewish clergy. It was later responsible for the establishment of the Jewish communal centre at Woburn House, the home of the first Jewish Museum.

One particular change in the West London Synagogue's own organisation was a forerunner of the movement towards Jewish women's 'liberation'; Miss Alice Henriques was elected to the Council, the first woman to play a part in the government of any synagogue in Britain, other than the role of Lily Montagu in the Liberal community. She spoke frequently at Council meetings, but it is interesting to note that in the Council minutes her name always appeared at the end of the list of those attending, regardless of the alphabetical order of the other members' names. She died in 1926, and expressing the Council's sadness the Chairman spoke of her as 'a valuable member whose gentle and pious character had won her the regard and affection of all who knew her.'[1]

The attention of the Council was turned to the East End work of Basil Henriques, and he was invited to attend a meeting at Berkeley Street to discuss his ideas on the establishment of a synagogue in the East End. The St. George's Jewish Settlement was established under the joint auspices of the

West London Synagogue and the Liberal Jewish Synagogue, with a Council of twelve members, six from each organisation, to include two Honorary Officers and one Minister from each. It was to be run on Progressive lines, with Capt. Henriques as the Warden of the Centre. Its first home was a disused hostel in Betts Street, though it later moved to more spacious premises. It remained the only synagogue in Britain affiliated to both the Liberal and Reform movements, and after two more moves was finally amalgamated in 1998 with the South West Essex Reform Synagogue in Newbury Park.

✡

The West London Synagogue did not change its ministers very often. Once they were appointed most of them came to stay until illness or old age compelled them to retire. David Woolf Marks, the first minister, served for fifty-three years, Albert Lowy for fifty, Isidore Harris for forty-four and Morris Joseph for thirty-seven. It was a great shock, though not entirely unexpected, when Morris Joseph resigned from his full-time ministry on health grounds in 1921. He wrote to the Council, 'I need hardly say with what reluctance and sorrow I have arrived at this decision, which portends the termination of a ministry which has extended over a period of more than twenty-eight years.'[2] He continued to serve the Berkeley Street congregation in a part-time capacity for another nine years. Morris Joseph was a Londoner born and bred, the son of the minister of the Western Synagogue, and had attended the Westminster Jews Free School and then Jews College. His early devotion to traditional Judaism soon evolved into a respect and then a love for a more modern attitude to religious life. His friendship with David Woolf Marks at Liverpool where they both served the Old Hebrew Congregation, an orthodox synagogue with a progressive outlook, encouraged him in his wish to serve a community with an enlightened view of his religion.

Morris Joseph's early confrontation with the Chief Rabbi and the United Synagogue resolved itself into an acceptance by the orthodox community of his integrity and scholarship, culminating in an invitation to give the eulogy at the funeral of Chief Rabbi Hermann Adler. He and Adler had sunk their differences and agreed to respect each other's differing concepts of Judaism, coming together in their anti-Zionist stance. Joseph was also involved with the Jewish Peace Society of which he was Chairman, an organisation founded in 1911, to try to deal with the militaristic ideals of many of the Jewish community. His involvement was continued by his successor Rabbi Harold Reinhart; the Society continued to play a valuable role during the Second World War, finally coming to an end in 1970.

As well as his attention to the congregation, leading it as a true shepherd who refuses to allow his flock to stray but comforts them when they are in trouble, Joseph was a fine orator. Several collections of his sermons appeared in print and he wrote on subjects as varied as current affairs, ancient Jewish poetry and the anti-Zionist view of a Jewish home in Palestine. The sermons earned a well-deserved place in the development of Jewish homiletics. When he died in 1930 the *Jewish Chronicle* praised his oratory, 'It was the brilliance of his matter and his polished style, his appeal to reason as well as to sentiment, that specially attracted his listeners.'[3] Nor was Joseph content to remain simply a parish priest with a large and distinguished congregation. He worked tirelessly both inside and outside the synagogue for the welfare of the Jewish people in England and abroad. At Upper Berkeley Street he established the West London Synagogue Association to widen the cultural and social interests of the congregation. Few synagogues in England offered any sort of activities to their members other than purely religious ones. But Joseph felt that there was an opportunity for debates on topical issues, lectures, social events, philanthropic ventures and a chance to bring within the community those who were lonely or disadvantaged. He was proved quite right, as social groups for young people, for women and for older congregants, Jewish education outside Hebrew classes, and the establishment of the synagogue as a social centre, soon attracted a wide audience. The Association continued to flourish through the Second World War and for many years afterwards. Morris Joseph was made Minister Emeritus after his resignation as Senior Minister and continued to give the synagogue the benefit of his scholarship, wisdom and oratory until he died.

Another change of control in the synagogue's government occurred when the synagogue appointed Henry de Metz as its *shammas* (beadle). The beadle of any religious organisation has in his hands far more than the weekly task of showing members to their seats. He is in command of much of the day to day running of the community's affairs, and Henry de Metz was a forceful character who served it for many years 'from generation to generation'. Large and imposing, with a strong voice which could be heard when necessary throughout the building, he could terrorise any recalcitrant congregant from choirboy to worshipper. Many older members of the synagogue remember him to this day; wearing a silk hat and gown, he gave much of his life to the congregation and was loved as well as feared.

The Council was now faced with a difficult situation. It was obvious that what was needed was a firm hand at the helm, and it was doubtful if either of the two Assistant Ministers could provide it. Rev. Isidore Harris was a capable speaker and a scholar but neither he or Rev. Vivian Simmons had the stature or command necessary for a rapidly growing community which played an important role in Anglo-Jewish affairs. The synagogue purchased in 1925 for £16,000 the freehold of the synagogue building, together with Nos. 29-37 Seymour Place (as it now was). It therefore owned a valuable property and had one of the largest congregations in Britain. Even this was not always big enough, for it was necessary to rent space for an overflow service for the *Kol Nidre* service, and if the West London Synagogue Association was to flourish it too needed room for an increasing programme of social events. For some time a desire had been expressed for some sort of Synagogue Magazine.

The Rev. Harris offered to cost out the venture and to edit the journal. The Council agreed to sanction it provided that its contents were supervised by a committee of three, one from the Council and two from the Association. The first issue of the *West London Synagogue Magazine* appeared in 1926, to become the *Synagogue Review* a few years later. All these ventures cost a great deal of money and a Senior Minister of the calibre the community wanted would not be cheap.

In the same year, the Rev. Isidore Harris tendered his resignation for health reasons, although he offered to continue to help out at services. He asked to be retired on full salary, but in accepting his resignation the Chairman would not commit the synagogue to this, bearing in mind that the synagogue would now need to replace two ministers. They agreed to pay his full salary until the end of January 1926. The pension schemes which had been put in place for retired ministers placed a heavy burden on synagogue finances. It was now extremely urgent that plans should be put in train to find a new Senior Minister, for Rev. Simmons could hardly bear the whole burden of leading the congregation by himself, whatever his abilities. Some regarded the succession as being inevitable – that the Assistant Minister would step into the shoes of his senior. But as the *Jewish Chronicle* put it, rather unfairly, 'Mr. Simmons with all his many advantages cannot wear the clothes of a giant without exhibiting himself as an absurd pigmy.'[4]

An Appointments Committee was set up consisting of ten members, five from the Council and five from the general membership, to consider applications for the post. The position was not an easy one. A new leader would need to contend with a widely differing congregation and try to please them all, an impossible task. Many long-time members clung bravely to their traditions and wanted no change. Other new and younger members, some with families, sought to break away from ancient practices. A Revision Committee tried to make improvements and put them in place before a new minister took up his post. One half-hearted attempt suggested that men and women should be allowed to sit together in the body of the synagogue during the afternoon service of the Eighth Day of Solemn Assembly. But even this somewhat patronising concession to a more liberal stance was turned down. When the editor of the *West London Synagogue Magazine* asked his readers, 'What is the greatest danger to our synagogue at this time?', one replied that the congregation was suffering from too much complacency – a kind of moral smugness. He felt it should be moving forward 'We have allowed the Liberal Jewish movement to steal our thunder.' It was certainly time to find a man who would lead them fearlessly into battle and fight just that kind of self-satisfaction.

In August 1925 the Ministerial Selection Committee reported to the Council that they were having great difficulty in finding 'the right man for the job'. No English applicant seemed ideal, and the congregation was always a little dubious about taking on a European candidate. So it was decided that Henry

S.Q. Henriques, K.C.,together with either Harold Marks (grandson of the Rev. David Marks) or Leonard Montefiore should be asked to go to America in order to interview possible candidates for the post of Senior Minister and that 'the expenses be defrayed out of the funds of the synagogue.' The envoys left that same month, deciding to extend their visit to Canada.

The Reform movement in America was far more wide-spread than in England. As early as 1875 Rabbi Isaac Wise had established the Hebrew Union College in Cincinnati as a theological college for training Reform ministers, and in 1922 Rabbi Stephen S. Wise founded the Jewish Institute of Religion in New York. The two were later amalgamated. HUC was the first college for Reform rabbinical training and is still in the forefront of Jewish education for the Rabbinate. The first stop for the West London envoys was Montreal. Here they received a warm welcome and sounded out the Rabbi of the Reform synagogue and a leading member of the congregation. Going on to New York they met many of the leading ministers and lay leaders, including Louis Marshall, Felix Warburg, Dr. Stephen S. Wise, Rabbi Dr. M. Harris, the Rev. H.S. Lewis, Dr. Cyrus Adler, Professor Richard Gottheil and Rabbi Dr. Schulman, attending many services, especially those whose leaders were possible candidates. In Philadelphia they met one very eminently suitable possibility but he did not wish to leave America. Their final stop was Washington DC, to see the President of the Conference of Reform Rabbis. After many weeks of interviews and recommendations, their choice at length settled on the only man who they felt was the right candidate, Dr. Joel Blau, the Rabbi of Temple Peni El of New York. They offered him the post, subject to ratification by the synagogue Council, at a salary of £1,500 per annum, with a pension scheme, and a sum of £360 to cover the expense of his coming to London.

Dr. Blau had been born in in 1880 in Hungary where he had attended the prestigious rabbinical college at Presburg. He came to America in 1905 and entered the Hebrew Union College and the University of Cincinnati, being ordained in 1908. While still a student he married an English girl, Raie Woolf. When she and husband came to live in London she became mistress of the Jewish Infant School. They had three sons. Blau's first rabbinic appointment, after receiving his PhD (his dissertation was on the Kabbalah), was at Temple Emanu-El in Brooklyn. He was a prolific contributor to Jewish and non-Jewish journals and wrote several books, mostly on Jewish law and belief. *The Wonder of Life*, a book of essays, was said by Israel Zangwill to be 'the most daring book on religion ever written by an American ecclesiastic.'[5] When the editors of the annual series *Best Sermons of America* wished for the first time to include a Jewish contribution, they chose one by Joel Blau.

Although showing signs of the debilitating illness from which he died less than two years later, Dr. Blau threw himself wholeheartedly into the life of his new congregation. By July 1926 he felt himself sufficiently at home to put before the Council some ideas for the future path of the West London Synagogue. Under the title *The Point of View* it recounted the position which the synagogue held in the Jewish community, taking the middle way between right and left. 'Benevolently neutral towards all parties in Anglo-Jewry,' he wrote, 'it nevertheless dares to put forward its belief that the future of Judaism in England is bound up with its own development and progress.'[6] He felt it had not realised its own potential, observing 'an attitude of well-bred reticence, not to say aloofness.' Its leaders, while playing an important part in the social, philanthropic and educational affairs of the community, had not taken up their religious responsibilities. 'The West London Synagogue must become the centre, intellectually and spiritually, of the Anglo-Jewish community.'[7] He was not the first leader to reproach the elders for failing to play their part in the religious work of the congregation. Nor was he the last.

Blau's suggestions for repairing the situation were far-reaching and innovative. He put forward the idea of regular Sunday meetings – a Community Forum – which would be under the control of the Synagogue Association. He spoke of the 'utter neglect' of the Friday evening services, which he felt should be attended by the wardens and the Council members, with perhaps a brief address by the minister of no more than ten minutes. He asked the Council for a 'Publications Fund', explaining that he had already been contacted by American organisations for publications from West London 'which do not exist'. This Fund would print and distribute sermons and addresses, involving a stenographer to take them down, as 'speakers do not always write out their talks, preferring sometimes to extemporise'. He asked for a weekly bulletin to be sent to all members containing notices, topics of sermons and matters of congregational interest, thus keeping in touch with members.

An entirely new idea was that of founding outer London branches, perhaps in the East End on Friday evenings and North London on Saturday afternoons. Here he was perhaps a little optimistic as he estimated that in the East End 'one thousand worshippers is fairly assured in advance.' The Annual General Meeting, he thought, should be more personal and less official, to take place in the evening instead of on Sunday morning, with the possibility of a banquet and dance afterwards to increase interest and attendance. He talked of a permanent Education Committee to deal with all matters concerning classes and adult education, with a qualified 'pedagogue' to run them. His final plea was for a speeding up of a Building Programme (already being discussed) to provide room for lectures and classrooms.

At a Special Council Meeting the Council discussed the report at length. On some points they were immediately agreed. The Friday evening services were accepted as inadequately attended and members of the Council felt duly rebuked. They stressed the insistence on an address of only ten minutes. As usual the answer to most of the subjects discussed was the setting up of more committees, one to discuss branch congregations, one for Education, and one for Publications. The idea for improving the Annual Meetings was immediately turned down, and the Building Committee was already enquiring into where and how additional space could be found. On the whole most members of the Council were delighted to find they had a leader who exercised himself not only in the religious matters of the community but on almost every other aspect of congregational life as well.

The Council was pleased to agree unanimously on making Dr. Blau's position a permanent one, and he was duly inducted into his post as Senior Minister of the West London Synagogue. A letter to *The Jewish Chronicle* from a Baltimore correspondent regretted his departure from America, but congratulated West London on obtaining his services, speaking of his Jewish tendency as 'a helpful progressive conservatism much needed in our times because it reckons both with the philosophy of Jewish tradition and the school of modern adaptation.'[8] His induction sermon, on 20th January 1927, recalled Moses' words, 'Here am I'. Speaking of his hopes for the future of Judaism in England, he spoke of 'a mighty stream, its feeble beginnings in antiquity that swell into a brook, and gradually broaden into a river. Can we become tributaries of that river and enrich it with our own life current?'[9]

Joel Blau's suggestions for 'branch synagogues' heralded the beginnings of a Reform movement, a federation of like-minded congregations which was to spread widely across Britain in the years to come. He had asked friends in America whether he was coming to a synagogue or a movement. He was in fact coming to both. But to the great sorrow of the West London Synagogue, their new dynamic young minister died at the age of forty-nine. He was cremated at Hoop Lane at a private ceremony (it was still unusual for a Jew, and certainly for a Rabbi, to be cremated) but the same evening a memorial service was held at Berkeley Street in the presence of a crowded congregation. Rev. Vivian Simmons led the prayers and gave the eulogy, telling his audience that Rev. Blau had specified that there should be no eulogy or special service. But the West London Synagogue, and indeed the whole of Anglo-Jewry, wished to pay tribute to the man who had been with them so short a time yet had made such a deep impression. Rev. Simmons spoke of his qualities as a writer and a preacher, and of his personal affection for Upper Berkeley Street. 'He loved every stone of this building ... he would come here day by day, so completely had he adopted our synagogue.'[10] Among those present were the Chief Rabbi, Rev. Morris Joseph, Rev. Israel Mattuck, of the Liberal movement and many other distinguished persons. Now the synagogue had again to search for a suitable candidate to be their Senior Minister.

Joel Blau hardly had the time in his short tenure of office to straighten out some of the problems of an active and rapidly growing congregation. The Education Committee reported to the Council its dissatisfaction with the synagogue's religion classes. Attendance was poor; rarely more than 40 children attended on any one day. The classes, sometimes four or five at one time, were all held in the body of the synagogue. His Honour Judge Alan King-Hamilton, a later Chairman of the congregation, recalled attending the Sunday School: 'The most junior class was in the two rows of seats immediately behind the Wardens' box … the next class was two blocks away and moving up the scholastic scale, there were two classes opposite on the other side. The Confirmation class was upstairs in the lobby outside the doors to the gallery.'

No reports were offered to parents and discipline was poor. No one teacher was in overall charge. The committee suggested several ways of improving the situation. Its hopes of employing a principal to take charge were dashed by the Council on grounds of cost. However, it did agree to employ another teacher and to divide up the classes and place them in different rooms in the synagogue, the teachers to act as supervisor in rotation. They also decided to make a small charge for each child, the money raised to be placed in a separate fund at the disposal of the committee. The parents were to be given an Annual Report on the progress of each child.

The Ministerial Selection Committee was by now going over old ground. All the possible candidates considered when Rabbi Blau was chosen were as unsuitable as they had been then. Rev. Vivian Simmons did not wish to be considered for the post and it looked as if another trip to America might have to be the answer. But the Hebrew Union College was putting out feelers, and on 23rd March 1928 a telegram arrived for the President, Philip Waley, from Sacramento – AM INTERESTED STOP AM WRITING YOU LETTER TODAY STOP. A few days later the letter arrived, explaining that Rabbi Harold Reinhart and his wife Flora were travelling on the SS Minnesota from Montreal (the first convenient passage they could obtain) arriving in Glasgow on 14th June. Addressed to Philip Waley it went on, 'I am now eager to see you and to learn more about the West London Synagogue. I am respectfully yours, Harold Reinhart.'[11] Clearly communication had been going on behind the scenes, though those involved had not so far actually met.

Philip Waley and his wife Mary were related to most of the 'Cousinhood' of Anglo-Jewry. The Raphaels, the Goldsmids, the Mocattas, the Montefiores, the Jessels, the Seligmans, the Sassoons, all appear in an intricate family tree put together by a later member of the family. Philip had tried for a place at University College, but was not accepted and instead went straight into the Stock Exchange. His father, Simon, had been a Warden at the time of the building of the Berkeley Street Synagogue, and was a distinguished musician, composing a setting for *Adon Olam* still sung in many synagogues on Shabbat. He had died at the early age of forty-eight, and after his death his wife became a Roman Catholic. At his funeral Professor Marks said, 'In every circle where human good is wrought and brotherly love and sympathy are cultivated, the death of the deceased gentleman will be deplored.'[12]

Philip too was a good amateur musician, and a fine shot. He loved horses and refused to have a car until after the First World War (unlike his son Frank who claimed only to have got into Cambridge because of his knowledge of the internal combustion engine). When they did get a car it was a dark-green Armstrong Siddeley, and their chauffeur wore a uniform to match. His wife Mary was an efficient and welcoming hostess, never ostentatious. Philip had helped in the preparation of a new prayer book 'with more English in it'. His splendid home in Gloucester Square had a private letter box at the front door, from which letters to be posted were collected by the postman every morning.

On 24th June 1928, the Council was informed, rather casually, that an American Rabbi was coming over to England shortly and it was decided to ask him to preach at Upper Berkeley Street on 30th June and 7th July. 'Mentor' of the *Jewish Chronicle* always had his ear to the ground, and reported in a short leading article on the 'mystery' surrounding the visit to the West London Synagogue of a young Rabbi from Sacramento, California, who was apparently *not* a candidate for the position of Senior Minister. He was introduced to the congregation and duly gave a sermon, but whatever plans were in hand for his future, Mentor 'never saw a cat in a dairy without knowing it was after the milk'.[13] The visitor, Harold Reinhart, had not so far met any of the Council, but certainly he was sounded out unofficially during the next few weeks. Waley replied at once, inviting the Reinharts to meet the Selection Committee at dinner at his house and later to spend a few days with him and his wife Mary. 'We have a lot to discuss and I look forward with great pleasure to making your acquaintance and have no doubt that whatever be the result of your visit in regard to the synagogue, you will find a ready and warm welcome among us.'[14] There followed a round of visits to some of the senior members of the synagogue's Council, introductions to other distinguished Anglo-Jewish personalities, London synagogues, as well as some sight-seeing, and by the time the American couple left for Paris to enjoy a short break, they must both have been exhausted. On 21st July another long letter arrived from France, thanking Philip Waley and his wife for all the hospitality shown to them. 'I am much richer for this experience – we found so much that is fine in English-Jewish life. I find that I have been writing a new *dayenu*, but I assure you it is as sincere as the one spoken by pious Jews on Seder night.'[15] He hoped that they would be able to go ahead with the project, noting that he was more than ever conscious of some real differences, that more problems would arise, but that 'with a congregation as nearly united as we can reasonably expect, I should be able to be of some service.'[16]

At the end of her husband's letter to Philip Waley, Flora Reinhart added a note to his wife Mary, thanking her for their kindness. 'Our own parents could not have been more solicitous on our behalf than were you and Mr. Waley. We feel for you gratitude and a very real affection.'[17] At a Council meeting at the end of that month it was agreed to call a Special Meeting of members as soon as possible after the High Holydays with a recommendation that Rabbi Harold F. Reinhart be elected to the vacant post of Senior Minister. Philip Waley's report of that meeting in a letter to Reinhart, showed his enthusiasm for the new minister. 'The meeting was well attended – rather unusual for us. The motion (to confirm the election) was proposed by Julian Lousada and seconded by Major Brunel Cohen. Sir Philip Magnus (the dear old man came up from the country on purpose) and Claude Montefiore both spoke.'[18] The meeting was unanimous in its election of the new Minister. He would receive a salary of £1,500 and be granted leave of absence every second or third year to return to the United States for a period not exceeding two months to visit his relatives there. Waley warmly looked forward to the Reinharts' arrival and invited them to stay with him until they found a home of their own. Reinhart's reply by cable read, 'MAY GOD HELP ME BE WORTHY OF YOUR CONFIDENCE STOP SHALL I EXPECT LETTER WITH DETAILS STOP I HAVE NO DOCTORS DEGREE BUT DEGREE RABBI FROM HUC 1915 GREETINGS.' A letter confirmed that they would sail on the SS Leviathan on February 27th from New York. Clearly worried about his form of address, Reinhart suggested 'Reverend' would be suitable and that he would wear 'civilian' dress outside the synagogue. He gave his hat size and the measurements for his gown ('the simplest sort available').

Philip Waley was anxious to complete all the formalities, asking Reinhart to get in touch with the three presidents of his former synagogues, Dr. William Feder, Mr. Henry Cohn and the Hon. Albert Enkus, to ask them for formal references. On his return to America he wrote saying he could now offer himself formally for the post with the official approval 'though not, I am glad to say, desire' of his present president. He felt he could not himself ask for recommendations – that should perhaps come from his new employers, and several very warm letters of commendation were duly received.

Harold Frederic Reinhart was born in Portland, Oregon, on 9th August 1891, one of seven children. He grew up in a home where music, literature and art were important and as a young man he showed a distinctive skill in drawing and design, wrote poetry and loved music. It was an observant Jewish home, though with a Reform inclination and his Rabbi there, who instructed him for his Bar Mitzvah, was Stephen S. Wise for whom he always had a deep and affectionate respect. He went to University in Cincinnati and Chicago and then to the Hebrew Union College in Cincinnati where he was ordained in 1915. His first post was in Gary, Indiana and while there he married a beautiful girl from a Russian-Jewish background, Flora Ruman. The Reinharts moved then to the synagogue in Baton Rouge, Louisiana, where they stayed for seven years, greatly enlarging the congregation and its buildings. It was here that he found and approved the 'open' system of seating whereby seats were unassigned, and congregants could sit where they wished, a system which he tried to introduce during his years in London without success. He was now well known and respected within the American Reform movement, receiving offers to minister to several distinguished congregations. He chose to go to Sacramento in California, but his stay there was short, only four years, before the call came to go to London.

✡

Harold Reinhart was inducted into office at the West London Synagogue on 16th March, 1929. The service was taken by the Rev. Vivian Simmons and the priestly blessing pronounced by the Rev. Morris Joseph, now over eighty. Rabbi Reinhart preached the sermon to a packed synagogue, but there were already indications that the 'new boy' was going to make changes. Naturally he took things slowly but there were clear signs that he would not be content to let matters drift. There were reports of a certain lethargy among the congregation. Many services were poorly attended and the great building was empty for much of the week. Young people felt little attraction in the religious life of the synagogue and there was not much for them to do. One of the new Rabbi's earliest difficulties – a contentious one, then and later – was the question of Bar Mitzvah versus confirmation. From its conception the West London Synagogue had favoured confirmation – for boys and girls –at fifteen or sixteen years of age, rather than the traditional Bar Mitzvah for boys only at thirteen. But over the years many parents had preferred to revert to the old ways even if it meant, as frequently happened, turning to another more orthodox congregation for the ceremony. By the time of Harold Reinhart's arrival Bar Mitzvah at West London was quite usual as families preferred to worship under the Reform banner, while turning to older conventions when they wished.

The new minister would have none of it. He drew up a reference paper which he presented to the Council stating his views. He understood the 'sentimental attachment' to Bar Mitzvah and that abolishing it entirely, as he would have preferred, would meet with considerable opposition. But he felt that certain abuses had crept in over the years and these were what he wished to abolish. Firstly, he suggested that all boys who wished to be candidates for Bar Mitzvah should be placed in touch with one of the ministers not less than two years before the proposed date, so that he could be assessed as to what instruction he needed. Then the parents should commit their son to continue his religious education and subsequently be confirmed. He was thus indicating two ceremonies and – most controversially – that the Bar Mitzvah ceremony should be at the age of fifteen, rather than the usual thirteen.

Reinhart explained that he had come across several cases – particularly with boys away at boarding school – where the candidate was hopelessly ignorant of Hebrew and of what he was required to do at the ceremony only a short time before it was due to take place. The parents of one particular child, whose knowledge was 'practically nil', asked if he might simply read the blessings over the *Torah*. This was felt by both ministers to be quite inadequate, so he was taken away to have the ceremony at a more orthodox synagogue where the suggestion was accepted. Reinhart went on to put the important point of the inequality of the sexes; that whereas previously both girls and boys were confirmed, the Bar Mitzvah arrangements precluded girls from entering into their religious coming-of-age with the boys. His general feeling on the whole vexed question was that the Bar Mitzvah ceremony should be regarded as the preliminary step to confirmation, and that 'the majority of parents who still desire to adhere to the Bar Mitzvah ceremony are very rarely indeed those who are conspicuous by the religious life they lead themselves, or by the religious example they set to their children.' Harsh words indeed to a Council who cherished the status quo of their synagogue regarding their children, and from a leader who had been with them only a relatively short time.

The Council was split in its reception of the proposals. These were that no boy be admitted to Bar Mitzvah after the beginning of the New Year 5691 (1931). It was minuted that l) a boy of thirteen is too young to grasp the meaning of a solemn religious rite; 2) only in rare cases are boys who have been Bar Mitzvah confirmed and regarded by their parents as having completed their religious education; 3) that Bar Mitzvah is contrary to the equality of the sexes, a quality stressed by the founders of the synagogue; and 4) that the confirmation service embodies the spirit of the Bar Mitzvah ceremony in the appropriate religious form of celebrating the attainment of religious majority. The debate rumbled on for many years, the Senior Minister gradually convincing the parents of new candidates to settle for confirmation – under whatever name they cared to call it – and always insisting on a continued period of religious instruction.

By the time he had been at Berkeley Street for a year, Harold Reinhart was feeling well established, and he and his wife had settled into the very different atmosphere of a London congregation. On the anniversary of his first year in office, the Senior Minister preached a sermon reviewing those twelve months. He felt he could now speak 'not only *to* the congregation, but *for* the congregation.'[18] He refuted the term commonly used to describe the position the synagogue held in the community at large, 'the middle way', feeling that this was too safe and sheltered for a dynamic and forward-looking congregation such as West London. 'In this age of mighty traffic,' he said, 'the middle of the road is not the safest place to be.'[19] A nice decorous service, which many members enjoyed so much, was not enough. He sought change and adaptation. 'Orthodoxy, with its completed code and its lack of living authority sufficient to deal with any matter of radical significance, must exalt conformity into the place of prime importance.'[19] This was not, he felt, what was right for West London, nor indeed for the rapidly growing Reform movement. Gone was the closely knit parish circuit – this was the hour for development!

CHAPTER VIII

A Sense of Growing Darkness

The death of Morris Joseph on April 17th, 1930 was greeted with the greatest sadness by all who knew him, and by many who did not. He was cremated at Hoop Lane on April 23rd and a memorial service was held at Berkeley Street the same day. Among the mourners were the Chief Rabbi and the Haham, as well as representatives of synagogues across Britain, and of course as many of the Berkeley Street congregation as could be crammed into the synagogue. Rev. Vivian Simmons conducted the service and Rabbi Harold Reinhart gave the address. He spoke with tenderness and sorrow of the man whom he personally held in high regard. As a scholar and preacher Morris Joseph had been admired in Britain and overseas. Although Harold Reinhart had never heard him preach, he had read many of his published sermons, and felt that his contribution to the West London Synagogue, his love of children, and especially his devotion to his faith, were examples which any rabbi would be proud to follow. The *Magazine* printed the address in full, together with memories of Joseph by Philip Waley, Maurice Myers, Rabbi Morgenstern of Cincinnati, the Union of Anglo-Jewish Preachers, the United Synagogue, church leaders and members of the congregation. A fund was set up in his name the proceeds of which were to be used to offer annual prizes in the Religion Classes for essays on Jewish themes.

Harold Reinhart was unwilling to lose his young congregants once they had achieved their confirmation, and in 1931 he established at West London a Junior Membership for young people over sixteen. The West London Synagogue Association was becoming more attractive for them, with programmes of music and dancing, visits, lectures and debates and it was felt only right that they should have the opportunity of meeting together, and of putting to the Council their points of view. At the inaugural meeting on April 12th it was explained by Leonard Montefiore and Harold Reinhart that the scheme proposed 'to bring to the enrichment of the Congregation a large and virile body of members, whose powers for Synagogue activity have hitherto for the most part lain dormant'.[1] It was decided to leave to the young people themselves to work out how they wanted the group to be run and they at once formed a committee of seven to start operations. Within a month they had written a constitution and arranged their first meeting for the beginning of July in the Goldsmid Hall. At that meeting Sidney Drage was appointed chairman (no adults were present 'not even in disguise'). It was resolved that 'a judicious mixture of social with intellectual activities was essential to success.' However, the Junior Membership was exactly what it said. It was not a Youth Group purely in the social sense – it was an association of the young members of the synagogue, and always maintained its position within the congregation. It traditionally took the service on *Hanucah*, stewarded on the High Holydays and provided as much help as it could in synagogue affairs.

The JM (as it was usually known) drew up a charter. Its objects were 'to give to young people a recognised status in the West London Synagogue so that they can express their opinion, and to provide a recognised body to whom Council, Honorary Officers and Ministers could consult where their interests were affected.' The age of membership was set at 16 to 23 (at first exclusively for the sons and daughters of members but this was later widened to include non-members). A Junior Council was set up with a quorum of twelve, with a Chairman, Treasurer and Secretary. This Council was to keep the synagogue Council informed and to submit to it the yearly accounts. The JM flourished for another fifty years, being the forerunner of the Reform youth groups, until contemporary life changed so completely that simple pleasures, such as rambles and debates, gave way to more sophisticated pastimes.

By the early 1930s only three Reform synagogues existed in Britain: West London, Bradford and Manchester, as well as the St. George's Settlement Synagogue in the East End. But West London had already expanded beyond its natural borders. It had no room for classes or meetings and was already offering overflow services on the High Holydays. An interesting assessment of members' homes showed that the majority lived in North West London (331), with 287 in west and central districts, ninety in the south west, forty-two in east central, five in the south east and four in the east. There were also 103 country members; a total of nearly a thousand individuals. So large had the congregation become that it was almost as if a ghetto had been opened in the West End of London. Its importance was sufficient to cause Selfridges to open a Jewish Book Department in July 1931.

It was suggested that north west London might form a centre of its own, for religious, social and educational activities, even at the risk of losing some of the members from Berkeley Street. In 1933 the North Hampstead Synagogue, later the North Western Reform Synagogue at Alyth Gardens, was founded and took a plot of land leased from the Hoop Lane Cemetery. Two years later, the Edgware and District Reform Synagogue came into being. The New Synagogue in Glasgow was also founded in 1933. These newly formed congregations joined the others under the umbrella of Reform synagogues in contributing to the West London *Synagogue Review* – its only form of inter-synagogue newsletter at that time – sending in a page or two of news, thus keeping all the congregations in touch with one another. Joining them, in June 1930, was the new Bernhard Baron St. George's Jewish Settlement. Opened by H.R.H. the Duke of Gloucester in a splendid new building, it offered under one roof an East End Reform/Liberal synagogue together with the boys' and

girls' clubs, and all the various welfare services so remarkably established by
Basil (later Sir Basil) Henriques and his wife.

It was becoming ever more obvious by now that the synagogue at Upper
Berkeley Street was too small for all it wished to achieve. The great sanctuary
itself was perfectly adequate for all normal Sabbath services, and for New Year
and *Yom Kippur* additional accommodation (usually the Wigmore Hall) could
be hired. But increasing office facilities, ministers' rooms, and expanding
classes, to say nothing of the social activities the congregation enjoyed, were
becoming impossible to house. Clearly a new building or at the very least a
better use of the present one, was essential. Classes were already being held
in members' homes and the various groups - Literary and Debating groups,
a library, a Needlework Section, The Berkeley Players, welfare groups and
the new Junior Membership - that were a part of the Synagogue Association,
were crowding each other out of the main building. It proved impossible to
move the tenants out of the houses the synagogue owned in Upper Berkeley
Street, so the choice fell on Seymour Place, where the synagogue owned
the whole site. The first estimate for the development of the site was put at
£32-34,000. But when the architects' ambitious plans were finally put out
to tender, the cost was considerably higher. It included £1,000 for a cinema,
subject to LCC regulations!

At a general meeting of members at the end of 1930, the Chairman, Philip
Waley, explained in detail the need for more space: a synagogue hall, classrooms,
better offices and library facilities. He made an appeal to the generosity of
members in providing for the work to be done. As early as November 1929,
the Editor of the *Magazine*, Harold Reinhart, who had taken over from Isidore
Harris, asked his readers: 'What is the greatest need of our synagogue in the
New Year?' One reply asked for men and women to sit together. Another
wrote anonymously (the Editor refused to print anonymous articles unless he
had the name of the author): 'Wanted – a Building. Adequate and convenient
headquarters accommodation for the activities of the synagogue.'

At the same meeting, Rabbi Reinhart's proposals for the abolition of Bar
Mitzvah in favour of confirmation were put to members. The Senior Minister
made a convincing speech in favour, but in spite of a long debate which 'waxed
fast and furious' for nearly two hours, the meeting voted for maintaining the
status quo. The congregation of West London seemed more in favour of its
new building than of changing the rules for the formal admission of its young
people to the Jewish faith. Members were enamoured of the idea for 'a stately
and adequate home' and began enthusiastically to subscribe to the request
for financial support. In the *Synagogue Review* (formerly the *Magazine*) an
appeal for suggestions for the use of the new building found several willing
supporters. One suggested the building should consist of only one storey and
proceeded to enumerate all the various uses to which it might be put. By the
time the synagogue hall was built – large enough for ambitious productions
by the Berkeley Players amongst others – with a library, a museum, seven

classrooms, cloakrooms and offices, it would have stretched over several acres. Another wished for a place to meet friends after the Service. This would mean a lounge, a writing room and a light restaurant. A third wanted to ensure that any additional construction would cater for all the synagogue's future needs. If this could not be done for financial reasons, a portion only should be constructed. Every possible need for the space had its devotees: a machine room for the sewing circle, the most modern stage equipment for the theatrical people, a parquet floor for dancers. Clearly the plans for the building could not be drawn up by a committee, let alone by the members in total. One correspondent brought the debate to a meaningful conclusion. Perhaps too much consideration was being given, he suggested, to the social affairs of the congregation and not enough to the religious ones. 'If external social life is an end in itself, it has no place in a synagogue, which, whatever it might have been in the past, is today a religious institution .'[2] It was a timely reminder.

Harold Reinhart's own attitude to the religious part of his work was uncompromising. Unlike some of his congregants, he saw the West London Synagogue as a religious institution of which the social side was purely incidental. His views were unequivocally on the side of equality for all and he was prepared to fight his corner to the end. Influenced by his ministry at Baton Rouge, Louisiana, he was rigidly opposed to seat allocation. First come, first served, with families sitting together, regardless of sex or age, was the way he wanted, with women able to take a full part in all aspects of synagogue life. The Council was prepared to listen but when the question of women reading in the synagogue was put to it (Reinhart wished them to be invited to read the *Haftarah*), the Chairman, Philip Waley, used his casting vote to refuse the motion. However, they were granted permission to be eligible to serve on any committee, to be Trustees or Treasurers, but not to serve as wardens. It was proposed that membership, formerly on the basis of 'seat-holders' should be replaced by an annual subscription so that no member should have a right to a particular seat. This was lost when put to the vote. Members still claimed a prescriptive right on the High Holydays to a numbered seat, in many cases the one which their family had 'owned' for generations. Full rights of membership were extended to all subscribing members over the age of twenty-one, male and female. But it was not until 1933 that the ladies could join the gentlemen in the body of the synagogue on Shabbat. Even then they were confined to the gallery during the High Holyday services for another fifty years.

On 5th February, 1933 the foundation stone of the new synagogue building was laid by Sir Edward Stern. It was a Sunday morning, and a short service was held in the synagogue. In his sermon Rabbi Reinhart spoke of it as 'a new house for the service of God', though he did concede that it would not be primarily for formal prayer. He mentioned the new classrooms which would enable the education of the children to expand and increase in efficiency. There would be a library and meeting rooms for study groups of all ages. 'These rooms will stand,' he said, 'as a permanent invitation to men and women to gather here, and, inspired by the ideal of Jewish culture, to pursue higher thought and deeper understanding, and to express in varied ways their mental and artistic heritage.'[3] During the singing of the 29th Psalm the Senior Minister, the Chairman and the Council walked in procession to the site of the new building in Seymour Place, where Sir Edward declared the Foundation Stone well and truly laid. Back in the Goldsmid Hall, he was presented with the gold trowel he had used to perform the ceremony. Sir Edward Stern, Bart., D.L., was a typical English country gentleman, who loved his horses and the pleasure of the hunt, and his fondness for children, in spite of his deafness or perhaps because of it, inspired his endless work for the Home for Deaf and Dumb Children. He was unwell at the time of the laying of the foundation stone, and he had already given a very handsome donation to the Building Fund. He sadly died a few weeks later. Edward Stern was educated at Kings College School and London University and went into the family banking firm of Stern Bros. He was for many years in the Territorials (the Berkshire Yeomanry) and involved himself in several organisations concerned with the Arts, with children's welfare and the upkeep of the countryside. He had been a long-standing member of the West London Synagogue and a warden for three years. When the new building was completed the principal room in the new wing, the communal hall, was named after him. As the work progressed the Council decided that other rooms in the new building should also bear the names of some of the generous donors. So the Library would become the Morris Joseph Library (many of his books had been offered to the synagogue), and four rooms on the second floor were to be named after the Mocatta, Montefiore, Sassoon and Waley families. Eleven firms had tendered for the work, and the contract was awarded to W.H. Gaze, at an estimate of £30,773.

The congregation itself was growing and flourishing under the leadership of Harold Reinhart, a dynamic and hardworking minister from the moment he arrived in London. The concerns over its descent into a boring and stagnant congregation, which refused to entertain change or improvement, were quickly dispelled. Watching the skeleton of the new building rising from the demolished old houses that had stood on the site, inspired the members to greater heights of activity, encouraged by a constant stream of information about the progress of the work in the monthly *Review*. However, Rabbi Reinhart's enthusiasm did occasionally overreach itself. Alan King-Hamilton (who himself remained a leader of the congregation until his death at the age of 105) proposed that the ministers should refrain from introducing politics 'either directly or indirectly' into their sermons, and should also refrain from introducing domestic politics unless previously approved by the Executive. Political discussion should be 'absolutely prohibited in the synagogue or in any part of the synagogue buildings, in the *Magazine*, or in any other publication or communication emanating from the synagogue or the Synagogue Association.'[4] However, the Council disagreed and felt that no action was called for. It clearly trusted its ministers not to overstep the mark.

✡

The domestic problems of the West London Synagogue – its new building, the behaviour of its ministers, Bar Mitzvah or confirmation – paled into insignificance in comparison with the horrors facing Jews in Germany and Eastern Europe. However much the English establishment might later profess ignorance of what was happening abroad, the Jews in this country were fully aware of the treatment meted out to their fellows (though not yet how appalling it was to become), particularly in Germany. The President of the Board of Deputies, elected only a few days before Hitler became Chancellor of Germany, was Neville Laski. He was still President when war was declared in September 1939, and his Presidency was marked by the terrible events in Germany, by the rise of fascism in Britain and the developments in Palestine. In fact the Board, as representative of Anglo-Jewry as a whole was generally considered to be slow to act in regard to Nazism. It was top heavy with committees and rent asunder with the private allegiances of the Deputies themselves. 'It considered it should not embarrass the government, which was tending to play down what was happening in Germany.'[5]

However, Harold Reinhart took it upon his broad shoulders to ensure that West London, at least, should do whatever it could to help. He made sure from the earliest days that his congregants were fully aware of the terror sweeping Germany. Articles appeared in the *Magazine* about the treatment of German Jews. One maintained, 'The joining of the vicious pure-race theory with the ascendancy of a reactionary militarist regime is a union of which anti-Semitism is the natural as well as the boasted offspring.' Meetings were set up at which eminent speakers, whose voice carried weight in the community, could explain what was happening. Leonard Montefiore, O.B.E., President of the Anglo-Jewish Association and Joint President of the Joint Foreign Committee, and of course a long-standing member of West London, addressed such a meeting on May 29th 1933, telling his large audience of the oppression of the German Jews. 'Though the German government may say it cares very little for foreign opinion, no country can ignore what its neighbours think.' He explained that it had been decided that no boycott – 'a double-edged weapon' – would be exercised against Germany. He said that practical relief could be obtained in three ways: by providing assistance to those Jews who chose to remain in Germany. (Few could foresee in those early days what would befall them.) Secondly, organisations were being established at home to provide help for those who emigrated to England, particularly in finding jobs for those previously professional Germans who could no longer continue in their former work; and thirdly to help in the relief of those who had left without possessions or income and sometimes without families.

A service of intercession for German Jewry was held at the Albert Hall, under the auspices of the Chief Rabbi, and organisations such as the Central British Fund and the Jewish Refugee Committee were quickly and enthusiastically established to organise the work. However, this was not enough for Harold Reinhart. With the help of his members, particularly the women, he set up the West London Synagogue Sub-Committee on Hospitality under the Chairmanship of Mrs. Julian Henriques (working with the Central Hospitality Committee at Woburn House), to offer hospitality to refugees, marrying up the members offering help with those coming from Germany in such desperate need. Financial help was requested – an advertisement in the *Magazine* read 'Thousands of pounds are needed – gifts of shillings will be gratefully received.' Leonard Stein, also a distinguished congregant, edited several pamphlets published by the Joint Foreign Committee on the situation in Germany: *The Persecution of the Jews in Germany, The Jews in Nazi Germany* and *The Religious Foundations of Internationalism*. They were reviewed in the *Magazine* and readers were encouraged to inform themselves as widely as possible about events in Europe. Donations to the Central British Fund were published each month. The intellectual needs of the refugees were not forgotten. 'Many of these refugees are cultured and sensitive people, Jews and Jewesses whom it is a privilege to know. Pity is the last thing they want.' It was the fate of the children that most exercised the minds of the congregation. A letter to the *Review* told how all schools in Germany at the beginning of term had to inform the children that Jews had no rights – they were only guests among them. One brave child dared to say that if Jews are guests they should be treated as guests in a friendly way. The girl was expelled. The members of Berkeley Street were particularly asked to provide homes for some of the young people coming to England, and if possible to teach them English.

The *Synagogue Magazine* (it became *The Synagogue Review* in December 1934) published a report from the High Commission in Germany to the effect that some 22,000 German Jews had emigrated, the majority to Palestine where they received training as artisans, though problems arose for professionals who found it difficult to pursue their original calling. Documents and papers were provided where possible by friendly countries, though there was great difficulty for stateless persons leaving Germany. There were restrictions there on property and pensions which were steadily intensifying. As regards their religion, Leonard Montefiore noted that in Nazi Germany 'the Old Testament is declared to be a book only fit for usurers, cattle dealers and white slave traffickers.' Such was the flood of refugees coming into Britain that the government had to review its immigration procedures. England had been considered as a small-scale temporary refuge, a country of transit for those refugees wishing to go to Palestine or the United States. But many wished to stay; some had relatives here or had always considered this country a sanctuary, as it indeed it was.

The British government had no legal responsibilities to refugees. It did not distinguish between immigration and the granting of asylum. It was concerned that any more generous policy might increase anti-Semitism in this country. Those who were unassimilated, who were easily identifiable by their outward appearance and those whose grasp of English was minimal or non-existent, were at the bottom of the selection list. Three senior officers of the Board of Deputies signed a declaration that no German Jew admitted to this country as a refugee would be a charge on the state. The three were the President, Harold Laski, Lionel Cohen and Leonard Montefiore – the last two were members of the West London Synagogue.

The refugees were divided, arbitrarily, into three groups. Group A were those of 'doubtful loyalty' Group B were of 'uncertain loyalty'; and Group C were of 'unquestionable loyalty'. But how such decisions were made was never made quite clear and many Germans coming to England changed group either on the whim of those in control, or because they fought for a change of status.

The events leading up to the elimination of Jewish life in Germany have been told elsewhere. The West London Synagogue played its part in the 1930s to rescue and re-establish as many of the refugees as it could. What occupied the thoughts of Harold Reinhart, too, was the fate of the German Liberal rabbis, many of whom had trained at the *Hochschule fur die Wissenschaft des Judentums* in Berlin. They could not hide from the German authorities, nor did they wish to. They felt their duty lay in staying as long as they could, to encourage and help their congregations in their terrible plight. Many were imprisoned, some were killed but Reinhart was sure that the future of Reform Judaism in England lay in enabling as many as possible of these brave and learned men to escape to a friendly land, find homes for their families and carry on the religious work that they had trained to do.

The head of the Jewish liberal movement in Germany was Rabbi Leo Baeck. He studied for the rabbinate at the eminent seminary at Breslau and was granted *semicha* at the *Hochschule* in Berlin. A gentle, scholarly man, he was respected by the Nazis and offered the chance to leave in 1938. But he refused, in spite of the pleas of his friends and family. He was elected President of the Representative Council of German Jews and remained to help his fellow Jews in whatever way he could until 1943 when he was sent to Theresienstadt. Here he was revered as a courageous example, insisting on taking his share of physical drudgery and giving lectures and talks to alleviate the terrible fate. His life was saved almost by chance. Another Rabbi, Rabbi Beck, died soon after he arrived. The authorities were informed that the great leader, Rabbi Baeck, had died, and made no further attempt to hunt him down. He continued to encourage and help the inmates of the camp – those who had not been transferred to Auschwitz – until the Russians arrived to rescue them. He refused to let them kill the German guards and finally agreed to travel to London to make his home with his daughter and her husband. Here he took a leading part in the life of the Progressive Movement, lecturing, preaching and trying to resuscitate the former glory of European Jewry. He became a British citizen. Many older members of the West London Synagogue will recall the slight, white-bearded figure sitting in a corner of the synagogue listening quietly to the sermon and the prayers. His name will always be remembered in that of the college for Progressive Rabbis.

Among the other rabbis rescued at this time was Dr. Bruno Italiener, who served for a while at West London. He had met Leo Baeck while they were both serving in World War I. Together they were responsible for founding Sunday morning seminars at Upper Berkeley Street for the refugee rabbis and teachers, conducted entirely in German. They included Gerhard Graf, who went first to Bradford, then Leeds and finally led the congregation at Cardiff, and Ignaz Maybaum, who came over with his wife and children on a *kindertransport*. He had been arrested by the Nazis in 1935 and served six weeks in prison. He was a distinguished theologian and became rabbi at the Edgware Reform Synagogue, making a considerable impact on the community at large, and on the training of young Rabbis at the College, because he was so traditional and at the same time so revolutionary. He maintained a strong German accent all his life, as did many of his fellows.

Another was Jacob Kokotek, who first taught at West London and then led the German based synagogue in Belsize Square. Charles Berg also assisted at West London and then went to Wimbledon on its foundation in 1950. Dov Marmur, born in Poland, fought in its war with Russia and finally led the Alyth Gardens Synagogue. Ernst Sawady went to the St. George's Settlement in the East End, and died at the early age of forty. The only Czech-born rabbi to come to England at this time was Arthur Katz, instrumental in founding the Association of Synagogues in Great Britain as the much enlarged group of Reform congregations was known. He became the first minister of the Hendon Reform Synagogue where he was succeeded after his death by his son, Stephen. Also an Assistant Rabbi at West London was Michael Curtis, popular for his quiet, shy charm, who became the Secretary of the Reform *Beth Din* when it was established in 1948.

The minister from Germany who perhaps was best known to the members of Upper Berkeley Street in Harold Reinhart's time was Curtis Cassell. He had stayed with his congregation in Germany until almost the last minute, when he and his wife Cecilia (they had been married in Berlin by Leo Baeck) together with their small son, decided to try to get to Sydney in Australia, where they had relatives and a post offered at Temple Emanuel. It was impossible to go straight there from Germany, but they managed to get to London. Here, in 1939, only a month or so before war was declared, no passages on planes or boats to Australia were obtainable, so they decided to stay. Curtis was conscripted into the Pioneer Corps, where most enemy aliens were taken at the beginning of the war, and his wife went into domestic service, the fate of many Jewish refugees from Germany. It was not until 1947 that the family, with a new baby, finally found a congregation to serve in Glasgow. A year later the Cassells came to West London, where Curtis was given a post first as Headmaster of the synagogue classes, then as Assistant Minister. However the German Rabbi who was eventually to succeed Harold Reinhart some twenty years later, though neither anticipated this at the time, was Rabbi Werner van der Zyl. Van der Zyl was born in Germany in 1902 and graduated from the *Hochschule* in Berlin. He was arrested by the Gestapo and imprisoned in Hanover. Lily Montagu was responsible for his release and Leo Baeck encouraged him to come to England where he was interned as an enemy alien. He became rabbi of the North Western Reform Synagogue in 1943.

These eminent and courageous men formed the basis for the rapid expansion of the Reform movement in this country. In 1942 it became the Associated British Synagogues and four years later the Association of Synagogues of Great Britain. Without them there would have been no more than a loosely-linked number of individual congregations. There was no training college for progressive rabbis and the few young men in this country who wished to go into the ministry. They brought with them Jewish scholarship and a tradition of serving their communities. The tragedy lay in the reasons for their coming.

CHAPTER IX

Berkeley Street At War

Just fourteen months after the laying of the Foundation Stone, the new building was ready to open. By means of continuing reports in the *Synagogue Review,* together with photographs, and of course what it could see with its own eyes, the congregation was kept fully informed. They watched as the brickwork rose among the old houses that fringed the site. By January 1934 the main structure was in place and the *Review* reported that plastering had begun. The Stern Hall filled most of the ground floor. It was a large room with big windows and a gallery, a spacious stage, suitable for theatrical performances, concerts or lectures, as well as for religious services when needed. It could seat 400 people. There were kitchen facilities in the basement, where the storage, heating and ventilation arrangements were. The building was heated by the panel system through electrical power. Upstairs on the first and second floors were the series of rooms which could be used for a variety of purposes; the Council Room and library, together with secretarial offices, were on the first floor while on the second floor were offices and classrooms and rooms for the ministers, as well as space for meetings and clubs. The offices for the Reform Synagogues of Great Britain were also housed there.

In March the opening of the annexe was announced for the coming May and the *Review* described it as 'sober, dignified and entirely suited to its high purpose' and printed the plans of each floor, including the mezzanine floor and the flat roof (a play area for the children and a suitable site for the *Succah*). Suggestions were invited for a name for the new building; the replies included: Berkeley House, Synagogue House, West London Synagogue House, Menorah House, Headway, the Synagogue Annexe, Beit Ha Kenesset, and The New Building. Finally it was decided to call it simply '33 Seymour Place' and so it has been ever since.

27th May was indeed a momentous day in the history of the West London Synagogue. Two separate ceremonies marked the occasion: a Service of Dedication was arranged for the morning, together with the Official Opening of the Building; and in the afternoon there was a Thanksgiving Service and Commemoration. Both took place in the new Stern Hall. The Rev. Vivian Simmons gave the morning address, mentioning in particular the welfare of the synagogue's children, hitherto doomed to try to learn in rooms totally inadequate for their use. He paid tribute to the President, Philip Waley, to the Treasurer, Alfred Belisha, to B.M. Woolf, the Secretary and of course to the Senior Minister, the driving force behind the project. Then the assembly was addressed by Samuel Instone, Chairman of the Building Committee. He congratulated the Berkeley Street children, who came 'unwillingly to school', where they were given lessons in 'overcrowded rooms, corridors, staircases and even in cloakrooms'. He told how the Ministers and staff were forced to work in conditions that would have been condemned under the Factories Act. But now, he declared, there would be 'proper and fitting accommodation' for them all.

The President formally accepted the key to the new building and welcomed the distinguished visitors, among them the Chief Rabbi, the Haham, Dr. Mattuck of the Liberal Jewish Synagogue, and Sir Robert Waley Cohen of the United Synagogue. Dr. J.H. Hertz, the Chief Rabbi, in a short speech, explained that, in spite of the differences that existed between Reform and Orthodox Jewry, he decided to be there that day because of his conviction 'that far more calamitous than religious difference in Jewry, was religious indifference.'[1] He congratulated West London on its participation in the community at large. Other religious leaders spoke, and then some hundred guests were escorted around the building. The afternoon's Thanksgiving Service was taken by Rev. Simmons, and the sermon given by Rabbi Reinhart. He viewed the house as a 'symbol of allegiance to a new standard of Congregational life, or rather to the old high standard which the fathers set when they raised the noble Shrine of which the extension dedicated today is the worthy complement.'[2] The Service included a new Dedication Hymn specially composed by Maurice Jacobson.

The new building was quickly put to good use. The telephone switchboard was enlarged and transferred to the cubbyhole just inside the new front door, rather grandly named the Porter's Lodge. This meant that the entrance was never left unmanned, and although security was by no means as tight as it is today, it did enable some form of control to be exercised on visitors to the building. The 'Little Chapel' on the first floor was renamed the Room of Prayer, and Rabbi Reinhart insisted that any Jew or Jewess who was in the building at 6.30 pm should attend there for a short ten minute service. The new Council Room was hung with portraits of former rabbis and Council officers with a plaque in memory of Morris Joseph after whom the room was named. Glass-fronted bookcases along two walls held the books from Morris Joseph's library.

The new facilities delighted all the various organisations which were part of life at Upper Berkeley Street. One particular new club was founded at about this time. Known as 'The 33 Club' it was aimed at the German refugees. Open every day, it proved to be a welcome relaxation for the many homeless visitors. Here they could find friends who spoke their language, enjoy music, play table tennis and enjoy tea or coffee. There were also language lessons for those who knew no English. The Board of Deputies had prepared a booklet *While You Are in England* given to all refugees, warning them to avoid speaking in German or reading German newspapers in public, to refrain from being conspicuous, and in particular not to comment on how much better things had been in Germany. The treasurer and moving spirit of the Club was Sir Sidney Drage. He sent a brief note about its activities to the *Synagogue Review* every month, always prefacing his words with a short quotation from the Bible or the Classics.

✡

The Junior Membership, who helped to run The 33 Club, entered into a friendly alliance with the youth groups of other synagogues to harmonise its work in the community at large. This led to the suggestion that the new building should be used as a focal point for what was eventually to become the Youth Association of Synagogues in Great Britain. The JM now had more than seventy members and offered a wide programme, including table tennis, mock trials, debates, lectures, dances and participation in synagogue events. Unlike the parent body, the younger members encouraged boys and girls alike to play a full part in congregational affairs. Many participated in social work at the Settlement in the East End, and invited young German Jews to come along to meetings. Several were to become important members of community life. The younger children founded a Scout Troop, the 25th St. Marylebone Troop, and also formed a Junior Branch of the League of Nations. The editor of the *Review* included a monthly children's newsletter within its pages. It invited comments on anything from fasting to the celebration of Christmas.

Changes were occurring in the synagogue services. For some time the congregation, and particularly the Ministers, had been dissatisfied with the Prayer Book. They were anxious to bring the Sabbath and the Festival services more closely into line, to make the services more modern and up-to-date by introducing variations. These would include participation by the congregation and modifying some of the old prayers and introducing new ones to meet the synagogue's religious needs. Among these changes were to have choral singing for *Mah tovu,* to put the Priestly Blessing at the end of the service instead of in the middle, and to read the *Kaddish* once only. Philip Waley also recommended that some of the prayers composed by Morris Joseph should be added, to be read aloud or silently. 'These prayers,' he said, 'are clearly composed to meet our present-day needs and aspirations, and may well help us to shape our daily lives on a nobler pattern.'[3] A *Kiddush* was introduced after the Friday evening service, though members needed reassurance that some portions of that service would be omitted so that it did not go on for too long.

Dr Rideout was becoming very concerned with the state of the organ. He expressed his feeling in strong terms to the Council, who felt that in spite of the heavy expense incurred by the new building, it was essential that West London should have an organ worthy of its name. Comprehensive repairs were ordered and the organist was soon able to write to the council, 'Most of the old pipes were retained and revoiced, additional stops to enlarge the range of tone qualities were added, and the entire action was pneumatically mechanised.'[4]

With the new building in full use, the daily work of the staff was much increased. The Beadle, Mr. de Metz, still commanded the ship, but in order to make it clear what the crew's duties should be, the Council drew up a list for him. He was taken on for one year at a time and re-elected at each Annual General Meeting. He was to open and close the synagogue and be present at all services. He was in charge of the synagogue and its ancillary buildings and was expected to live close by. He was to attend at all Council meetings and General meetings, all marriages and burials and at private houses if a Minister was in attendance. He should make all arrangements for funerals and not claim any fees without the consent of the wardens. He was to take no commissions. He should comply with all orders and if he should transgress in any way he could be suspended. A lesser man than Henry de Metz would have quailed under such a task but he took it all in his stride, kept the staff under his personal control, and like a butler of an aristocratic establishment, brooked no disagreement from anyone. During the war he became an ARP Warden and was instrumental in dealing with a fire that had broken out on the synagogue premises before too much damage could be done. He had become a part of the larger family and his son Sidney was elected Chairman of the Junior Membership. The congregation's membership continued to grow, though there were still fairly strict rules as to who might be admitted. When a certain gentleman applied to join, it was found that he was by profession a moneylender. He was refused, though some of his illustrious predecessors continued to be members as City money brokers, surely the same profession.

A motion was put before the Council in October 1936 to consider closer co-operation with the Liberal movement. It was suggested that five representatives from West London and five from the Liberal Synagogue should come together to see what further association between the two might be beneficial to both. The proposal stated that 'whilst differences existed in rituals and methods of procedure, there was general agreement between them and their respective congregations on religious principles.'[5] Claude Montefiore, the leader of the Liberals and a staunch member of West London, was strongly in favour. Both organisations stood for Progressive Judaism and any such move would not interfere with local autonomy. The Council resolved to consider how some form of co-operation might be achieved, but with three instead of five representatives of each body. A year later the talks broke down because West London viewed its affiliate synagogues as completely independent, but Liberal synagogues were controlled by their governing body, which seemed to fetter their full freedom of action. Relations remained cordial, but many at West London felt that they might have had a narrow escape!

In the summer of 1937 Harold Reinhart was taken ill. It seemed serious – he was away from his duties for some time and likely to go away to recuperate. The synagogue was not well placed for ministerial assistance. Rev. Simmons was the second minister but he needed help (the congregation by now numbered some 1,700 persons). A young Oxford scholar, Chaim Rabinovitch had been a temporary Assistant Minister for a while and the synagogue offered him a permanent post, initially for three years. But he turned it down. Chaim Rabinovitch later changed his name to Chaim Raphael and is known for his Hebrew and Jewish scholarship, though he wrote several books on non-Jewish themes, including an autobiography, *Memoirs of a Special Case.* The Council decided to do its best to find a new incumbent specifying that they would prefer an English-born candidate as at least a temporary assistant. There were, in fact, two possible candidates in the United States and it was decided to try to obtain the service of one of them at a total cost of £650 (to include the cost of his fare to England). The young man chosen was Rabbi Louis Cashdan, who came to England in 1939 to help out. He was appointed to a regular post as Assistant Minister and stayed until 1942. He explained that he had then to return to prevent the loss of his American citizenship if he stayed away too long. He finally went first to Des Moines and then to Canada as Rabbi at Temple Emanu-el in Toronto. While in London he proved to be a great friend to the congregation, especially to the younger members and many of the Junior Membership kept in touch with him after he left England.

By the early months of 1938 Jews more than any were aware of the terrors that the National Socialists in Germany were inflicting on minority groups in Europe. The war clouds were not dispelled by Munich, in spite of the optimism of Mr. Chamberlain. The *Synagogue Review* published a letter signed by two Junior Members (who were encouraged to contribute to the journal each month) which was virulently anti-war. It urged the community to play its trump card - 'the absolute refusal to fight.'[6] The young idealists continued 'Unhappily, unaided by glamorous uniforms, stirring music and adulation of fools and cowards, man has not the courage to use this godly power.' The letter was followed by others from irate older members of the congregation, disputing the reasons for war set out by the original writers. Major J. Brunel Cohen, with a distinguished war record from the first World War, wrote, 'It seems lamentable that young men should arrive at even their obviously, tender age without realising that as strong a reason as any for fighting is the wish to defend one's own.'[7] In the same issue Harold Soref contributed an article defending the nation's right to go to war. 'If the democracies of the world were to disarm, the forces of the swastika and the fasces would have a free field for oppression and injustice.' Soref was a right wing polemicist, later a conservative MP and member of the Monday Club, who battled with most establishment bodies at one time or another, including the BBC, the Anglo-Jewish Association and every synagogue he joined. He founded the *Jewish Monthly* and only his sharp sense of humour prevented him from quarrelling with everyone he met. Perhaps at the age of thirty-one he was cutting his journalistic teeth in the *Synagogue Review.*

At home, too, danger signals were obvious. Sir Oswald Moseley addressed a meeting at Olympia in 1934. His speech was a full-scale attack on Jews 'a foreign, antisocial menace, exploiting British Society and exerting disproportionate, deleterious influence.'[8] The Board of Deputies, always reluctant to interfere in politics, kept its collective head down and limited its stance to thanking MPs for raising the matter in Parliament. The *Jewish Chronicle* was very critical and as the Fascist involvement grew, the Board became more willing to be involved, forming the Jewish Defence Committee, responsible for dealing with all anti-Semitic attacks in this country. However, even though the initiative had come from the Board itself, it condemned the 'unauthorised activities' of the Committee in dealing directly with HMG, and distanced itself from the Committee, many members of which were members of the Communist Party.

West London was warned, like all other public places of worship, to consider taking Air Raid Precautions. It was hoped that members of the staff would take up some form of National Service. Already Mr. Woolf, the synagogue secretary, had been granted leave of absence for three months to carry out relief work in Austria, where his family had come from. With the outbreak of war he rejoined his regiment with the rank of 2nd Lieutenant. He refused the synagogue's offer to make up his salary. When Hitler moved into Austria that year, the steady stream of refugees needing help increased. The Hospitality Committee, charged with the task of administering help to those Jews managing to get to London, was inundated with requests, particularly for young people. Pleas for money appeared regularly in the Jewish Press, and the West London Synagogue, like other synagogues and churches throughout the country, held a special service of solemn intercession for Jews and all who suffer persecution.

The Council, however, seemed rather more concerned with the centenary celebrations due to take place in 1942. They planned for a special service to take place on the evening of 27th January (the date of the very first service one hundred years before). They asked Cecil Roth to produce a history of the congregation, with an introductory chapter by Harold Reinhart, and appointed a Centenary Committee to submit recommendations for the celebrations.

In the early months of 1939 Rabbi Reinhart was hard at work on behalf of the Jewish refugees coming to England from Germany and from Eastern Europe. He sent money to enable them to get to London. All immigrants had to have a sponsor, to affirm that they would not be a drain on the state, and many of these sponsors were not Jewish. The Quakers, in particular, were exceedingly generous with practical as well as financial help. Harold Reinhart called in many favours (and few could resist his beguiling requests), to find domestic posts, educational facilities and comfortable homes for the new arrivals. He was also dealing with West London's usual administrative work, answering letters and replying to questions. One mother, whose son was to be Bar Mitzvah at an orthodox synagogue wished him to use the Sephardi accent as she had grown up with it at Berkeley Street. The Rabbi explained the differences in the vowels and the one consonant (the letter 'taf'). 'As you know, the Ashkenazim are careless about the authentic Hebrew accent,'[9] he wrote, and went on to explain the stress that each pronunciation used. Always tolerant of non-Jews who married into the faith (sometimes more so than of those who were born Jewish), he refused to countenance a wedding in the synagogue where one partner had not converted, though he would always perform a blessing after the ceremony. Approached by the comedian Bud Flanagan on behalf of Val Guest, the writer and producer whose wife was not Jewish, he agreed to bless their baby daughter at the latter's home.

In spite of itself the West London Synagogue was moving into the modern age. The Rev. Cashdan proposed that 'any woman member of H.M. Forces may, with the approval of the Wardens and Ministers, read the *Haftarah* at the Sabbath Service.' This was agreed without contention. Already women were being asked to play a more active part, not only in the Jewish community, but in national and international affairs. The President of the synagogue circulated a message from Sir John Anderson (Lord Privy Seal, after whom the wartime Anderson shelters were named). Every man and woman in Britain was asked, 'Will you volunteer for National Defence? Will you pledge yourself to serve your country according to your age, physique and special skill?' The response was heartening, especially from the women. The foundation of the Women's Voluntary Service in 1938 was to prove a vital part of the running of Britain once the country was at war. The Chairman was the Dowager Marchioness of Reading, the second wife of Lord Rufus Isaacs, the second Marquis, whose family had long been members of Upper Berkeley Street. The Chairmen of almost all the various committees affiliated to the West London Synagogue Association were women.

✡

In the first issue of the *Synagogue Review* after war was declared on 3rd September 1939, the Editor, Rabbi Reinhart, printed a poem he had written at the ending of the High Holy Days. It began:

> We prayed the New Year's healing for bruised humanity
> Instead it broke in, dealing relentless agony.
> We sought a token given by Heaven's holy light;
> Instead we're snared and driven, bewildered by the night.
> We looked for indication of truth and peace in store;
> We're met with desolation of treachery and war.[10]

He suggested that members of the congregation should possess 'a little armoury' consisting of the English Bible, the WLS Calendar giving the Sabbath readings, and the Daily and Sabbath Prayer Book. Two days after war was declared the Council called an Emergency Meeting. The Executive had been considering various measures regarding the holding of services and the administration of the synagogue during the war. The London Fire Brigade advised discontinuing the use of the synagogue for services. This was in line with the government's wish to limit the number of people assembled for public worship. The attendance at any one meeting was limited to 250, so several services were held over the High Holydays to permit all those who wished to attend. A scheme was prepared for the conduct of the services and circulated to members, and the Council (which usually met only every three months), agreed to extend the Executive's powers so that any decisions could be expedited. Two months later, during the 'phony war' it was suggested reverting to holding services in the synagogue. But this was felt to be premature and the Stern Hall continued in use as a temporary synagogue. By the spring of 1940, with full blackout arrangements in place, and heating no longer needed, the synagogue reopened for services. Men and women sat together on the High Holyday Services because of the risk of families being separated during air raids. The National Anthem was sung at the main services on all Festivals, on the first Sabbath of every month and on any special occasion. Amid protests, the synagogue's beautiful iron gates were taken away for the 'war effort'. In view of the name of the congregation – Gates of Righteousness – this was particularly unfortunate.

Two months after the beginning of the war, with many of the younger members of West London enlisting or being called up, Harold Reinhart wrote a series of short pieces called *War Time Prayers*. They appeared first in the *Synagogue Review* and then were reprinted on tiny pages which could be kept easily in a uniform pocket and carried about. Another series, *Worship in the Fortress*, appeared a few months later and many men and women in the armed forces found them of great comfort at a time when they had no opportunity of attending congregational services.

Very aware of the worsening hostilities the Council had postponed the ideas of celebrating the centenary of the foundation of the synagogue. They did eventually commemorate the occasion, but not in the way they had wished. No book was written by Cecil Roth, no celebrations with music and laughter took place and no-one felt like having a good time. Quietly and with restraint the *Synagogue Review* carried a series of short articles remembering the troubles encountered by the founders of the congregation, the reasons for their actions, the *cherem* issued by the Chief Rabbi and the trials and tribulations they had gone through before the West London Synagogue of British Jews came into being in 1840. The anniversary did coincide with the congregation's return to worshipping in the synagogue itself, and a special service was held there on the day. Rabbi Reinhart led the service and several members of the Council took part. The worshippers prayed: 'Let not the treasure of all the vision and hope, joy and zeal, yearning and devotion which has mounted through these hundred years of our congregational life - in the first council chambers, in Burton Crescent, in Margaret Street and here - pass away, but

may the stores of spiritual power remain and continue to grow, to bless our
and future generations.'[11] In his address the Senior Minister said, 'This hour
of celebration is no time for giving details for our religious necessities. But
the need cries out. Our religious life lies about us in ruins, especially in these
tragic times…as our fathers wrought in their day may we strive to perform in
ours; and through continuing piety may this dear "Berkeley Street" be now,
and in the years to come, a centre of light and of life, of aspiration, of comfort
and of hope.'

In October 1940 the West London Synagogue was damaged by a bomb
which fell at the back of the synagogue building. Many of the beautiful stained
glass windows were blown out, there was damage to some doors, with holes in
the roof and some internal disruption, particularly to the annexe. No-one was
hurt either within the building or in the basement which had been turned into
an Air Raid Shelter. As many as one hundred people a night took refuge there.
Many of those in the building at the time had lucky escapes. Fortunately the
synagogue itself was closed, having reopened for the summer, with services
taking place in the Stern Hall. Mr. and Mrs. Reinhart's flat in Bryanston Court,
backing on to the Upper Berkeley Street synagogue, also suffered damage.
So did both the synagogue's cemeteries, though the government paid for all
damage to gravestones.

The Council widened its remit on admitting non-members' children to
religion classes, so that the sons and daughters of refugees could receive
instruction. When it was suggested that for funerals of refugees a special area
of Hoop Lane should be set side, Rabbi Reinhart refused, insisting that this
would lead to 'an invidious distinction.' After the fall of France all enemy
aliens were interned, to be released where such release 'would involve no
danger to the public'.

Many of the wealthier members wished to send their children abroad to
America or Canada to escape the bombing, but some were evacuated with
thousands of non-Jewish London children to safer homes in Britain. The
little evacuees had the advantage of their contemporaries in the East End
in that they often had some experience of country life. They usually spoke
good English, rather than Yiddish or a mixture of East European dialects, and
were less 'foreign-looking'. But war made equals of them all and they were
as home-sick as their fellows, for there were few Jews in the areas where they
were sent. The Central Committee for Problems of Evacuation was set up by
the government and the Jewish community did its best to offer some form
of communal life including Hebrew lessons, services for the Sabbath and
the Holy Days and seders at Passover. The Board of Deputies appealed to
all synagogues for assistance in providing religious education. However the
request was turned down by West London when it realised that the teaching
would follow orthodox lines. It requested that Reform synagogues should
be allowed to offer their own form of education (Sephardi pronunciation,
English prayers and Jewish history). The Board refused, but the problem had

an unforeseen result. Upper Berkeley Street called a Conference in Manchester to which all five Reform synagogues (West London, North West London, Manchester, Bradford and St. Georges) sent representatives. This was the first meeting of the nucleus of a Reform Movement.

Called originally to discuss religious education, it was decided to establish a Standing Conference which would meet once a year (or more frequently if necessary) under the title Associated British Synagogues. The first affiliated synagogue to include the word 'reform' in its name was North West London (Alyth Gardens). Twenty-six delegates met at the Midland Hotel in Manchester under the chairmanship of Harry Marks, grandson of West London's first minister and president of the synagogue. They agreed to organise a system of education for the children of Reform Jews, but the importance of the meeting lay in the coming together of five synagogues with similar ideas on the way they wished their religious life to be interpreted and the possibility of future association in other spheres of activity. They also decided to arrange a meeting with the Liberals to see if any mutual benefit might ensue. Sadly, the Park Place synagogue, the home of the Manchester Congregation of British Jews, was completely demolished by German bombs not long afterwards. No one was hurt but the synagogue's collection of scrolls and appurtenances was damaged beyond repair. West London, with other members of the Association, offered its help. Another synagogue that had to close for very different reasons, was the Edgware and District Reform Synagogue in London. Its Council decided that in view of the fact that many of its leading members were called up or leaving London, it could not maintain services or other congregational activities and it closed down for the duration of hostilities.

Some of the small communities established outside the cities during the war became thriving congregations, where Reform or Orthodox affiliations became less important than keeping a Jewish atmosphere and a Jewish home for the children. The appalling bombing of the East End virtually brought to an end the Jewish presence there, culminating in the destruction in 1941 of the Great Synagogue in Duke's Place, the first and biggest Ashkenazi synagogue in Britain. Almost all the tiny synagogues in the streets around Whitechapel, Stepney and Hackney were destroyed (at the height of the Jewish immigration into the East End there had been one on almost every corner) but a few did survive, including Fieldgate Street, Princelet Street, Sandys Row, East London and the Voice of Jacob in Commercial Road. The St. George's Settlement Synagogue also came through almost unscathed although it moved twice and eventually in 1997 merged with the South West Essex Synagogue in Ilford.

A young boy whose school was evacuated from London to the country gave an interesting account of how he and his fellow Jews were coping, so far from any traditional Jewish education. He described their meetings, discussions and an amended form of service, and went on to say, 'We have some boys from the West London Synagogue and some from the Orthodox and some from the Liberal, but we have managed to create our own service and decide on our own policy without any friction at all. If we, as boys, can co-operate in such a fashion, we should be producing the right type of person to assist in Jewish affairs. There are still some misguided souls who think that by professing their Judaism they are increasing the possibility of anti-Semitism. This is far from the truth, for when the Jew shows how proud he is of his own religion, he cannot help being respected by others.'[12] Another fifteen year old West Londoner, evacuated to the depths of the country where she helped out on the farm, showed something of the calm determination of many Jews at this time. 'For the adolescents, we who will have to make a new world after the war, it is necessary to learn all we can and prepare ourselves to take the places that would normally be filled by the generation now fighting. It is ignorance of beauty and art that causes such horrors as the Nazi regime. I think it is most likely that England will be invaded and that the Nazis may try to rule. They will fail. They cannot break our spirit,'[13] she wrote to the *Synagogue Review*.

The East End of London, with its large Jewish population, was greatly in need of help. The Board of Deputies put out an appeal for clothing and tinned food, and for help with billeting homeless families, working in rest centres and caring for children made homeless by the bombs. Some school teachers kept the schools open during the holidays as many children had nowhere else to go. The West London Synagogue was not slow to respond. The Hospitality Committee worked tirelessly to obtain clothing, especially shoes, toys for the smallest children and for funds to care for the ninety-three children it had taken under its particular care. It was managing with a much reduced staff – all voluntary – as helpers joined the forces. It still manned its office at Berkeley Street every day of the week. In January 1941 it was noted that the Committee had managed to find work for 'two girls training as dressmakers, living in a hostel; one girl apprenticed to a milliner, living with her sister; two boys training for Engineering; four boys in Hotel work; one girl out of work, in a hostel; one boy awaiting training as an Engineer.' The report ends sadly, 'The boys in hostels get a day off a week and have nowhere to go. The girls in hostels get wary of being in a herd and often long for a little peace and privacy.'[14]

There were appeals for binoculars for the fighting services and for help for Polish Jewry, whose need was equally as great as that of the German refugees. A refugee camp begged for a piano to provide concerts – some of the inmates were skilled musicians. The ladies knitted and sewed for the troops, bemoaning the dreaded khaki colour of wool, the only one they could use for socks and mittens. The Needlework Section of the WLS Association continued its work in a country vicarage. Lady Nathan of Churt (the Nathan family had been members of West London for some time and Lady Eleanor Nathan served on the London County Council) made a special appeal which she thought might be devoted to the 'ground-defenders' of London, those who manned the Anti-Aircraft guns, the searchlight crews and the men of the Balloon Barrage (the huge inflated balloons intended to trap low-flying aircraft). In the event it was decided instead to fund mobile canteens manned by the YMCA, which could quickly be on the spot to provide hot drinks and food for forces or civilians, particularly in bombed areas of London during the Blitz.

By now the Junior Membership, which flourished in the warmth of the friendship of West London in wartime, had sent many of its members to fight in the armed forces. In 1941 it introduced its own magazine *Focus,* a small but well-written and interesting journal. The Council congratulated the editors on the appearance of the magazine and suggested it should be sent to all serving members of Berkeley Street, young and old, as a means of keeping up with the youth of the congregation. The third issue included an article – 'Focus on Berkeley Street' which invited the reader to stand back and look at the synagogue. 'You will see the jagged skeletons of buildings, the torn out window frames, the rubble, the dust. Then there is the synagogue, intact and apparently unscathed. Inside, if you look hard, you will see the battle scars: a piece of cardboard or even just an open space where once was a stained glass window.'[15] A remarkable piece of on-the-spot reporting from a young amateur newspaperman.

Members, staff and ministers at Upper Berkeley Street were determined to continue with as many activities as possible during wartime – 'business as usual', as Mr. de Metz put it. One letter to the *Synagogue Review* suggested that the magazine should cease publication for the duration, in view of the cost and energy expended in keeping it going. The Editor replied that he felt sure that its value to members at home and abroad, in civilian and military life, was worth any amount of effort. The Junior Membership, too, refused to give in and played an important part in keeping its members in touch with one another, though it was now beginning to report in *Focus* some of the casualties brought to its notice. Its activities differed somewhat from those it had enjoyed in peacetime. Debates centred more on problems of Jewish life during hostilities: should women be conscripted for 'war work', for example. Much of the news it printed in the magazine was news from the front, activity in Home Defence or achievements of its members. But the congregation kept going, sure that this sense of continuity was vital in keeping up the morale of its members. It offered hospitality on the Festivals to those who were far from home, or who had no home at all. Subscription income was considerably down on usual levels; some members had left London and resigned from the synagogue, some were unable to pay due to their changed circumstances, others had joined congregations nearer to where they were living. Staffing levels were cut and those who were left had to work harder than ever to maintain standards.

The welfare of those members of the synagogue who were engaged in the fighting overseas was a subject of much concern to those left at home. Complaints were being made in the daily press about the quality of care that might be expected from the chaplains, and Jewish chaplains were no exception. A letter from 'A Private' to the *Synagogue Review* examined the changes that inevitably occurred when Jews joined the forces. 'Religion is no longer the synagogue and the congregation, the festivals and the lovely atmosphere of the Jewish home,' he wrote, 'but a church parade, the not attending of which may bring them into trouble and an Army Chaplain to whom they have to pay military compliments.'[16] He urged those on the Home Front to 'adopt a number of Jewish soldiers to whom you send your greetings on Jewish festivals, to whom you open your home when they are passing by.' In the First World War Rev. Vivian Simmons had acted as chaplain to the Jewish forces with considerable success, but he was now too old for active service. He left Berkeley Street in 1939 to go to Alyth Gardens, and then served several other Reform and Liberal synagogues. He died at the age of 83 in 1970. A.S. Diamond wrote of him, 'He was tall and fair; he read the prayers with grace, dignity and clarity in a well-modulated voice; he had good knowledge of the music and a taste for Jewish scholarship.' Not a bad obituary for a man who never quite made it to the top of his profession. Other correspondence on the subject of Jewish chaplains followed, and the ministers assured their congregation that their sons and daughters did have access to Jewish chaplains - three in the Middle East, where the bitterest fighting was - and that all efforts were being made to increase the number available.

In 1942 the United States came into the war, and many American Jewish servicemen found themselves stationed in or near London. Harold Reinhart's links with America were still strong and he let it be known that these soldiers and airmen, far from home, would always find a welcome at Upper Berkeley Street. It was Samuel Golden, the father of a later warden, Lewis Golden, who established, with Reinhart's encouragement, the West London Services Club for British and Allied Servicemen and women. Thousands of lonely Jews (and some Christians) came regularly to Upper Berkeley Street, in uniform, where in the Stern Hall they could find companionship, refreshment and a chance to relax from the horrors of war. The Club was open every day between 3 and 9.30. An advertisement in the *Synagogue Review* in January 1943 asked for gifts of furniture and equipment as well as books and periodicals. Apart from the Stern Hall for larger gatherings, there was a canteen, a reading room and a room for music and games. It was not long before word of this 'home from home' got round and the building was soon teeming every day with men and women of many nations and many religions. Many women of the synagogue were happy to serve as hostesses and a 'captain' was in charge of each session. Dances, concerts, billiards, table tennis and darts were arranged and by popular request special Sunday afternoon tea dances with bands from the RAF and from the American Services. Not all the allied soldiers were aware of what was going on. One, seeking entertainment, wandered into the synagogue on the Day of Atonement and asked, 'What sort of a show have you got here? Is it any good?' The reply was, 'It ought to be – it's been running for nearly six thousand years!'

CHAPTER X

A Hard-Fought Peace

The Second Conference of the Associated British Synagogues took place in London in November 1942. It set up a central fund for financial assistance to any congregation needing it and its aim was to advocate the cause of Reform in areas where there was no progressive synagogue. It was also anxious to set up both a *Beth Din* and a Central Committee of its own Rabbis. The ministers and congregants of the Reform Movement refused to allow the enthusiasm they had engendered to fall by the wayside just because the nation was at war. A congregation was formed at Leeds and other towns and cities were showing interest in having a progressive synagogue of their own. This expansion of Progressive Judaism was partly due to the Liberal influences coming in from Germany. The Belsize Square Synagogue was established almost entirely by and for liberal German immigrants. Their sermons were, at least to begin with, in German, and their Rabbi from 1957 was Jacob Kokotek, who had been brought over by Harold Reinhart in the 1930s.

As the weary years of fighting rolled on, the West London Synagogue began to worry about its future. The danger from bombing in London and the welfare of its members overseas were its principal preoccupations, but the Council was beginning to express doubts about the future administration and control of the congregation when the war ended. The Synagogue Association met infrequently and before long its young people would be returning home, needing a lively and invigorating organisation. Meetings of the Council and Annual General Meetings had been virtually abandoned during hostilities and it was felt that it was time to tighten up the administration to cater for a new generation of Jews whose lives had been turned upside down by what they had been through. A new committee was set up under Harry C. Marks, grandson of the first minister, to establish what was needed under circumstances the congregation had not experienced before. Rabbi Reinhart was overwhelmed by the work that he had undertaken and Rabbi Charles Berg (previously in the Pioneer Corps) came to Upper Berkeley Street to help out. Col. Robert Henriques was upset. 'To have people with German accents is deplorable,' he told the Council, 'He would not be the type of man we should want.'[1] Rabbi Berg proved to be an admirable Rabbi and administrator, liked by all. He became minister of the Wimbledon Reform Synagogue when it was established in 1950.

Many members of Upper Berkeley Street saw action during the war. Some lost their lives and the congregation mourns their loss every Remembrance Day Shabbat Service in November. A register of all members serving in H.M. Forces and in Civil Defence was drawn up and members of the congregation were asked to pass on to the Senior Minister the names, ranks and branches of service of their families who served. A Youth Conference was held at Seymour Place at which nearly all Jewish and Christian youth organisations were represented. Most of those who came home spoke little about their experiences, but it is known that they acquitted themselves with honour and courage. Alan Tyler, son of a former President, became a Lieutenant Commander in the Royal Navy, Leo Bernard joined the Royal Marines and went over to France on D-Day, and his sister Gladys became a V.A.D. nurse. When the war was over she joined the Jewish Relief Unit to help at Bergen-Belsen. Joan Ansell, Helen Keen and Joan Lewis enlisted in the WRNS. Lewis Golden, son of Samuel Golden who had started the Services Club, became adjutant of the 1st Airborne Divisional Signals and landed at Arnhem. He later wrote a book about his experiences, *Echoes from Arnhem*. Murray Lewin was wounded at El Alamein; he wrote an article, called 'These Above All', recounting some of his memories of war which was published in the Junior Membership's *Focus*. 'I remember …the sinking feeling I had when the ambulance arrived to pick me up and it was discovered that there were no stretchers inside, so that it had to return to the forward dressing station three miles away to get one, and every minute counted.'[2]

✡

One young man who was destined to play a vital part in the affairs of the West London Synagogue was quite unknown to anyone in London at the time. He was better acquainted with the tragedy that had consumed Europe than any of his fellows at Upper Berkeley Street. This young Hungarian boy of fifteen was Hugo Gryn. He had been taken with his family from his home in Berehovo and sent with his father to a prison camp. He survived the horrors of the concentration camps. His father died two days after their release but Hugo reached his home where he managed to find his mother. The story was afterwards told in his own memoirs, written with his daughter Naomi, *Chasing Shadows*, but it was not until several years later that anyone at Upper Berkeley Street knew of his existence. Nor could they know what an influence he was to bring to bear on their affairs. When he did come to England, in true West London tradition, he met and married a girl from West London's Junior Membership, Jacqueline Selby.

The West London Services Club continued throughout the war to offer a 'home from home' to servicemen and women from many nations (and religions) who found themselves in London. One particularly enjoyable event was a visit from E.N.S.A. in the Stern Hall. It was recorded by the BBC and transmitted to troops abroad. Another was the visit of comedienne and singer, of music hall fame, Nellie Wallace. Wounded servicemen were invited to attend special entertainments, were given presents of cigarettes and took back to hospital some of the flowers that had decorated the synagogue. The congregation, which had also formed an Activities Committee and a Symphony Orchestra, determined to maintain as far as possible a semblance of normality. The younger members of Upper Berkeley Street were also becoming wary of their future. 'Will the JM be the same in the future as it was in pre-war days?' an editorial in a 1944 issue of *Focus* asked. It went on to suggest that the older members would answer 'We hope so', while the younger members would probably answer 'We hope not.' They formed a new group, the Berkeley Reunion Group, for JM members returning home.

In May 1945 came the end of the war in Europe. For the Jews it meant that democracy had won and the iron fist had failed. But, as the *Jewish Chronicle* wrote in its first edition after peace was declared, why did it have to happen time and time again, that a tyrant dragged down peaceful, innocent peoples before a rescue could be mounted to save them? Nevertheless the country celebrated joyously. The Anglo-Jewish establishment arranged days of thanksgiving, the Board of Deputies called a special meeting to welcome the peace, and the King and Queen visited the East End, to the site where the last V2 rocket had landed in Vallance Road, killing 150 people, mostly Jews. Thousands turned out to greet them, though the East End would never again be the home of such a large Jewish community.

At Upper Berkeley Street the congregation was struggling to re-establish itself. Harold Reinhart himself, an ardent and active pacifist from his youth, had worked ceaselessly to support refugees, fighting men and women and had done all he could to promote peace in his adopted country. He had been associated with the Jewish Peace Society and the League of Nations for some years, and now he lent his energy to the National Peace Council and the Campaign for Nuclear Disarmament. He was also active in fighting for the abolition of Capital Punishment and took some of the members of the congregation to a meeting at the Albert Hall, where the principal speaker was Victor Gollancz. Reinhart remained an American citizen all his life, and could have returned to the United States when England went to war. But he was by then a part of the life of the West London Synagogue and had absolutely no intention of leaving it in its hour of need.

The Council called a Special General Meeting in October 1945 so that it could discuss with the membership the best ways of proceeding in time of peace. The Chairman, Owen Mocatta, explained to the meeting that it considered the synagogue should revert to normal practice as far as possible, and that 'there must be a transition period while this end is reached.'[3] He gave a brief account of the fortunes of West London during the war; how Air Raid precautions were put in place; correspondence lessons were arranged for children away from home; of the 'great stores of energy' of the Senior Minister,

and the help given by Dr. Italiener and Rabbi Arthur Katz. He thanked the
Wardens for keeping the services running and Mr. de Metz for maintaining
the efficiency of the building. He spoke of the Services Club and the Junior
Membership, and condoled with those who lost family and friends during
the conflict. But his outlook for the future was vague, and seemed to look
forward to 'everything as it was before.' Every member present must have
known that this could not be so. Lives had changed, young Jews had grown
up and Berkeley Street could no long maintain its cosy niche in Anglo-Jewry
with little heed for the outside world.

The West London Synagogue was now the leading member of a growing
group of like-minded congregations. The Associated British Synagogues, as it
was in 1942, with six constituent members, became in 1946 the Association of
Synagogues in Great Britain which within a few years had doubled in size. It
now had a Youth Association and in 1947 established an Assembly of Ministers.
At Conference that year it was suggested that the Reform movement should
have its own *Beth Din*. Rabbi Reinhart was firmly in favour. He understood
that many young people were returning from the war wishing to marry and
settle down, often with non-Jewish girls who might very well want to convert
to their husband's religion. Conversion by orthodox means was a lengthy and
often difficult path, and it seemed the time had now come when a Reform
court should be set up to deal with this, as well as having power to arbitrate
on other matters of Jewish law. Not all his fellow rabbis agreed. Some thought
this a retrograde step – a return to 'rabbinical authoritarianism' – as a leading
account of Reform Judaism put it.[4] Would the traditional 'government by
laymen' have to submit to a greater power? Would those ministers who were
not rabbis be excluded? What interpretation of Jewish law would rule over
decision-making?

Rabbi Reinhart decided to go it alone if necessary, and set up a Reform *Beth
Din* at Upper Berkeley Street. Conversion certificates were issued in the names
of individual synagogues, rather than of the Association itself, and Rabbi
Michael Curtis was appointed Clerk (later Convenor). Without the refugee
rabbis from Germany (as Michael Curtis was) there could have been no *Beth
Din*. They were to form the bulk of those who sat at its sessions and almost
all took part at one time or another. Rabbi Leo Baeck himself frequently sat
as a member of the Court. He had come to London in December 1945 and
Upper Berkeley Street welcomed him as an Honorary Member, voting the
sum of 250 guineas towards a pension that had been set up for him. At his
death it was said that he was called from the *Beth Din* below to the *Beth Din*
on high. It was not only in the matter of conversion that the Reform *Beth Din*
acted. The question of the *Agunot*, the 'chained' women who could not obtain
a *Get* (religious divorce), cross-communal problems, difficulties with proving
Jewish descent, all these matters came before the court. 'The object of the *Beth
Din* is to help,' wrote Rabbi Curtis, 'it does not judge people, nor condemn

those who transgress.'[5] It was established to enable Reform Jews to live their lives according to Jewish law as interpreted in the way they chose to follow.

✡

Life in England once the war was over was not always as rosy as those on active service had thought it would be. Right wing movements were founded to 'give England to the English' and Fascism was not dead simply because Hitler and Mussolini were no more. In April 1946 several ex-servicemen joined the newly established 43 Group. This was set up (named after the number of those attending the first meeting at Maccabi House) by Morris Beckman and Gerald Flamberg to counteract the increasing number of Fascist attacks on Jews in the East End. The British Union Party was among the right-wing groups who continued to demonstrate, sometimes very violently, against Jewish homes, shops and offices. Little action was taken either by the Board of Deputies or the Home Secretary, James Chuter Ede, but many members of AJEX, the Association of Jewish Ex-servicemen, took an active part in countering the attacks, feeling, as they explained to the *Jewish Chronicle,* that this was not what they had fought for. They set up meetings across Britain to fight for their democratic right to peace and clashed on many occasions with the black shirts of Moseley's men and the other right-wing agitators. Berkeley Street members were much in evidence, perhaps because of their English background. It had been 'their war' and they were not about to let the victory be ruined by the peace. Leo Bernard and Jessica Blooman (née Kemper) were speaking on a platform in Derby, when it was overturned by a group of violent demonstrators. They were not badly hurt – Jessica was more concerned about her ruined nylon stockings and her dignity, but when Marks and Spencers heard of the incident they insisted on replacing the stockings! Several other members of Berkeley Street, particularly those who were helping their friends in the East End, were similarly treated by these right-wing agitators. The Jewish establishment frowned on their counter measures. 'The Board's leaders deplored the illegal tactics of the 43 Group and resented its challenge to their claim to represent communal opinion.'[6]

The Board itself was now very much under the control of the Zionist movement in this country. The President throughout the war and for a few years afterwards was Selig Brodetsky, an ardent Zionist, and a brilliant mathematician and physicist. In his opening speech as President, he tried to reassure the Deputies of his intentions, hoping that it would be possible 'for a convinced Zionist to be just as impartial and objective and fair in the conduct of the affairs of a mixed body as a convinced non-Zionist or a convinced anti-Zionist.'[7] Upper Berkeley Street had never been too concerned about affairs in Palestine. Now they could not avoid it. It was a British problem as well as a Jewish one and a conflict of interests made it difficult to take sides. Many of those who were liberated from the concentration camps felt Palestine to be their real home, but the British tried to prevent wholesale immigration into the Mandated Territories. After the Holocaust the Jews were learning to fight back, and the British forces in the Middle East responded in kind.

In July 1947 the King David Hotel in Jerusalem was bombed by Palestine Jewish extremists, with appalling loss of life, and the terrorism of the Irgun and the Stern Gang against British soldiers caused an uproar among British Jews whose loyalties were divided. They felt that nothing could excuse the murder of Jewish civilians by other Jews, whatever their feelings towards the Zionist cause. West London called an Emergency Meeting of the Council and put out the following statement: 'We, the Council of the West London Synagogue of British Jews, condemn without reservation every act of terrorism and violence carried out by Palestinian extremists; we regret these outrages as a betrayal of the most sacred teachings of our Faith. We express these sentiments the more strongly because we are mindful of the traditional friendship of the British people towards Jews of all nations. We call on all other synagogues and responsible organisations in Great Britain, powerless though they may be to repress these activities, to use such influence as they can upon the Jewish community in Palestine to suppress gangster methods to the utmost of its power.'[8] The resolution was sent to the press, but the *Jewish Chronicle* published only a very short précis in the following week's edition. The following year the Council made known its 'unbounded condemnation' of the murder of the UN peace negotiator, Count Bernadotte. The Swedish diplomat had done so much to help the Jews of Europe, rescuing many by diplomatic means and facing up to Germany's leaders in their defence. He was murdered by the Stern Gang in Jerusalem because they felt he favoured the Arabs in peace negotiations. Other such incidents were the assassination of Lord Moyne in 1944 (this was in Cairo - where he was the British Minister in Residence - apparently at the instigation of the Stern Gang) and the murder of two British sergeants in 1947. Many Jews in England, having fought beside British soldiers during the war, were torn in their allegiances between their religion and their country. Most of them deplored violence on both sides.

It was hardly surprising therefore that when, in 1949 in the course of preparation for a new Prayer Book, the suggestion was made that a Prayer for Israel should be included, it did not meet with the immediate approval of the Council. It was agreed that a draft should be prepared, but many of the West London 'aristocracy' were against it. Rabbi Reinhart himself could see no reason at all for its inclusion. Finally the matter was put before a Special General Meeting who voted in favour. The new Prayer Book was already at the printer when the subject came up. It was said that Rabbi Reinhart had phoned the printers and asked them to 'hurry it up' so that it could not contain the new prayer. It was indeed printed without the prayer, but having agreed the wording with Rabbi Reinhart's acceptance, a small slip was stuck into every copy. It was not read in the synagogue until January 31st, 1953. Rabbi Reinhart was himself very much against the Zionists and what they stood for. When the Junior Membership held dances at the synagogue it was the custom to finish the evening with God Save the King and *Hatikva* (the Israel National Anthem). On one occasion Rabbi Reinhart heard the music and angrily instructed those in charge to stop. 'We do not play that song here,' he said. Perhaps he felt that the energy and affection bestowed on Israel would replace that for Judaism.

West London Synagogue's efforts to help the Jews looking for sanctuary in England after the Holocaust were particularly concentrated on the children. The unimaginable traumas that they had experienced at such a young age would take years to abate. Rabbi Reinhart spoke privately to many of his members. This was not a job for a committee; it needed a personal touch. What was essential, Reinhart felt, was a house in a quiet neighbourhood, not too far from London, with a capable, caring woman to act as Matron, where these damaged boys and girls could begin to pick up the pieces of their interrupted lives. The Council agreed to vote the sum of £6,000 for the purchase of a hostel, but it was Sir Benjamin Drage who came to the rescue. He offered his beautiful house, Weir Courtney, near Lingfield in Surrey, for the use of some of these war-torn children. It was a large house set in fine gardens and it came to represent safety and sanctuary for the refugees. The British government had decided, even before the war was finished, to allow some 1000 children who had survived the camps, to come to Britain under the auspices of the Jewish Refugee Movement and the Central British Fund. 850 were chosen to come and assembled at Prague Airport, where nine British bombers were waiting to take them to safety. They landed at a remote airfield in Wales, where they were met by Alice Goldberger and Leonard Montefiore, and were cared for to begin with at Troutbeck Bridge near Windermere in the Lake District, when it was felt that small groups of houses or hostels would be more suitable.

The children who came to Lingfield were very young, from about four to nine years, many of them very damaged. They had been on the last bomber to leave Prague; two or three had come from Displaced Persons Camps, where they had hoped to be found by relatives, and some had spent their first years in Terezin. They came from Czechslovakia, Hungary, Germany, Austria, Italy and Poland. Most had lost their parents and were totally without any means of comfort or support. Harold Reinhart found in Alice Goldberger the perfect answer to their needs. Born in 1897, she was a German refugee herself and had worked there before the war in several child centres. She came to Britain in 1939 and was interned as an enemy alien on the Isle of Man where she set up a children's facility. When released she was appointed superintendent of Anna Freud's War Nurseries, helping to look after the children of British working mothers. As Matron of Lingfield she gave the children the affection and care they so badly needed. She was helped by a Catholic refugee, Sophie Wutsch, who became her right-hand woman and stayed with her for most of their lives. Sophie learned to cook Jewish food (the home was strictly kosher).

The children were taught English, kept pets, enjoyed music and acting, sports and games and were taken on seaside holidays. At first it was for

Alice an uphill task to gain their trust and confidence. Sdelka Husserl, one of the very youngest, now living in London, tells of her life-long fear of Alsatian dogs, even when seen from a bus, because they remind her of the guard dogs at Terezin. Their early drawings, many of them preserved in the Holocaust Museum in New York, show distress and misery, but after a very short time they were painting pictures of themselves playing, singing and dancing, looking after their animals and obviously enjoying the happy times at Lingfield. They reported their progress frequently to the Lingfield Committee at Berkeley Street who passed on their stories to the Council. One such account announced that during the previous year the twenty Lingfield House chickens had laid 2,212 eggs! Soon they were well enough settled to attend the local school and some were reunited with their families. Two of the children married and went to live in Australia.

At West London funds were urgently needed to maintain the home – it was the only one not under the direct control of the Central British Fund - and a Hostel Committee was now established under the chairmanship of Mrs. Gladys Pinto, which established the yearly Lingfield Bazaar, a joint effort which took place every November in the Stern Hall, raising many thousands of pounds. When Lingfield House finally closed, the Annual Bazaar continued raising funds for the charities supported by the congregation. Alice Goldberger stayed with 'her' children, and in 1948 they took a house nearer London at Isleworth in Middlesex and renamed it Lingfield House. In October 1978 she appeared on BBC Television's *This is Your Life* with Eamonn Andrews as host, when several of the children appeared on the programme. Hugo Gryn also took part. He had not lived at Lingfield but had often visited and took a particular interest in the children. Many tears were shed by those who took part in that programme and by those who watched. Two Italian sisters were rediscovered by their mother because of the publicity. Alice brought the children to worship at West London every Sabbath and High Holy Day Festivals, and will always be remembered, not only by the children she cared for but by all those who knew her. When the children were older and began to disperse, West London installed Alice (and Sophie) in a large flat in Hampstead. She moved finally to Osmond House, the Jewish care home, and died at the age of eight-eight in 1986. In the obituary printed in the *Synagogue Review*, Rabbi Hugo Gryn wrote of her that she became parent, teacher, play leader and 'best friend' to all of the Lingfield children, and to the end of her life she stayed in touch, worried about and, more than anything else, loved them.

Those who believed that the Zionists at the Board of Deputies might introduce a breath of fresh air into the Board's control of Anglo-Jewry were sadly mistaken. This time it was the Liberal side of the Progressive movement which caused the problem. Just as in the previous difficulties experienced by the West London Synagogue, it was the appointment of marriage secretaries that provoked an acrimonious situation. Several Liberal congregations applied to the President, whose right it was to agree to such an appointment for 'a synagogue of persons professing the Jewish religion'. He acted as the spokesman for the Chief Rabbi or the Haham, his ecclesiastical authorities. He had agreed to such appointments as long ago as 1935 for the principal Liberal synagogue at St. John's Wood. Now, more than ten years later, he seemed to regret his action, claiming he had been pressurised into it by Sir Robert Waley Cohen. The new Liberal synagogues had assumed that they would be included under the umbrella of their leading community. The 'ecclesiastical authority' certainly had no control over the Progressives, so a small sub-committee of the Board proposed that the phrase 'or in the case of a Liberal synagogue by the President of the Liberal Jewish Synagogue in St. John's Wood Road' be used. This was exactly the same formula as had been applied in the case of the Reform movement, when West London was granted the right to appoint marriage secretaries for all its sister synagogues. The committee was not unanimous and decided to consult with the orthodox *Beth Din*. It refused and they tried to invoke the new Marriage Consolidation Bill going through Parliament, all to no avail. The Liberal synagogues withdrew from the Board.

The members of West London were due to elect their new Deputies, but upset by the Liberals' action and the reasons for it, decided to postpone elections 'to a Board that is not primarily interested in Anglo-Jewry' – a reference to the Zionist presence at the Board. The final straw was the withdrawal of the Spanish and Portuguese Deputies, which prompted the Council of West London to consider not holding elections at all. A vote in Council resulted in six for and six against, with the chairman's casting vote for. However, it did decide eventually not to hold elections, as did most members of the Association of Synagogues in Great Britain, and the Union of Jewish Women. Representatives of Manchester, both Reform and Sephardi, remained with the Board. The new Chief Rabbi, Dr. Israel Brodie, together with a new chairman of the Board, Dr. Abraham Cohen, was not able to resolve the problem. Dr. Brodie, the first Chief Rabbi to have been born and educated in Britain, was always considered to be one of the more tolerant and forward-looking to hold the office. A good friend of Harold Reinhart, he was not afraid to visit a Progressive synagogue, nor to hold views outside the Jewish establishment.

Percy Cohen, one of West London's Deputies, wrote an account of the fracas for the *Synagogue Review*, published in September 1951. He claimed, correctly, to have participated in 'probably every single phase of the long controversy'. He explained that West London's role had been to work 'quietly and unobtrusively' for all that time, and maintained that under Dr. Abraham Cohen's predecessor, Selig Brodetsky, the Board had lost its representative character and the 'caucus' of Deputies who ruled without democratic methods, and with an autocratic control, had come close to ruining the purpose for which the Board had been founded. He mentioned the 'sweep to the left' which was prevalent in Britain as a whole and the difficulties experienced by the middle-of-the road Deputies in putting their point of view. Percy Cohen sat on the ill-fated Feldman Committee, set up without success to examine the Board's constitution. He felt that West London could act as mediator and at a meeting with the new President, Dr. Cohen, showed him a memorandum drawn up by the Council, expressing its feeling that the Board's 'policies should reflect the largest possible measure of common agreement.' Each side in the dispute consulted its adherents; conferences were held by all interested parties (mostly at Upper Berkeley Street), and finally in 1951 came peace and a satisfactory solution to all the difficulties. West London acknowledged its gratitude to Mr. Cohen for all his work in achieving this.

In 1948 Rabbi Curtis Cassell came from Scotland to West London as Assistant Minister. He and his wife Cecilia with their two sons, Charles and David, took one of the houses the synagogue owned in Upper Berkeley Street. Rabbi Cassell proved a stalwart and loyal supporter of the Senior Minister. He played a full part in the affairs of the ASGB, wrote for the *Synagogue Review* and lectured on occasion to the Jewish Historical Society. He never lost his German accent, but loved everything about England, his adopted country, from its history of the Jewish population to its food and particularly its national sport, cricket. He was well-known for his terrible puns and his joyous sense of humour, and greatly endeared himself to the congregation.

In his book *The Boys*, the story of 732 young concentration camp survivors, Sir Martin Gilbert writes much of the early experiences of Rabbi Hugo Gryn. After his release from the concentration camp, Hugo managed to get to England. Unable to make himself understood in English, he was labelled 'Green' instead of 'Gryn' by the immigration officer, and sent to a farm in Scotland. He lived for a while at Polton House in Glasgow, and then came south to London (speaking English with a Scottish accent) and decided to become a rabbi. He originally wanted to go to America to study at the Hebrew Union College (there was then no such college in England) but decided to stay in England as West London, together with the Jewish Refugee Committee, was willing to sponsor him. When he did finally get to America he returned with a strong American accent much to the delight of the children. He visited Lingfield House on many occasions, helping the children and giving them a useful male influence in their lives. When Leonard Montefiore lectured to the Cambridge Union of Jewish Students about the refugee children in 1949, he had told his audience that there was no likelihood at all of any of the refugees becoming a part of the Reform movement in the future! But he did report to the West London Council a few months later that 'Mr. Hugo Green had made remarkable progress in his secular and semitic studies in this country.'[9] The Council agreed to take a larger share in his education. He helped out by teaching Hebrew at Upper Berkeley Street, and was sent to the Hebrew Union College in Cincinnati, partly financed by the synagogue's Women's Guild.

Another German refugee student rabbi, who came to England in 1939, was Jacob Petuchowski. He also went to study in Cincinnati and came over to England, with his wife Elizabeth, to help at West London. The synagogue paid their return fares, and offered a salary of £1,000 a year. They were to stay for six months, with the possibility of a further six months if they agreed. Jacob was very popular with the younger members of the congregation and many kept in touch with him and his wife when they finally returned to America. There had been rumours that Jacob might stay on as a rabbi to the congregation but he and his wife preferred to return to the States. Jacob was a prolific writer and several of his books became standard works for rabbinical students and others interested in Judaism. André Ungar was another young man of considerable scholastic ability who was taken under West London's wing. He was regarded as 'the type of young man who should prove suitable for our Ministry'.[10] He was later appointed an Assistant Minister, after which he left for a successful career in South Africa which he was forced to leave after he stood against apartheid. He finally went to America, being one of the Rabbis who marched with Martin Luther King.

Owners of buildings damaged by enemy action could claim reparations from the War Office, and the Berkeley Street synagogue was badly in need of repair. The Building Committee drew up elaborate plans for restructuring and redecoration, but Rabbi Reinhart was not pleased. He felt that such a massive rebuilding programme was not necessary. He suggested that a perfectly good restoration could be achieved by cleaning the poor paintwork and re-using it. But the Council wanted a complete redecoration, repainting the ceilings 'with a mosaic colour scheme resembling the existing scheme but similar in design.' Walter Schwab, father of Rabbi Julia Neuberger, told the story of how the Council believed that only the President of the Royal Institute of British Architects could decide on the colour scheme. Together the President and the Rabbi climbed the scaffolding to the cupola and examined the colour chart which the President had brought with him. He said, 'This will do'. 'Nonsense,' replied the Rabbi, 'this is my synagogue and I shall decide on the colours!'[11] But when it came to the elaborate ceiling, Reinhart resigned from the Committee in protest. However, his misgivings were valid, and it was decided that the funds allocated to the repainting of the ceiling should be awarded instead to the Lingfield Committee for their work, and the ceiling was painted in a plain colour. It is now admired with much pride when the story is told, precisely the kind of ethical decision which governs much of the work of the Reform Movement. The work went ahead and from March to September the synagogue was closed for repairs. Services continued as usual in the Stern Hall, and on September 15th, 1952 the sanctuary was reconsecrated with a special service. In a prayer composed for the occasion, Rabbi Reinhart said, 'Happy are we to possess this gracious shrine! Privileged are we to serve in it!'[12] In his address he welcomed the visitors and members to the splendid new building, addressing in particular the members of the West London Synagogue of British Jews. 'For us,' he finished, 'may the renewal of this house be a token of the renewal of our love for "Berkeley Street" '.[13] Present were representatives of the Spanish and Portuguese Synagogue, the United Synagogue, the Federation, the Western Synagogue, the Liberals and of course the Association of Reform Synagogues, as well as those of the state of Israel, other Jewish bodies, and the Christian Church. The *Jewish Chronicle* gave due prominence to the occasion, recalling the divisions in the community when the West London Synagogue came into being, the part it had played in communal activities since that time, and particularly its hospitality to American service personnel during the war and since.

The synagogue's reputation for caring for its own members as well as outsiders was well deserved. Ruby Jones, the sparrow-like little 'commander' of the entrance lodge in Seymour Place, known to all as 'Ruby' – her surname lost in the mists of time - was taken ill. The synagogue saw that she was well cared for in the Jewish Hospital until she was well enough to return to work. She knew everything there was to know about the synagogue, its members and its visitors, though they knew little about her. But she performed her duties to perfection and was much loved by all who encountered her. She continued to work at the synagogue for many years and died in 1976. The *Synagogue Review* remembered her, 'She knew more about Jewish dates and festivals than a calendar compiler ... she was incapable of even harbouring unkind thoughts. We shall miss her always with affection.'[14] Another synagogue servant, the Beadle Henry de Metz, celebrated his golden wedding, his seventy-fifth birthday and his retirement at this time. He had supported the synagogue throughout many difficult years, saved it from destruction when as an A.R.P. warden he had discovered and extinguished a fire, and seen generations of young Jews grow up under his watchful eye. Montague Calman, who wrote a column 'The Jew Within Me' for the *Synagogue Review,* missed his presence in the synagogue. 'How Israel Zangwill would have rejoiced over such a personality,' he wrote. 'May Mr. de Metz continue to blossom forth with his idiosyncrasies for many years to come!'[15]

Always delighted by anniversaries, the congregation also celebrated fifty years' service by the synagogue's organist, Dr. Percy Rideout. It was commemorated by a recording of some of his synagogue music and a concert in the synagogue. Dr. Rideout, apart from his work at Berkeley Street, played an important part in the Guild of Organists and the Royal College; he was a great gardener, and one of his proudest moments occurred in 1918 when he showed the King and Queen around his allotments at Wimbledon. Rabbi Cassell, in a note about Dr. Rideout at his Golden Jubilee, explained how the organ music had become an integral part of the synagogue service. 'Rideout succeeded,' he wrote, 'in integrating the sound of his majestic instrument into the frame of Jewish devotion.' Towards the end of Percy Rideout's time at

West London a young assistant organist was appointed. Arnold Richardson was a distinguished organist, working at St. Albans, Holborn and then at Wolverhampton, where a blue plaque marks his name. In the Berkeley Street tradition, each organist has appointed his successor and when Rideout retired Richardson took his place. He later married Daphne Kaner, who was a long-time member of the synagogue staff.

Another important anniversary occurred in 1954. Rabbi Harold Reinhart celebrated twenty-five years in office. Montague Calman, in 'The Jew Within Me – Extracts from a Jewish Occasional Notebook', his column in the *Synagogue Review,* wrote, 'Much of Dr. Reinhart's work is seen behind the closed door of his crowded study: crowded as it is with books, papers, and above all else with the numerous human problems confronting him daily. Yet despite the frightening turmoil of a busy Minister's life, he has always found time to blend wisdom with humour, perception with humanity.'[16] The same issue, which was dedicated to Rabbi Reinhart, its Editor, included tributes from the President of the ASGB, Leo Baeck, the President and the Senior Treasurer of the synagogue, Owen Mocatta and Leonard Montefiore, and from the President of the Hebrew Union College in Cincinatti, Nelson Glueck. Rabbi Reinhart, with an abiding love for children, probably gained as much pleasure from the displays and presentations of the children of the synagogue, followed by a Jubilee Service and a ceremony in the Stern Hall. Owen Mocatta presented Rabbi Reinhart with a testimonial; the presentation was followed by a tea for members. A dinner was held at the Trocadero when a small presentation was made. The money collected for the rabbi was put into a special fund, at his request, for charitable causes. Few present at that very successful weekend could have imagined that within three years they would be saying goodbye to their beloved rabbi for good.

CHAPTER XI

The Second Schism

The Ministers of the Association of Synagogues in Great Britain had been concerned for some time about the shortage of rabbis to continue their work. The German-born rabbis who were the backbone of the Reform Ministry in this country were mostly in their sixties or seventies and few young men were coming forward to take over. Even if they did wish to become rabbis there was little opportunity in this country for them to take up training. Jews College might help, but ministerial preparation there was entirely under the orthodox banner and not sympathetic to those who wished to enter the Reform movement. The subject had been discussed at Conference on several occasions but no practical suggestions had been made. Some young men had gone to the Hebrew Union College in Cincinnati under the auspices of the Society of Jewish Study, founded by Dr. Leo Baeck in 1949 in which Rabbi Reinhart played a leading part. The Society had a Collegium of three Rabbis to supervise a programme of study for ministerial training, but candidates were seldom well educated enough to be able to cope with the rigorous curriculum.

The synagogue at Wimbledon, under Rabbi Berg, tabled a resolution at the 1952 Conference that a seminary for training ministers should be established. It was felt that the Reform movement alone could not undertake such a move, but that, perhaps with the cooperation of the Liberals, a college along Progressive lines might be possible. Rabbi Reinhart, always a little wary of bringing West London too close to the Liberals, was not in favour. Another possibility was a college at one of the older universities, and the Association set up a Ministerial Training Committee to investigate further. It was Rabbi Werner van der Zyl, Minister at Alyth Gardens, who seized the reins, and drove the matter forward. Alyth offered to fund a scholarship for a suitable candidate and West London gave its support. The chosen candidate obtained his BA degree, was funded for two more years and joined by another graduate to pursue studies in Hebrew at University College and with the Society for Jewish Study. The two candidates were Lionel Blue and Michael Leigh.

A newly formed Leo Baeck Scholarship Award Committee, in honour of Dr. Baeck's eightieth birthday, supported the two fledgling rabbis. They, and any others who joined them, would never be obliged by the Committee to pledge themselves to remain in the Reform movement, nor to repay any of the bursaries they received if they left it or went abroad to work. Gradually it was becoming clear that a fully supported College, with a comprehensive programme of study, supervised by ordained ministers and scholars, was a distinct possibility. What were needed urgently were a Director of Studies, qualified teachers, a syllabus and a home for the College. The moving force in all this was Rabbi van der Zyl. He called it 'a great venture which would affect the whole life of the Association'.[1]

The Ministers' Training Board consisted of Rabbis van der Zyl, Reinhart and Maybaum, together with Leonard Montefiore and Albert I. Polack from West London. A.I., as he was affectionately known, was the Housemaster of Polack's House at Clifton College, following in his father's footsteps. He was much respected both in Jewish and non-Jewish educational circles, having provided several generations of Jewish boys with a first-class education while, with his wife Betty (née Cohen) giving them a warm Jewish home background. As a classicist and an all-round scholar, he was an ideal member of the committee. Its task was to appoint an Examining Authority of three Rabbis to award ministerial and rabbinical diplomas, to prepare curricula which must have the approval of the Examining Authority, to interview and advise prospective ministerial students and to appoint examiners for special subjects.

The rabbinical training of the two young men continued for three years and in 1954 Rabbi van der Zyl asked the Conference for a more formally organised system to bring into being a fully accredited College. The two students had nearly finished their training and wanted to plan for their future, but first they needed to obtain *semicha* or at least a diploma which would enable them to become Rabbis and to minister to a congregation. The Chief Rabbi had refused to allow them to qualify through Jews College and neither they nor the ASGB wanted them to go to America. It took another two years before Rabbi van der Zyl was appointed Director of Studies (part time). Six eminent scholars (not all Rabbis), agreed to teach and five new students enrolled, the majority of them from the Reform youth movement. Dr. Baeck gave them his blessing and the Jewish Theological College came into being. The inauguration of the College took place on 30th September 1956 at Upper Berkeley Street. The ceremony was to have been under the direction of Dr. Baeck, but sadly he was ill and unable to attend. Dr. Reinhart took the chair instead. More than two hundred people were present to hear Leon Roth give the opening lecture, in which he addressed the present students and those who would be joining when the College started its term a month later. 'He who wants to learn,' he said, 'will be welcome; the use of his learning will depend upon his conscience.'[2] Dr. Baeck died only two months later, and the College was renamed the Leo Baeck College.

✡

In 1954 the Council of West London created a new position in the congregation, that of Religious Education Adviser, and appointed the Rev. Alan Miller to the post. He was at the time serving as Chaplain to the Forces and had often been seen at Berkeley Street, as well as helping out at the summer school of the Youth Association of Synagogues in Great Britain, the young people's wing of Reform Judaism. Son of a Rabbi, he joined West London at the age of twenty-eight after graduating at University College with a first-class degree. He then went on to Jews College and to Oxford. Soon after his arrival he instituted a series of popular weekly lectures on Judaism, a weekly Talmud study circle and a course of addresses on the Bible. He quickly became very popular, particularly with the younger members of the congregation, playing the guitar at their gatherings and leading discussion groups at conferences and seminars.

Harold Reinhart was due to retire from his post in August 1956. He had been ably supported in his work at Upper Berkeley Street by Rabbi Curtis Cassell. They made an excellent leadership team, working together in harmony, their mutual qualities fitting together to the lasting benefit of the congregation. This was not always true of their wives; Cecilia Cassell was overshadowed by the personality of Flora Reinhart who nevertheless admired her; they never allowed their differences to impinge on their work for the synagogue. Cassell's affection and respect for the Senior Minister had an important bearing on the events which were to come. Their work for the synagogue continued unabated.

In the year 1656 the Jews had been readmitted to England, ready to play a full part in the nation's affairs. Three hundred years later, Britain commemorated the anniversary with a comprehensive programme of events. West London was well to the fore, acknowledging as they always had, both their Englishness and their Jewishness. A special service for the Tercentenary was held in the synagogue on 7th January and the congregation participated with their fellow Jews in enjoying a magnificent concert at the Royal Festival Hall, a banquet at Guildhall, where the guest of honour was the Duke of Edinburgh, a garden party at Lambeth Palace, as well as parties, lectures, exhibitions and entertainments of all kind. There were essay prizes for the children, and many members of West London took a leading part in the celebrations.

Law 73 of the Laws of the Synagogue stated that 'every Minister shall retire on attaining the age of sixty-five, but may be invited by the members to continue in office for a further period or periods.' Leonard Montefiore asked the Council to extend every 'courtesy, facility and opportunity' to the Senior Minister to state his views on certain matters which were in his mind. Leonard Goldsmid Montefiore was the son of Claude Montefiore and spent his whole life in the service of the Anglo-Jewish community and in particular of the West London Synagogue. He was academically brilliant and had an aesthetic yet practical outlook on life which endeared him to all. Those who were close to him will still remember the private letters on sheets of bright blue paper which he used to communicate his thoughts. He was President of the Anglo-Jewish Association, and participated in the affairs of the Board of Guardians, the Bernhard Baron Settlement in the East End, the Wiener Library and the Central British Fund. As Chaim Bermant put it, 'He attended them all, gave money to them all, offered guidance to them all.'[3] He was a very dear friend of Harold and Flora Reinhart.

It was agreed in the early months of 1956 to invite Rabbi Reinhart to attend a private meeting and that a Special Meeting of the Council should be arranged to follow it to discuss the implications of Law 73. A long time had elapsed since his last meeting with the Council. Addressing the members of it, he said that he felt that the congregation was being deprived of its central driving force. He had a personal relationship with every member, convinced of their confidence and goodwill, and felt strongly that the Council should 'make the congregation effective for the purpose for which it was established.'[4] He went on to suggest that there was a barrier between the Council and the Minister, and not only the Council but the Executive as well. The Ministers were consulted on matters that were 'quite unimportant.' He drew up a list of how matters might be improved. There should be more communication between the lay and the religious leaders, for the Ministers were more in touch with the congregants than any individual member of the Council. 'Every cause should have a champion and a spearhead. Ministers should have the vision and courage, a "sacred fire", without which meetings degenerated into routine; tardy, face-saving and not really constructive. There were "ways and ways" of using laws. Members of the Council should leave meetings singing.'[5] The Senior Minister explained his misgivings as to the way in which the synagogue was controlled – his opinion, not shared by many on the Council, was that everything to do with the synagogue was the concern of the Ministers. It was obvious from the way he spoke that he had the close co-operation of Rabbi Cassell. They felt that they were being side-lined when it came to knowing the deliberations of the Council.

It was clear that communication, or rather the lack of it, was a large part of the problem. Minutes of Council meetings were uninformative and often turbulent. When one member of the Council addressed the Treasurer as 'Mr.Pinto' he was reprimanded. 'Major Pinto, if you please' he was told. As Editor of the *Synagogue Review*, Rabbi Reinhart felt he was given insufficient information. One member suggested that 'cooperation is a two-sided affair'. Perhaps Dr. Reinhart's idea of cooperation meant subordination and the speaker appealed for his help. Another said that many routine matters, including financial affairs, did not concern the Senior Minister, and that 'the chaff should be divided from the grain.' Edward Henriques felt that the meeting had been a waste of time – Rabbi Reinhart did not agree.

When the Senior Minister had left, Leonard Montefiore reported to the Council on his private meeting with the Minister. He had explained that the Law in question could not be ignored, but he sought a 'Golden Bridge', a compromise. Rabbi Reinhart could continue as Minister Emeritus, but when he had been offered an extension of one year, it was turned down. Both Montefiore and Owen Mocatta, the synagogue's President, had the impression that the Rabbi felt that Law 73 should be regarded as inapplicable in his case.

When the problem became more widely known many considered that Rabbi Reinhart's attitude showed an arrogance not in keeping with his ministerial character. But the real truth lay in the fact that when Harold Reinhart came to Berkeley Street in 1929 no such Law existed. In legal terms therefore, he was in the right. He could not be expected to concede to something he had never agreed to in the first place.

All those present knew that there was tension between the Minister and the Executive Committee, particularly when the subject of the Ministerial Succession was raised. He felt himself to be in his prime and certainly there was no question as to his energy, both mental and physical. Those present all agreed that Harold Reinhart was an idealist and a perfectionist, that he had given almost all his professional life to the synagogue, that he was a good, sweet man but 'baffling in his waywardness'. He would be a hard man to replace but the situation had to be faced. The Treasurers, Edward Henriques and Major R. Pinto, had tried to see a way out but had been rebuffed. They felt it impossible to ask Harold Reinhart to continue in office.

The discussion raged this way and that. Some members of the Council held their Rabbi in great affection and recognised his qualities, but felt that it was not in the interest of the synagogue to ask him to remain, that congregational life should not be driven by one man. One said, 'We could not look for a successor while the Senior Minister was in office.'[6] The problem of appointing younger rabbis was also debated. Rabbis Alan Miller, Jacob Petuchowsky and André Ungar experienced difficulties in working with him and the latter two had left the congregation after a short while. One Council member likened it to a 'Romish church' where the Pope had supreme authority. Support for Reinhart came from Albert Polack who felt it would be a disaster if the Senior Minister were not invited to continue, perhaps on a yearly basis. During the course of 1956 three Special Meetings of the Council were held; the attendance was very high, showing the level of concern for the future welfare of the synagogue. Finally the resolution was put that 'In view of Law 73 this Council recommends to members that Mr. Reinhart be invited to remain in office, subject to one year's notice on either side.'[7] The motion was put to the Council and defeated by eighteen votes to six. In case the Rabbi saw this as a vote of no confidence, he should be informed that the Council was unanimously conscious of his good service. It agreed to commend to him the Council's conclusion.

Before any further decisions could be made, another quarrel arose. The Council had decided to appoint a Ritual Committee to consider changes to religious services. It was to be composed of a representative of the membership and of the Council, the wardens and one Minister. The Rabbis felt they should both attend. The Committee agreed but at the first meeting Rabbi Cassell was out of London and Rabbi Reinhart did not appear. On being questioned he said that he had not been consulted before the meeting was set and that he objected to the Chair being taken by Louis Littman, a devoted and scholarly member of the synagogue. It was therefore held by the Committee that Mr. Reinhart seemed to view it with disfavour and was unlikely to cooperate. It decided to go ahead even without the Senior Minister and report to the Council. It had apparently sent a note to the *Synagogue Review* explaining why it had been set up but this had not been published. This contretemps did nothing to allay the bad feeling that was growing within the management of the synagogue.

The three Wardens at this time were men of great integrity, intelligence and common sense. They were all experienced in community affairs. Bob Toeman had a very quiet, sweet disposition, and he and his wife Iris had been members of West London for some years. Sam Ansell had been a Brady Boy, brought up in the East End under the guidance of Basil Henriques. He had married Joan Berman in the first wedding at Berkeley Street after the war and their two sons attended religion classes there, as their mother had done. Lewis Golden, an accountant, had a distinguished war career, an acute financial brain and refused to entertain any idea of bending rules to achieve his ends. He, too, was a devoted admirer of Harold Reinhart.

Much has been said about the appointment of Rabbi Alan Miller as Education Officer. The candidate for this position was chosen by the Synagogue Council, with the Senior Minister consulted only as a formality. Rabbi Miller's two-year term of office was due to end in July 1956 and a six-month extension was suggested. This was felt to be unsatisfactory. He was not brought in, one Council member said, as a temporary stop-gap and should not be affected by ministerial differences. A twelve-month extension was finally agreed. Rabbi Reinhart was greatly upset by the decision to confirm Rabbi Miller in the post, less because he disapproved of him as a minister and a teacher, than because he felt slighted by being almost ignored in the process of appointment.

The next Annual General Meeting was called for 12th June, 1956. A draft Agenda was sent out to Council Members which included a recommendation that, in relation to the present Senior Minister, the operation of Law 73 should be suspended until August 1957. But the chairman revealed that 'there was a further development in the matter' (what this meant was not mentioned) and it was agreed to send out the Agenda without that item. Meanwhile the Council was arranging Special Meetings to try to sort things out before it had to face the members. It was told that Rabbi Reinhart 'wished to remain in office unconditionally'. He addressed the Council for over an hour, mentioning again that he accepted Law 73 but felt that it did not apply to him. The Council appointed a Ministerial Selection Committee and tried to find some sort of compromise, consulting Lord Cohen on the legal questions that arose. Lionel Leonard Cohen, Baron Cohen, came from an Orthodox background but had found himself more at home in a Progressive synagogue, joining West London when he married. He was a distinguished barrister – 'his advice, shrewd, practical and authoritative, and his excellent judgement, put him in the first rank.'[8] But by May his lordship's efforts had not led to an amicable solution and he recommended extending the Senior Minister's term of office until the end of December, 1958, another two and a half years. But the Council stood firm and decided on an extension to 31st August 1957, just over a year.

Rabbi Reinhart told the Senior Warden, Bob Toeman, that this was unacceptable and was asked to put his objection in writing. On 10th May he told the President that 'unless he received a vote of confidence he would retire on the due date'.[9] This was 9th September 1958. He explained that the only offer he would accept was a five-year extension; this was refused by the Council by nineteen votes to eight. The Council decided to inform the membership accordingly.

The Annual General Meeting of 1956 took place in the Stern Hall, with Owen Mocatta in the Chair. A small paragraph appeared in the *Jewish Chronicle* under the headline 'West London Synagogue Dispute – Differences with Senior Minister', which referred to Mr. Henriques' presentation of the synagogue accounts, during which he spoke of the 'virulent attacks' on him by Rabbi Reinhart. But the meeting then went into committee and the press was excluded. No mention of any such complaint appeared in the report of the meeting in the *Synagogue Review*.

However, a Special General Meeting was called for 2nd July and the Council met beforehand when the President asked members to express their feelings 'in as gentle terms as possible.' This meeting took place at Friends' House, the Quaker headquarters in Euston where a larger room was available for the numbers of members expected to attend. It was hotly debated in Council as to whether the Senior Minister should be invited to be present; some felt he should be able to put his views forward, others that it was invidious to discuss him before his face. It was decided to ask Leonard Montefiore to present an Opening Report, the Rabbi would then put his case and retire. The ballot would be secret and the chairman would take the vote at 9.45 pm. Ballot papers would be issued only to those entitled to vote and scrutineers were appointed. A Ministerial Selection Committee was set up, consisting of Julius Hart, Leonard Montefiore, the Hon. Roger Nathan, A.I. Polack and Sefton Temkin. Mr. Polack said that if his motion (to extend the period of office) was defeated he could not serve on the committee, and the Senior Warden would take his place. 389 members of the West London Synagogue attended the meeting, which was long and bitter, and after a somewhat violent discussion the matter put to the vote was that the Senior Minister should be invited to remain in office until August 1961. It was carried by a majority of four votes, and Rabbi Reinhart agreed to the terms.

No report of the meeting appeared in the papers (the press was excluded), but a small paragraph did appear in the *Synagogue Review* the following month reporting the meeting in sober terms, and recording Mr. Polack's proposal that 'in view of his 27 years' devoted service to the West London Synagogue, which has so largely contributed to its present reputation and the position it holds as a religious force in the Anglo-Jewish community, and his undoubted capacity to continue such service with unimpaired vigour, the Senior Minister be invited to remain in office until August 1961 so that a further period may be secured during which our congregation may enjoy the benefit of his spiritual guidance.'[10]

The whole matter seemed to have been settled, but it was the lull before the storm. Nothing had really changed. The problem was succinctly put in a memoir of the Senior Minister published after his death. 'Upper Berkeley Street's administration, he felt, had drifted towards a commercialism which could not be reconciled with the aims of a religious community.'[11] The problems revolved, not for the first time, around Rabbi Alan Miller. The Senior Minister made in clear that he did not wish to allow Rabbi Miller to take part in the forthcoming High Holyday Services. Edward Henriques put a resolution to the Council that 'this Council desires to see the services of Rev. Miller utilised in public worship in the Synagogue.' At this time a new Reform synagogue was being founded in South West Essex, and Mr. Miller had been helping the congregation which at that time had no rabbi. It was suggested that perhaps he might be seconded from West London and as he was working towards his PhD it suited him well to have the opportunity of a part-time post with plenty of time for his studies. South-West Essex was offered the sum of £750 towards his salary, though West London would not be committed to any arrangement beyond the agreed term of his contract which was due to terminate in July 1957.

By the end of the year there was a fragile peace. The Ministerial Selection Committee advertised in the *Jewish Chronicle* for an Assistant Minister, determined to ensure that any man appointed to the post would have a formal written Service Agreement! Owen Mocatta, the Synagogue's President, was becoming old and frail and both he and Leonard Montefiore were finding it difficult to give much attention to synagogue affairs. Consequently A.S. Diamond was elected Vice-President and Deputy Chairman of the Council. Abraham Sigismund Diamond, usually called Siggy, was the son of a Rabbi and had been brought up as an orthodox Jew. He won the Military Medal in World War I and was a pioneer of western Zionism. He had later turned to the West London Synagogue, was called to the Bar and had a distinguished legal career, becoming Master of the Supreme Court, Queens Bench Division. He was for some years the Head of British ORT, chaired the Council of the Leo Baeck College and was the President of the Jewish Historical Society. He was a Deputy representing West London, chairing the Law, Parliamentary and General Purposes Division.

The winter of 1956 was overshadowed by the death of Dr. Leo Baeck in November. His leadership of the Reform Movement in Germany, and after the war in Britain, had moved and humbled Jews of all denominations. The *Synagogue Review* printed many tributes from rabbis, scholars and laymen, and a Memorial Service was held in the Synagogue. On that occasion the Rabbis of most of the ASGB synagogues were present, as well as representatives of the Archbishop of Canterbury, the Free Church, the Council of Christians and Jews, and congregations across the world. Leonard Montefiore wrote, 'He taught us by example to prize those great virtues that ennoble man: courage, humility, piety and forgiveness.' The Chief Rabbi of Denmark, Dr. Marcus Melchior, speaking in German, addressed the congregation and referred to Dr. Baeck as a mild man of a goodness that knew no limits, in whom Liberal and Orthodox, Zionist and non-Zionist, *Hassidim* and *Mitnagim*, could find a common expression of all the various trends. Dr.Baeck was buried at the Golders Green Cemetery, Hoop Lane.

The Council decided to appoint Alan Miller to the post of Youth Education Officer. At a Special Council Meeting in May 1957, it was suggested that if such a post were created, the two Ministers should be given the opportunity to air their views. They joined the meeting, making it clear that no appointment should be made without their consent. Their joint opinion was that 'the Ministers must be responsible for the spiritual and educational work of the Synagogue, and it is not in the interests of the congregation for this appointment to be made.'[12] They were informed that the appointment of Rabbi Miller had already been made and a formal binding contract signed. The notice convening that Meeting had not included any mention of rescinding the contract; it was called simply to hear the views of the Ministers. Master Diamond found Alan Miller 'a young man with promise, with a proper respect for Rabbi Reinhart.' He asked the Senior Minister if it was not possible for him to agree to Alan Miller to be in the same building. The Rabbi said it was not possible and asked the Council to rescind its appointment. The meeting dissolved to consider the matter further.

That same month Owen Mocatta died. He had belonged to one of the oldest Anglo-Jewish families, among whom were several of the Founders of the West London Synagogue. He had held the offices of Warden, Treasurer, Chairman and President and had presided over the affairs of the St. George's Settlement, the Council of the Anglo-Jewish Association and the Jewish Historical Society. Leonard Montefiore, speaking to the *Jewish Chronicle,* attributed to him 'a well-balanced judgment and a shrewd though kindly appraisal of men and affairs.'[13] In the *Synagogue Review* the Rev. Arthur Barnett wrote, 'He was always quiet and unobtrusive. Some there are who imagine that in religious organisations good character can be taken for granted. Alas, alas, such an assumption is not borne out by the facts ...throughout he kept his integrity and honoured the high office he held. He was neither ingenious nor deft; he was incorruptible, a man of the highest principles, activated by the noble beliefs of his religion and a man whom one could trust implicitly.'[14]

At the end of May, Bob Toeman, the Senior Warden, read to the Council a resolution: 'that the Council, having heard the objection of the Ministers to the appointment of Rev. Alan Miller as Youth Education Officer, and the unanimous opinion of the Wardens, Bob Toeman, Lewis Golden and Sam Ansell that in this instance the Ministers' advice should be decisive, and having regard to the resolution of the Council passed on 2nd May, 1957, to give further consideration to the matter, it is hereby resolved that Alan Miller be not employed by the Synagogue after 31st July, that any contract for such employment which may have been entered into, be determined and that by way of compensation therefore a contribution of £750 per annum towards the salary of a Minister be made to the South West Essex Synagogue for two years, commencing on lst August 1957'.

Bob Toeman explained that in spite of the misgivings of the two Ministers, three Wardens and Chairman of the Education Committee (A.I. Polack) concerning the appointment, proper consideration had not been given. Instead a glowing account of Mr. Miller's work led the meeting into discussing Mr. Miller's qualities. The Youth Education Officer could not run his own department separately from the overall control of the Rabbis. 'Into this team, so the Ministers maintained, Mr. Miller did not fit; not because his outlook was immature, his scholarship inadequate or his manners lacking, but because he and the Ministers were incompatible. To them he was *persona non grata*. He did not want to be part of the team. They did not want him as part of the team. They would not have him!'[15] The Senior Warden felt that there was a fundamental principle that no man, however great his qualities, should be foisted on the Ministers against their will. He went on to forecast what might happen if the resolution was lost. Both Ministers would resign, as would the wardens, the Head of the Education Committee, the next warden (Leo Bernard) already elected, and many of the members. There would be lasting harm to Rev. Miller if he were to be the centre of 'an unsavoury drama'. The vote was lost by sixteen votes to nine.

Immediately the three wardens notified the Council that they and the Ministers would resign on 20th June (the date of the Annual General Meeting, postponed in the event until 4th July). The Ministers' resignation would date from 31st July. A compromise was suggested by Lady Nathan that Rev. Miller should be employed at West London and carry the title of Visiting Lecturer. The Annual General Meeting took place at Friends' House. The room was packed, by Harold Reinhart's supporters, by those who felt he was in the wrong and by those who simply wanted to know what was going on. Master Diamond was in the Chair. After a few matters of business, the Chairman put forward to the meeting three Resolutions for its consideration. The first was that which had already been put to the Council and rejected. This was that the contract to employ Rabbi Miller should be rescinded. It was put forward in the names of Mr. Justice Karminski, the Hon. Roger Nathan, A.I. Polack, Leonard Stein, Harold Benzimra. Sidney Craft, Arthur Tasher and Vera Levi. An amendment was added calling on the Chairman to convey to the Ministers the desire of members that they withdraw their resignations. It was also recorded that the passing of such a resolution in no way reflected on the character or ability of Rabbi Miller.

The second resolution, in the names of Cecil Speelman and E.A. Michaels, called for a Private Court of Enquiry to go into the matter. And the third was the one previously put forward by Lady Nathan, suggesting that Rev. Miller be employed as Visiting Lecturer and West London pay a yearly sum to South West Essex for that synagogue to make use of his services. It was this compromise that won the day, by 287 votes to 187, with thirty-five abstentions. The hope was expressed that Harold Reinhart and Curtis Cassell would accept it and operate it in the spirit in which it was put. But the meeting was contentious, bad-tempered and very noisy. It became very clear which side the Chairman favoured – many of those in favour of the original resolution were denied the floor. Some were cut off as they were speaking. It had been made very clear what would be the outcome if the first resolution was lost – that West London would find itself without a religious leader. Families looked at each other in dismay as their loyalties were split. No conclusions could be drawn from the way the voting went. It was not young against old, or traditional against modern. The argument was quite simply for Harold Reinhart or against him. Many members of the West London Synagogue left the meeting in shock.

After the meeting a telegram from Rabbi Reinhart and a letter from Rabbi Cassell confirmed their resignations. The Wardens and the Warden Elect resigned, as did the Chairman of the Education Committee, A.I. Polak, and in the following weeks many of the members of the West London Synagogue relinquished their membership. Rabbi Cassell had been offered the post of Minister to a new Reform congregation in Bulawayo, which he now accepted, and arranged to sail on 1st August. A letter was sent to Rabbi Reinhart with a list of his possessions which should be removed from the synagogue. The *Jewish Chronicle* gave front page coverage to the news, heading their story WEST LONDON CRISIS – Ministers and Wardens Resign, with Synagogue members, including Sir Seymour Karminski, Leonard Stein and Frank Waley. There were photographs of the two Ministers and Rabbi Alan Miller.[16] A leader the following week made the point that no public declaration or statement was issued by Berkeley Street, which showed, it felt, a lack of good Public Relations.

Frank Waley wrote to Rabbi Reinhart: 'I don't know what to say to you after that beastly meeting'[17] and many letters expressed the view 'we can't imagine Berkeley Street without you.' Some were from Rabbis, colleagues and friends, from the Council for Christians and Jews, from Judge Alan King-Hamilton asking him to withdraw his resignation, and from Lady Susan Karminski, on holiday, which read 'Sitting by an open window looking out at the sea, so vast and peaceful, I can hardly realise I was involved in an episode which for its sordidness, misery and injustice will never be able to be erased from my memory.'[18] The letters continued to pour in, from many who had no connection with the events, such as Rabbi Livingstone, from those who had not been a part of Harold Reinhart's community and those who had, such as

Sidney de Metz, son of the former beadle, Jacob Petuchowski, Rabbi Curtis, Harry Moss a long-standing member who wailed, 'You can't go – you mustn't go – I'm having sleepless nights – oh dear! oh dear!'[19]

In the August edition of the *Synagogue Review*, its editor, Rabbi Harold Reinhart, said his farewell. Using the editorial 'we' the first paragraph started rather awkwardly as 'We, the Editor, are the Senior Minister of the West London Synagogue. Since I have resigned my office as Minister, we must leave our editorial chair.'[20] But he thanked all those who had helped to achieve such a continuous and successful run of a journal which had always achieved a high scholarly yet friendly standard. This was followed by a poem written by him, remarkably appropriate for the circumstances, about the Ninth of Av, the Jewish commemoration of sorrow, which fell at that time:

> But what is man to fathom God's intent?
> Mayhap, 'tis whispered, Temple walls prevent
> The piety they purposed to protect.

In the same issue a letter appeared above the names of Harold Reinhart and Curtis Cassell. It dwelt less on the events leading up to their resignation, than on the 'goodwill and confidence which have been shown us through the years by the vast majority of the members.' It ended 'We have striven long and unremittingly for the truth as we see it. Now we resign because this is the only course remaining to us whereby we can contribute to the eventual reassertion of the true character of our great Synagogue.'

CHAPTER XII

A Change of Leadership

In the weeks following the upheaval at Upper Berkeley Street and Harold Reinhart's resignation, members of the congregation were often asked why. Why did he resign? What was really behind the second schism to affect the West London Synagogue? What made so many distinguished members of the congregation follow his lead? What did they know that we didn't? More than fifty years later these questions are still being asked. Those who knew the Rabbi well were better able to understand his reasons. They stretched deeply into the relationship he had with his flock. He was a man of unswerving principles, a man of integrity who was impatient with those who could not match up to his very high standards. He found many of the leaders of the community too materialistic, too concerned with their balance sheets to attend synagogue services. Their attention to the social problems faced by the synagogue could be met by signing a cheque. But for Harold Reinhart this was not enough. He felt that the idealism of his younger days, when he had followed in the footsteps of David Woolf Marks and Morris Joseph and swept along with him the principled, high-minded members of his new congregation, had diminished to a point that he could hardly recognise it as the same synagogue. The whole matter was clearly put by Kershen and Romain in their book about Reform Judaism. 'His departure was due to disputes over synagogue policy and the direction of the congregation, with Reinhart feeling that elements in the congregation who lacked spirituality and vision were taking over, while many members considered Reinhart was becoming increasingly autocratic and out of touch with their needs.'[1]

Whatever may have been the rights and wrongs that led to the meeting at Friends' House, it was very clear that Harold Reinhart had no intention of disappearing from public view. He had to resign his posts in the ASGB and the Leo Baeck College, but within two weeks he was invited to a meeting to discuss with some of his supporters the possibility of establishing a new congregation which might carry on the aims and principles which had motivated the West London Synagogue in the beginning and which he and his friends held so dear. He refused to accept the invitation to minister to any emerging community until it had established itself as a viable congregation, as he was contemplating a possible return to America. The new synagogue which was founded then was called the New London Jewish Congregation, later to become the Westminster Synagogue, and Harold Reinhart became its Rabbi, though he would not take a salary while he received a pension from

The old West London Synagogue cemetery at Balls Pond Road, Dalston

The Chapel at the cemetery at Hoop Lane

The Hoop Lane Cemetery

The Edwarebury Lane Cemetery

The Wedding of Philip Waley and Mary Raphael at West London

Reception at the House of Lords before the Seder in 2008

Lingfield House

A card from the children at Lingfield to Alice Goldberger
(by kind permission of US Holocaust Memorial Museum in New York)

Berkeley Street. The President was Sir Seymour Karminski, the Chairman Frank Waley, the Vice Chairman A.I. Polack and the three Wardens the same three who had served at Berkeley Street. Some eighty families from West London became founder members of the new community, and when the first High Holyday services were held in September 1957 in the Rudolf Steiner Hall, some 300 people attended.

✡

The first issue of the *Synagogue Review*, after its former Editor had departed, appeared in a new format. Clearly if there was to be change at Berkeley Street, it must be thorough and far-reaching. Its leader explained that although details of the editing of the journal were not complete, the Magazine Committee was alive and well. It invited readers to contribute their views as to what such a journal should set out to achieve and how that might be done. The congregation, still in shock after the events of the last months, was inevitably anxious to know what measures were being taken to fill the gap caused by the departure of its Ministers. Much of Jewish life is measured, as it has been for centuries, by the seasons. The autumn was coming with its yearly round of festivals, and the leaders of Berkeley Street were anxious to reassure the members that everything was under control for the conduct of the forthcoming High Holydays.

Leonard Montefiore wrote to Rabbi van der Zyl, 'In some ways I could have wished our Friends' House meeting had gone the other way, and I could then have retired gracefully from the scene. However, I am now faced with the problem of *Yom Kippur;* mercifully it falls late this year, and I am looking for help. Arthur Barnett was at Alyth for a bit, I believe, last year. Now I venture to ask, could you visit him? Truly I am not a conspirator. I said to HFR, "Think what happened to Bismarck – the chancellor kept sending in his resignation until finally it was accepted. And Randolph Churchill too, another famous case. As for LBC and the Liberals: Mattuck and Lily versus HFR – agreement hopeless! We must see Blue and Leigh through and that is an A1 priority.'[2] The Assembly of Ministers of the ASGB were taking immediate steps to ensure that its flagship synagogue would have the benefit of its Rabbinate, and that it would experience no break in continuity.

Rabbi Curtis Cassell and his family had departed for Southern Rhodesia, and were much missed by members of the congregation. The *Synagogue Review* gave an account of his life and achievements and went on to devote four pages to those of Rabbi Reinhart, describing Rabbi Stephen S. Wise's comments on meeting Harold Reinhart: 'He is very fine and manly and devout, a lofty-souled person of whom I am proud to think that I gave him the first impulse to go into the ministry.'[3] This was a warm and generous account of the Minister's remarkable work during the twenty-eight years of his ministry, of his contribution to the rescue of the German refugees, his devotion to the members of West London, his 'inspiration and driving force' which helped the congregation to achieve so much. Referring finally to the events which had led to his departure, the article compared those events to 'the tragedy of the over-possessive parent, the parent who gives all for the child, little realising that although father knows best, the child grows up and must loose the yoke if it is to develop normally.'[4] The issue also contained, for the first time, an article by Rabbi Alan Miller on prayer and where it should take place, entitled 'Praying in Bedrooms'.

It was a complex task for the Synagogue Council to arrange to cover all the many activities that had previously been led by Rabbis Reinhart and Cassell, particularly the Sabbath Services. A visiting Rabbi from America gave the address on one occasion, so did Rabbi Maybaum from Edgware and Dr. André Ungar, now back in England from South Africa. For the High Holydays it invited three Rabbis from America; John Levi was an Australian studying at Cincinnati; Dr. Bernard Heller was American, having graduated from the Hebrew Union College and the third, Dr. Ernst Appel, was German born but working in the United States. It also asked Rabbi Wolfe Kelman to come from Canada to London for three months to act as guest Minister. The Ministerial Selection Committee convened at once to find a replacement as Senior Minister. With a number of vacancies on the Council it needed another five members to make up its number. A.S. Diamond, now the Synagogue's Chairman, took the Chair. The ASGB requested that no offer of an appointment should be made to any of its members without first consulting that member's synagogue officers.

At the first Council meeting, held as soon as possible after the Friends' House meeting, three new Wardens were elected: Julius Hart, R.M. Norton and S.G. Schwab. The Chairman expressed his conviction that the new Council 'would soon achieve a spirit of harmony in the affairs of the synagogue.'[5] Harold Reinhart's pension was arranged and a new editor for the *Synagogue Review* was appointed, S. D. Temkin. Sefton Temkin, born in Liverpool, was a barrister whose stammer impeded his success at the Bar, but whose scholarship and knowledge of the Anglo-Jewish community came to be of great benefit to the synagogue. He had edited the *Jewish Monthly*, an English journal of high repute, and later went to America where he became Professor of Jewish Studies at the State University of New York at Albany. He was the acknowledged authority on Isaac Mayer Wise, the founder of Reform Judaism in America.

The High Holyday services of 1957 were considered extremely successful, both from the point of view of attendance (more congregants were present at the Synagogue and the additional services than ever before recorded), and in the quality of the leadership. The visiting Rabbis were happy to conduct the services in accordance with West London's usual practices and were warmly welcomed. They were assisted by other Rabbis of the ASGB, among them Dr. van der Zyl and Rabbi Curtis, and some of the student rabbis at the Leo Baeck College. The Association itself, always a little reluctant on the part of some of its constituents (including West London) to include the word 'Reform' in its title, now decided to do so and at its Conference in May 1958 changed its name to the Association of Reform Synagogues of Great Britain. Dr. van der Zyl had always disliked labels of any kind, and could not see the need to explain what was already evident, but he submitted to the majority view. It was in fact a West London delegate who proposed the change, although Berkeley Street, from its earliest days, had maintained that it had never wished to 'reform' Judaism at all. At the same meeting the 'Association' part was dropped and it became simply the RSGB. The Ministers' Assembly of the movement recommended that no ministerial appointments should be made without consulting with it first, and also that no minister should use the term 'rabbi' without permission, *semicha* only to be granted by a recognised rabbinical authority.

Another important problem occupying the minds of the Association was the future of the Leo Baeck College. It was still small (seven students) and very under-funded, with West London providing the bulk of its income. Talks with Jews College were no more fruitful than they had ever been, and the only way out was to invite the Liberals to share the burden of financial support, in return for including prospective Liberal ministers in its ranks. Many of the members of the Association had set their faces firmly against such a partnership. It was suggested that half the classes would take place (as they did then) at West London and half at St. John's Wood Liberal Synagogue. As the Editor of the *Synagogue Review* put it, 'If an institution conceived on these lines ever acquired a soul of its own, it would find a neutral resting place (midway between the two headquarters) in the waiting room of Baker Street Station!'.[6]

The two young ministers who were instrumental in keeping the West London Synagogue going while a Senior Minister was being sought were Michael Leigh and Lionel Blue, the first two students at the Leo Baeck College. Their backgrounds were dissimilar, but they formed a good balance. Leigh was born in London in 1928. He took his first degree at Oxford and then went to University College London where he studied Hebrew and Semitics. He was a family-oriented traditionalist, whereas Blue was a single man with progressive ideas. He came from a modest East End family with a background of rabbis, and also went to Oxford. His troubled early life led him first to Marxism and then to a rabbinical career. He had sent to the College a document stating his reasons for wanting to join the Ministry in which he affirmed his attachment to tradition while at the same time wanting to apply its principles to the changed circumstances under which he lived. His down-to-earth spirituality, accessible to everyone, is expressed in his various books, and he is today as well known and loved by the non-Jewish community as by his fellow religionists, mainly because of his humorous contributions to the BBC's 'Thought for the Day'.

Now that the storm had died down and the congregation seemed to be sailing through calmer waters, the Council set its thoughts on improving the way the synagogue was run. It was too large and too dispersed to function as efficiently as it should, so a Membership Committee was set up under the chairmanship of Lady Nathan to examine what could be done. Its findings were that it should continue to encourage new members to join a local congregation, but that no steps should be taken actually to limit the membership. Contact should be maintained with distant members through occasional gatherings in the suburbs, and all the synagogue committees should try to offer opportunities for service to a wide circle of congregants. The Education Committee agreed to establish branch classes in North Middlesex, where many members lived, and the Ministerial Selection Committee was asked to bear in mind the importance of a minister's pastoral duties and close contact with members. Finally this committee, which had been convened on a temporary basis, became a permanent Membership Committee to continue paying attention to the needs and desires of the congregation as a whole.

The Selection Committee was hard at work to find the right man to fill the post of Senior Minister. It had under consideration twenty-five persons, coming from four continents, and pursued the majority of them vigorously. After much consideration and many hours of discussion, it reported to the Council that its choice had settled on a home-grown, if not home-born, candidate, well-known to the members, who had all the qualities needed for such an onerous and responsible post. This was Rabbi Dr. Werner van der Zyl, then minister of the North Western Reform Synagogue, Alyth Gardens. Rabbi van der Zyl was born in 1902 in Schwerte, Germany and studied at the *Hochschule fur die Wissenschaft des Judentums,* serving as Rabbi in two Berlin congregations before being rescued by Lily Montagu and brought to England. He was interned first of all in Richborough in Kent, and then on the Isle of Man where he became Camp Supervisor. His wife Anneliese and little daughter, Monica, joined him, and in 1943 he was released to serve as Rabbi at Alyth Gardens. It was Werner van der Zyl who was the moving force behind the establishment of the Leo Baeck College for the training of ministers for the Reform movement. Liked and respected by all who knew him, he was offered the post of Rabbi in Santa Monica in California. Annaliese would have enjoyed the exciting life that Hollywood promised, but this was not what Werner wanted. He decided instead to take on the difficult task of leading a community, bereft of their former leader, who prided themselves on their Englishness and their long history. He himself said, 'A minister in his teaching must think and act in a true sense always in generations, from generation to generation.'[7] He took up his post on 1st August, 1958.

In his service contract he promised faithfully to perform such duties as were set out in the Laws of the Synagogue. He accepted a salary of £2,600, with an expense allowance of £400 per annum, a pension and six weeks' holiday, the term of his appointment to expire at the end of December 1967 when he would be 65. In Germany the salaries of Ministers of religion, Jewish as well as Christian, had been paid by the state; they were regarded as civil servants.

It took Werner a little while to understand that he was now an employee of
a small Committee, acting on behalf of a widely differing group of Jewish
congregants, whose personality must have some bearing on his Terms of
Office. He retained his German accent and his congregation enjoyed hearing
his pronouncement of the priestly blessing, ending in 'May you have deep
fai-ce.' But his modest, gentle personality smoothed his path, even though
he could on occasion be quite stubborn. He and Annaliese wanted to stay
in their house in Temple Fortune, opposite their former synagogue, but the
Council preferred them to live nearer to Berkeley Street. The van der Zyls
stayed where they were.

Dr. van der Zyl was warmly welcomed. The *Synagogue Review* said that 'he
brings to his task the very qualities most needed and he and his congregation
can look forward to years of growing mutual affection and trust.'[8] The
Induction Service for the new leader of the West London Synagogue took
place on 28th July 1958. In his sermon on that occasion, Dr. van der Zyl spoke
of the relationship between the rabbi and his congregation. 'In order to fulfil
his obligation the rabbi must stand within his congregation, not above it.
Judaism does not know of a task which belongs to the Minister alone. If he
is a trustee of the *Torah*, of the whole teaching of our religion, so also is his
congregation.'[9] He asked, too, for greater mutual understanding within the
larger community. The service was conducted by Rabbi Katz and many local
dignitaries were present, including the MP, Sir Wavell Wakefield, and the
Mayor and Mayoress of St. Marylebone. Many religious leaders were there,
Christian as well as Jewish, and the congregation numbered more than 900
persons. It was, of course, quite impossible for the new Senior Minister to
speak to all of them, so a series of receptions was arranged so that he might be
introduced to more of the community.

These numbers were not achieved just on special occasions; Sabbath Service
attendance was increasing, as was that for the High Holydays. In fact to find a
hall big enough to take overflow services was a difficult task. Only the Central
Hall, Westminster, the Royal Festival Hall and the Royal Albert Hall could
accommodate these huge congregations. When the synagogue itself was
full some difficulties were experienced with the sound system, and a new
system of amplification had to be installed. Several members enquired why
women were not reading the blessings over the *Torah*, or the *Haftarah*, or a part
of the service. There was nothing in the Laws of the synagogue, they were
informed, to prevent this, but when a young lady read part of the service in
the synagogue during a YASGB Service, the appointed Membership Liaison
Officer, Major R. Pinto, resigned. The Ritual Committee was also concerned
with the synagogue services, and recommended that the *Kaddish* be said in
Aramaic and read before *Adon Olam*, that Blessings should be read before and
after the reading from the Scroll, and that there should be a regular *Havdalah*
Service at 6.30 on the Sabbath. It was not only the service itself that came
under the scrutiny of the Council and its Committees. On some occasions

when a Bar Mitzvah was celebrated, it was felt that the behaviour of the boy's relatives constituted a 'lapse from the usual decorum'.

The question of the Aramaic version of the *Kaddish* was an interesting one. It dated back to Babylonian times when Aramaic was the everyday language of the people. By tradition that was still the version recited in the synagogue. But at the suggestion of Professor Marks when the first West London prayer book was compiled, it was changed to Hebrew, perhaps because his inclination was to make the service as comprehensible as possible to his congregation. It did not seem suitable to use English, but Hebrew was the next best thing. Traditionalists of West London had long wanted to return to the old familiar wording and welcomed the change.

So many committees had by now been established at Berkeley Street that it was felt that the West London Synagogue Association was superfluous and it was disbanded. The Association, now under the leadership of Vera Levi, had been instrumental in providing many different social and religious outlets for the members, but now each had its own controlling committee; the newly-formed Women's Guild had taken over many of them and the Members' Activities Committee was responsible for others. A new group for the 20 – 30 year olds, the Berkeley Group, offered a wide social programme for the younger members, after their initiation into congregational allegiance in the Junior Membership. With the membership now numbering some 2,400 souls, the synagogue was yet again running short of space. The children's classes were overflowing, the various activities found themselves fighting each other for room, and the Leo Baeck College, occupying the old Council Room over the synagogue, was trying to increase its rabbinical student facilities while at the same time offering opportunities for study to Hebrew and Biblical scholars. Rabbi Michael Leigh, having graduated from the College, was appointed Assistant Minister to Rabbi van der Zyl, Rabbi Lionel Blue, after a period with the World Union of Progressive Judaism, became Convenor to the Reform *Beth Din,* and Rabbi Alan Miller went to the United States, joining the Reconstructionist Movement there, founded by Rabbi Mordecai Kaplan.

The only answer to the space problem was a new building adjoined to the present one, via the 33 Seymour Place entrance. It was suggested that the old houses owned by the synagogue on the corner of Upper Berkeley Street and Seymour Place should be demolished and the site redeveloped for the use of the synagogue. The plans were for a spacious building to house the Leo Baeck College (and classrooms on Sunday mornings) a flat above and possibly shops on the ground floor. The architects chosen were Yorke, Rosenberg and Mardall, with Hamptons to act as Estate Agents to advise on the commercial and residential properties. The College was to pay rent to the synagogue, parking space would be provided according to local authority regulations, and an Estates Committee was set up to prepare plans and costings with proposals for financing the new building. The little Room of Prayer on the first floor of the synagogue was also refurbished and redecorated, with better lighting, and improvements to the layout of the room. Nowadays the new building, still known as the Leo Baeck Wing, is opening as Halcyon, an international comprehensive school.

The West London Synagogue was now established as the largest congregation in Britain, had been in existence for 120 years and commanded the respect of most of Anglo-Jewry and the wider world, but this did not mean that in some quarters it was not still regarded as a rebel organisation, whose secession from main-stream Judaism was unacceptable. The RSGB 'viewed with sorrow and concern' pronouncements concerning the 'illegitimacy' of children whose parents, though 100% Jewish, had married in a Progressive synagogue. The Board of Deputies was asked to investigate and to arrange a meeting with the United Synagogue to try to improve their attitude. At the Conference of European Rabbis in 1959, the Chief Rabbi, Dr. Israel Brodie, the Convenor of the Conference, held in Amsterdam, issued a 'clarion call' against the 'wrong ideologies' of the Progressive Movement. The *Jewish Chronicle* published a report of a letter sent by Dr. Brodie to all Rabbis and religious organisations in the diaspora. Written in Hebrew it was headed 'How to Remove a Stumbling Block', in terms reminiscent of the *cherem* 120 years earlier, he wrote, 'There exists an organisation known as Reform Synagogues', and referred to the *Beth Din* of the RSGB. 'They deliberately mislead the public to believe that this is a real *Beth Din* ... all their actions are in sharp contrast to the Laws and principles of the *Torah* ... their actions have no validity and are completely worthless.'[10] Much of the hostility was aimed at the West London Synagogue as the first and largest community in the RSGB, and considerably distress was caused to its members by these diatribes, particularly those who were married to non-Jews and had children. However, the Association decided that it was better to keep silent than to prolong the dissension aroused by the Orthodox leaders in this country.

There was also some disagreement in the ranks of RSGB members. The association had decided to withdraw its membership of the World Union for Progressive Judaism. This close association with Liberal Judaism was a running sore within the ranks of the two groups. Louis Littman, a member of the committee drawn up to advise the Conference of Reform Synagogues on the advisability of continued membership, wrote to the *Synagogue Review* to justify the withdrawal. Many members were unhappy with some of the religious practices of the Liberals, he explained, and also with the fact that the leaders of the St. John's Wood Liberal Jewish Synagogue formed the leadership of the World Union. Many RSGB rabbis were at odds with those leaders and did not believe that they were in sympathy with the aims and ideals under which Reform Judaism had been established. Members of Reform Synagogues hardly knew what went on in the affairs of the Union and there was a fear that if the Association continued its membership there might not only be a rift in its ranks, but that some synagogues might defect to Liberal ranks. This was the main reason for the withdrawal.

The Hon. Lily Montagu, Hon. Life President of Liberal Judaism (sometimes referred to as 'the first British woman Rabbi' though she never received *semicha*) replied to Louis Littman's letter. She maintained that officers of the World Union were not chosen for their affiliation to either Reform or Liberal Judaism but for their competence in doing the job. She expressed her pleasure that the subject of the link between the two was appearing in the journal. 'In the past', she wrote, 'we have pleaded in vain for assistance in explaining and publicising our work'[11] – a reference perhaps to Rabbi Reinhart's antipathy towards the Liberals. She hoped that in the future Reform congregations would help in trying to 'satisfy the spiritual needs of large numbers of Jews who have never had a Jewish education or who are now breaking away altogether from Judaism.'[12]

Another interesting contribution to the *Synagogue Review*, published in September 1959, was an article by Rabbi Gerhard Graf of Cardiff, He explained that in his home town the Lord Mayor was a lady. So was a leading Cardiff barrister whom he met at the inauguration of the Mayor. This was about the time when the Church of England was discussing the ordination of women ministers. 'I feel the time has come,' Rabbi Graf wrote, 'for Reform Judaism to encourage women to train for the rabbinate.'[13] This daring point of view was not entirely new. Rabbi Regina Jonas had received *semicha* in Germany as long ago as 1935 and, as Rabbi Graf put it, 'Equality of the sexes is a recognised and basic principle of Reform.' Needless to say, not every reader of the *Review* supported him. One referred to his feeling of 'consternation and apprehension' at reading the article. 'There really must be some limit to the wild aspirations of some of those whom we trust to lead us in the right direction,' he said, referring to the pulpit as 'the last prerogative of man.' A lady, not ruling out the suggestion of women ministers, reassured him that 'there will be no queue of eager ladies outside the Leo Baeck College clamouring to be admitted.' Another, supporting Rabbi Graf, envisaged that 'only the best types would aspire to it and only the ablest of the best would succeed.' Rabbi Graf himself replied to his irate correspondent, ' The place of the Jewish woman as a professing Jewess is not only in the kitchen to prepare "*gefilte fish*". Her place is wherever she can teach and guide the children of Israel, including the pulpit.'[14] It took another sixteen years before the first English woman rabbi was ordained.

The plans for the new building at Berkeley Street fell foul of Town Planning restrictions and modifications had to be drawn up. It was decided not to make use of the houses in Upper Berkeley Street, but to erect the new building on the corner with Seymour Place. Two houses had to be pulled down, but the space available was enough to create new premises for the College as well as classrooms and a Library, and outline planning permission was obtained. An appeal was made for £150,000 to finance the project, and although contributions would come from other RSGB synagogues, the burden of raising the money would inevitably be West London's. Special events were organised: a Supper Party followed by an impromptu debate, a Guild Fair, and several minor functions, all of which helped to achieve the sum required. The funds took some time to accumulate, and it was not until 1965 that the new extension was completed and consecrated. Master Diamond, as President, led the congregation at the opening, performed by Mrs. Leonard Montefiore (her husband had died suddenly in 1961). The building included a lounge and office accommodation, the Leo Baeck College Library, a Youth Centre as well as a small cafeteria and two staff flats. The flats were taken by the Caretaker and by Sidney Pettle, the Beadle, and his wife, with access from the third floor of Seymour Place.

Several of the rooms were named after generous donors to the Building Fund: the Library by Louis Littman, after his late father, the adjoining Students' Room of the College by Mrs. Montefiore for her husband, Leonard, the Lounge on the ground floor after the Henriques family as well as several others in the new annexe.

✡

During the war it had not been feasible for West London to celebrate its one hundredth birthday, but it was certainly not to be deprived of a second chance when, in 1963, the 120th anniversary of the first service of the congregation took place. On 10th June a dinner was held at the Hilton Hotel. The price of a ticket was three-and-a-half guineas, a great deal in those days, and a glittering guest list included Lords Longford, Cohen and Nathan, with their ladies, Viscount Chandos, Sir Barnet and Lady Janner, Sir Seymour and Lady Karminski, Sir Louis and Lady Gluckstein, Sir Wavell and Lady Wakefield as well as numerous Rabbis and other guests of note. The Editor of the *Jewish Chronicle*, William Frankel, attended and the paper printed a four-page supplement to mark the event. This included an account of the first 120 years of the synagogue by its President, A.S. Diamond, which was later expanded into a booklet and published as *The Building of a Synagogue*. In the same year S.G. Schwab had asked the Council if consideration could be given to publishing a history of the West London Synagogue. During the following fifty years, apart from an unpublished account of the first eight years by Rabbi Cassell, no such account has been published until now.

The *Jewish Chronicle* Supplement also included an article by Rabbi van der Zyl on 'Our Religious Tradition', and a charming account of 'A Day at Berkeley Street' by the Secretary Alan Silverman, in the form of his tour around the synagogue in the company of an S.I.M. (Somewhat Inactive Member!) who could not see the need for keeping the synagogue open during the week. After his visit, when he saw the innumerable purposes for which the building was used, he changed his mind and donated handsomely to the Building Fund.

During the course of the next year or two, the Senior Minister found himself with too little support for his huge task of keeping the congregation running. He needed at least one assistant, preferably two. However when the question of a third minister was raised in Council, it was felt that financially this was almost impossible. Then Rabbi Leigh was appointed to be Rabbi of the Edgware and District Reform Synagogue. This deprived Berkeley Street of its principal assistant, and the Council looked around for a replacement. An American Rabbi, Leo Abrami, was appointed, and a Rabbi from South Africa, Michael Elton, was recommended to help out on a temporary basis. But Mr. Abrami was 'unable to fulfil his duties satisfactorily' and Rabbi Elton's term of office ended and was not renewed. The difficulty was acute and the Ministerial Selection Committee had to convene again. This time it interviewed a young man it had met before. It found him eminently suitable and offered him the post, at a salary of £2,250 p.a. with a four-bedroom flat near the Synagogue.

Known to many members, either from their early days in the Junior Membership, or as a frequent visitor during his visits to England, Rabbi Hugo Gryn was destined to play a vital role in the history and development, not only of the West London Synagogue, but in that of Anglo-Jewry as a whole. After his tragic experiences in pre-war Germany, and a brief spell in Scotland, he had won a scholarship to King's College, Cambridge, to read mathematics and biochemistry. He went to Israel to serve in the army, but contracted jaundice and came home. Dr. Leo Baeck was a leading influence in his decision to train as a Rabbi, as was Lily Montagu, of the Liberal Synagogue. He went to the Hebrew Union College in Cincinnati on a scholarship partly funded by the West London Women's Guild and by the World Union for Progressive Judaism. There he obtained his first degree, as well as a Masters and a Doctorate, and in 1957 was awarded *semicha*. Earlier that year he married Jacqueline Selby at West London, and together they went out to India where Rabbi Gryn spent two years, under the auspices of the World Union, travelling and lecturing. Their eldest child, Naomi, was born in India and three more children were born in New York where Gryn had taken his family when he was appointed Executive Director of the WUPJ. He became Director of the American Joint Distribution Committee, charged with the responsibility of helping Jewish people in Eastern Europe. But he was always anxious to become Rabbi of a community, was offered a post at Waco, Texas (where the appalling siege and deaths of the followers of David Koresh took place many years later) but preferred to accept the call to come to London.

Rabbi Gryn (known to most as Hugo) was inducted into office in October 1964 at Upper Berkeley Street in the presence of more than 700 people, among them the local M.P., Quintin Hogg, and the Mayor and Mayoress of St. Marylebone. The service was conducted by the Senior Minister, Rabbi van der Zyl, who led the procession, followed by the three Wardens and the President, Master A.S.Diamond. Hugo gave the address, expressing his confidence that the 'great past' of the congregation would prove a prelude to an even greater future. 'It is not the ministers who make a congregation great and venerable,' he said, 'but the congregants. The lay leaders of this congregation have not only given me a cordial welcome, but have made a great impression by their sincerity and undisguised devotion to the congregation.'[15] The family moved into a flat at York House, where Jackie Gryn lives to this day, playing a full and welcome role in synagogue life.

CHAPTER XIII

The Synagogue in the Seventies

During the years 1963-5 the Synagogue remembered with great sadness three distinguished leaders, two non-Jewish and one of their own members. On December 1st 1963, Dr. van der Zyl addressed the congregation during a Memorial Service for the late President Kennedy. 'The death of John F. Kennedy,' he said, 'has united all well-meaning people into one great family of mourners'.[1] He referred to him as 'a man of faith, a God-fearing man', and quoted the President's own words, recalling perhaps something of his own commitment when inducted at West London; 'the energy, faith, the devotion which we bring to this endeavour will light our country and all who serve it, and the glow from that fire can truly light the world.'

Just over two years later the congregation again mourned a great man, not directly connected with the West London Synagogue but without whom, perhaps, it would have ceased to exist at all. This was Sir Winston Churchill, a man much admired by Dr. van der Zyl. He died on 24th January, and the Synagogue held a Memorial Service a week later, when again Dr. van der Zyl led the service, assisted by the chairman of the Assembly of Ministers, Dr. Michael Leigh, Rabbi Berg from Wimbledon and Rabbi Hugo Gryn. Apart from Dr. Leigh, all the three Rabbis had good reason to believe that their very presence was due to England's ability, under Mr. Churchill (as he then was) to keep the free world safe from Hitler's attempts to enslave it.

Nearer to home occurred the sad death in 1965 of Edward Henriques, O.B.E., the former Synagogue Treasurer, whose father and grandfather had been members of West London from its earlier days. He had been associated in various capacities with the Anglo-Jewish Association, the Bernhard Baron Settlement and the Joint Burial Committee of West London and the Spanish-Portuguese Synagogue, apart from the different offices he had held within the congregation. A new President had just been elected to succeed Master A.S. Diamond, who resigned as he felt a younger man should take over. Another distinguished lawyer took his place. His Honour Judge Alan King-Hamilton, Q.C. had been a member of Upper Berkeley Street throughout his life, attending Religion Classes before his confirmation, and marrying his wife Rosalind Ellis there. He was a Bencher of the Middle Temple and a Freeman of the City of London. He presided over many notorious trials, including the *Gay News* trial for perjury. He died in 2010 at the age of 105.

In October 1967 Rabbi van der Zyl suffered the first of two serious heart attacks. He was ordered to take time away from his duties, and the synagogue was capably led by its Assistant Minister, Rabbi Hugo Gryn and by Rabbi Jacob Weinstein, the immediate Past President of the Central Conference of American Rabbis, who came to help out over the High Holydays. The van der Zyl family went for a time to Majorca, where they had always enjoyed refreshing holidays.

At this time the *Synagogue Review* had been subsumed into the journal of the RSGB (it had always carried news of all the associated synagogues) and the congregation had been making do with a monthly bulletin, giving the bare news of what was going on. But in 1967 it was revived, this time as the *West London Synagogue Review,* and was able once again to include news and articles of its own.

Unlike its stance in earlier days, Berkeley Street was by now much more involved, as were most English Jews, with the State of Israel. Even before the outbreak of the Six-Day War, members were showing a greater interest in Israel and its problems; visits and holidays were more frequent, and Israeli visitors, especially young people, were finding in England a warmth and hospitality somewhat lacking before, certainly in the Reform community. Rabbi Gryn had always felt himself closely allied to the Israeli cause and deteriorating relations with Arab countries had caused him much distress. On his return from a visit there he spoke to a very large audience of members (the numbers were so great that they had to be taken down to the Stern Hall, unable to fit into the Council Room). In his talk – 'Israel after the Six-Day War' – Rabbi Gryn emphasised how little hatred the Jews in Israel felt for their Arab neighbours and confirmed that the gap between Israel and the Diaspora was closing fast. He had attended a court case where two Arab boys were defended by an Israeli lawyer, and saw for himself how some of the soldiers at the checkpoints were giving fruit to the children. He felt Israel to be a civilised place, where there was respect for human life, with everyone equal before the law.

The Leo Baeck College, too, was reaching out towards Israel with a programme of visits, exchanges with students and a greater awareness of that country's problems. The College was no more firmly placed financially than it had ever been, and Rabbi van der Zyl, now its President, was concerned for its future. Its reputation stood very high in academic circles. Doctor Samuel Sandmel, the distinguished Professor of Bible and Hellenistic Literature at the Hebrew Union College, came as visiting Principal for a year, and the College welcomed students from all over the world, not only to train as Rabbis but to study Hebrew, Jewish history, philosophy and bible studies. As early as 1952, the Reform movement had discussed with the Union of Liberal and Progressive Synagogues the possibility of training Rabbis for Liberal as well as Reform congregations. Rabbi Reinhart had been against any such move, so had Rabbi Selvin Goldberg of Manchester, referring to the proposals as like trying to arrange a marriage where the bride could not provide a dowry. It was not only a question of further funding for the College – it needed lecturers of the highest quality, and these could not be found if opportunities were stretched over two different Progressive sources

Finally, in 1963, after many years of sometimes acrimonious discussions, the Annual Report of the College to the RSGB Conference made specific reference to the collaboration of the two bodies for the joint administration of the College and the setting up of an Academic Committee. Dr. van der Zyl spoke of the College as 'the only undogmatic, non-Orthodox Jewish theological institution in Europe, and the first to be maintained by Jewish Progressive movements ... All studies are free from indoctrination, in the spirit of the Hochschule fur die Wissenschaft des Judentums in furtherance of Judaism, regardless as to Progressive or Orthodox viewpoints'.[2] When Dr. Immanuel Jakobovits became Chief Rabbi in 1967, he was in many ways as intransigent towards Reform as any of his predecessors, but he did lecture on occasion at the College and consulted it in connection with advice given to the government of the time regarding body transplants. The next problem to face the College was the question of women rabbis. Several women were already studying there, taking Hebrew and Bible classes, but none had so far tried to acquire a rabbinical diploma, let alone take on the responsibilities of leading a congregation.

Rabbi van der Zyl returned to the synagogue in January 1968 and resumed his duties as vigorously as ever. But he was by now sixty-five years old and due for retirement. In view of his health and in spite of his unfailing energy, he decided to retire after the coming High Holydays. He had been elected Chairman of the newly formed Council of Reform and Liberal Rabbis, a position which led the Jewish Chronicle to consider him the Chief Rabbi of the Progressive movement. He hastened to disillusion its readers. In a letter to the paper he wrote that the spokesman for Progressive Judaism differed from the Chief Rabbi of the United Synagogues in that he was 'elected by his fellow Rabbis; had no jurisdiction over his fellow Rabbis; was elected for two years, and officiates as the Council's spokesman in consultation and agreement with his colleagues.' [3] In pointing out these differences Dr. van der Zyl was drawing attention to some of the very difficulties which faced the Chief Rabbi and which throughout the establishment of that office had returned time and time again to plague the holder.

In view of the forthcoming retirement of its Senior Minister, the Council took on a new Assistant Minister, another face well-known to the younger members of the congregation. For Michael Goulston had been an active member of the Junior Membership at Berkeley Street. After graduating from the Leo Baeck College he became Minister at the Middlesex New Synagogue, and was made very welcome in his new post at West London. The Synagogue Review of October 1968 devoted its whole issue to Rabbi van der Zyl's retirement. Judge King-Hamilton recalled the difficulties in which the synagogue found itself 'without benefit of clergy' and how well the new Senior Minister had fitted in with the traditions of Berkeley Street. He mentioned the close cooperation of the two ministers, the establishment of a 'wonderful team.' 'He is a most unassuming person, with a genuine sense of modesty, a warm and friendly nature, a quiet sense of fun,'[4] he wrote. Rabbi Gryn followed this with his own tribute referring to their work together as 'one of the most harmonious associations in my experience.' Other contributions came from Rabbi Lionel Blue, of the Leo Baeck College and Raymond Goldman of Alyth Gardens and the RSGB. The *Jewish Chronicle* combined its account of Rabbi van der Zyl's departure with a welcome to his successor, Rabbi Hugo Gryn. In keeping with Rabbi van der Zyl's habitual low profile, his farewell party was a tea in the synagogue at which he and his wife were presented with a silver-topped crystal jug, presented by the Chairman of the Women's Guild, Mrs. A.S. Diamond. The van der Zyls had decided to make their home in their beloved Majorca, returning to England whenever they could to see their many friends. Berkeley Street had not traditionally been in the habit of promoting its Assistant Rabbi to the post of Senior Minister. It had usually preferred to seek elsewhere for a successor, but in this case there was little doubt that Hugo would accede to the throne in due course, to the acclamation of its members and the world outside.

Happily settled in Majorca, Rabbi van der Zyl helped to establish a synagogue in Palma; there had been a thriving Jewish community there in the fourteenth century, but it had been destroyed and the site occupied by a church. In 1973 he led a Friday night service, the first held on the island since the Jews were expelled from Spain in 1492. For a while the new community flourished, a mixture of Reform and Orthodox traditions, but gradually the Orthodox took over and the van der Zyls decided to bow out. Werner van der Zyl died at his home in Majorca in 1984 at the age of eighty-two. He was buried at Hoop Lane, not far from the grave of his beloved mentor, Leo Baeck. The obituary in the *Jewish Chronicle* quoted his breadth of scholarship, his oratory and the work he did for Jewish youth. The paper quoted the words of Rabbi Hugo Gryn, his assistant and then his successor, 'He was a Rabbi who loved the *Torah* of German Jewry, its *Wissenschaft* and traditions of *Menschlichkeit*, and whose mandate was to keep it alive and to enhance it. He never wavered from his purpose and succeeded in it.'[5]

✡

The West London Synagogue of British Jews had chosen its name in 1840 with very good reason. It wished to avoid the distinctions in the community between Ashkenazi and Sephardi Jews which had caused much animosity in the early years of its foundation. More than 120 years later that distinction was hardly noticed, prompting a lady to write a letter to Judge King-Hamilton which was published in the *Synagogue Review* suggesting a change of name. The writer felt that the concentration on 'British' Jews might make members who came from Eastern Europe or Germany feel that they did not belong.

However, having discussed the matter the Council did not agree, was proud of the synagogue's name and felt it should remain as it was.

Although West London was now under the leadership of a young and very active Minister, who was happy to introduce new ideas, the synagogue still clung, not only to its original name, but also to much of its old traditions. In an article, Master A.S. Diamond, former President of the Synagogue and now a Life Member of the Council, reviewed the changes that had come about in his lifetime. He bemoaned the fact, as had so many of his predecessors, that so few members appeared in the synagogue on the Sabbath. Some felt the service was 'too orthodox', some that it was 'too liberal'. He recounted the old traditions of the reading of the Ten Commandments, a relatively modern practice, with Berkeley Street reading a shortened form, even more modern, though it dated back to ancient times. He recalled that in earlier times, members never bowed to the *Torah* or touched it with their *tallit*. The Wardens never bowed to the Ark when they closed the doors, nor were members called up to the Law. There was no Kiddush on a Saturday morning after the service. Perhaps this earliest of Reform synagogues was turning towards Orthodoxy. Another member also wanted change, noting the swing of the pendulum from the early departure from orthodox practice, through reform, and back again. He felt that 'we are in danger of having too much decorum and too little heart'[6] in the services. He wanted more Hebrew and less English. What would the early fathers of Reform have said to that? The new generation of Rabbis now training at the College did not appear to agree. Rabbi Goulston, at the RSGB Conference, showed delegates audio-visual aids for education, including a synchronised film strip and a video-tape made in the Berkeley Street synagogue.

In August 1969, the West London Synagogue was saddened to hear of the death of their former Senior Minister, Harold Reinhart. He had served Berkeley Street for twenty-eight years and had been Minister at Westminster Synagogue with some of his old congregants. The sad circumstances of his departure in 1957 had not prevented him from continuing his long affiliations with many of his old friends and colleagues, and he was remembered for his energy, his integrity, his work for Jewish refugees, and his love of children. The *Synagogue Review* noted particularly the part he had played in the establishment and growth of other synagogues, leading to the founding of the Reform Synagogues of Great Britain.

By 1970 another problem had arisen, not just for West London, but for the whole Reform movement. The Hoop Lane cemetery was almost full. West London's original estimates for burials at its ground in Golders Green had not taken account of the huge expansion of Reform congregations in London, and the matter was now urgent. It was obvious to all religious organisations that ground for interment in or near London was at a premium. Even with the increasing inclination towards cremation (not a possibility for Orthodox Jews) the necessity to make burial available for those who wished it, meant journeying quite a distance out of town, a problem for relatives and administrative staff. Perhaps the elders at West London who agreed to share the sixteen acres of land at Golders Green with the Spanish and Portuguese Synagogue should have been more farsighted, and held on to the whole plot. After much searching to the north and west, where most Reform synagogues lay, they finally agreed to buy from the London Borough of Camden a large acreage of land off Edgwarebury Lane and share it with the Sephardim, a cooperation which had worked so well in the past.

The journal of the West London Synagogue, the *Synagogue Review*, had been published almost without exception, every month since it began as the *West London Magazine* in 1925. Right through the war it appeared regularly bringing news as well as comfort to those oppressed by what was happening to them and their families. The same complaints by members of the congregation reappeared from time to time over the years: a dearth of attendance at Sabbath Services, a refusal to join in the singing, disturbance on the High Holydays when late arriving members claimed 'their' seats, already occupied by others. In July 1970 the format of the *Review* changed again, this time into something more like a newspaper format, easier to read, perhaps, but much more difficult to file away. What did not change was the high quality of the articles and reports, written almost entirely by members and their Rabbis, and it was clear from letters to the Editor and the comments expressed in the paper that it was much valued as a form of communication, enabling the congregation to keep in touch. For those who were confined to their homes for much of the time it was a lifeline. For the leaders of the community it served as a way to inform, to teach and to express their intentions.

The first edition in the new format contained an article by Rabbi Gryn entitled 'The Synagogue in the Seventies'. It was the keynote speech at the RSGB Conference of that year. Rabbi Gryn felt that the Reform Movement was ideally placed to provide innovation and experiment, so badly needed in the modern world. At that time anti-Semitism, as earlier members of the community had known it, was being replaced by anti-Zionism. Pressure from within, particularly on modern youth, was one of the enemies the movement had to fight. 'Membership of a synagogue,' he said, 'is too often merely a passive method of securing seats for the high holydays and a burial plot.'[7] He saw the ideal synagogue of the next decade as a sanctuary, surrounded by a centre, with classrooms, a library, a place for leisure time activities where a sense of community could develop. He felt that Progressive Judaism had the greatest opportunity of welcoming in the next generation of active Jews. 'We are not rigid in our interpretation,' he went on, 'there is no religious computer which, when all the right buttons are pressed, will come up with oracular answers to all the problems confronting the world ... but our voice must not be denied.'[8]

The following month was an important occasion in the history of West London, and the *Review* devoted a whole edition to commemorating the one hundred years of the synagogue's existence in the Berkeley Street building. A special service was held, at which 700 members were present, together with many Jewish and non-Jewish celebrities, including Lord Hailsham, Lord and Lady Janner, Lady Henriques, Robert Carvalho and the representatives of most Jewish organisations. A special anthem was composed by Samuel Solomon, set to music by Sidney Fixman, the Synagogue's choirmaster. Rabbi Gryn gave the address, in which he paid tribute to the beauty of the synagogue building, its organ and those who had helped in so many ways during the hundred years of its existence. He felt that it should not be 'a storehouse of prayers but a power-house, created by a thriving community centre where religious faith would be expressed through a host of life-giving and life-saving activities.'[9] Sadly, the Chief Rabbi saw fit to reprimand those Jews under his control who attended the service, describing this as 'contrary to Jewish law'.[10]

The congregation also had the unusual honour of playing hosts to the Royal Philharmonic Orchestra, conducted by Sidney Fixman, in a performance of Bloch's *Sacred Service* in the Synagogue itself. This was the first time the work had been performed in Hebrew in Britain. The choir was formed from the choirs of the metropolitan synagogues of the RSGB. The synagogue was crowded to overflowing, as the orchestra, in full white tie and tails, took its place in a cleared arena. The musicians had their backs to the Ark, facing the audience, and the *Jewish Chronicle* commented particularly on the 'glistening bells and colourful mantles of the *Sifre Torah* in the Ark, providing a brilliant if unusual backcloth for the orchestra.[11] The choir was composed of forty singers, with Kenneth Ash, baritone, as soloist. Much of the work consisted of the familiar words of the Sabbath Service, set to Bloch's touchingly beautiful melodies. The story of how Bloch came to write the piece, is as fascinating as the music itself. Born a Jew, but with no Jewish affiliations in his early life, the composer was overwhelmed by the idea of writing sacred music for the synagogue, and had learned Hebrew in order to be able to understand the words.

The annual winter Bazaar, originally instituted to help Lingfield House and now contributing towards the synagogue charities, was expanded into a 'Centenary Bazaar' to include stalls for toys, stationery, a 'flower bower', cosmetics and several others. It made nearly £8,000. A special Centenary Appeal was launched to help with the essential repairs to the synagogue building which needed 'a new roof, new lighting, better amplification and new furniture'. On its front page the *Review* reproduced a picture of the synagogue as it was in the nineteenth century, all the male worshippers resplendent in silk hats and tailcoats, flowers and palm trees around the Ark. No women appear in the picture – at that time they were hidden away in the gallery.

Several other events took place during these celebrations. Rabbi Michael Goulston organised an Arts Week which included an evening with Donald

Swann, with the first public performance of his *The Story of Bontzye Schweig*, poetry readings, an exhibition of paintings and lithographs by contemporary Jewish artists, and a panel discussion with Al Alvarez and the Cultural Attaché at the Israel Embassy among others. The evening, under the title of 'Nationality and the Creative Process', was introduced by Lord Goodman. During the course of the discussion the speakers, although Jewish, disclaimed their attachment to Judaism, prompting a letter to the *Review* from L.T.S. Littman, asking why these 'atheists of Jewish ancestry' should be qualified to act as ambassadors of the Jewish community. 'Surely,' the letter asked, 'these are fallacies we would do well to put aside.'[12] The letter prompted an angry reply from the organiser of the panel, Anthony Rudolf, describing its 'narrow-mindedness as symptomatic of the malaise he purports to deplore.'[13] Several members felt that the dispute was a worthy example of West London's refusal (over one hundred years) to accept the obvious and to question what had hitherto been accepted. All the Arts Week events were well attended, and the Synagogue had every reason to feel it was well set for its next one hundred years.

However, in spite of West London's pride in its long and unselfish service to the Jewish Community, its insistence on a modern outlook and its refusal to submit to many ancient traditions, there was one element where many of the congregation felt it was letting them down. At any average Sabbath service the attendance was composed of some 60-70% women. Girls at their Bat Mitzvah read from the scroll, women were very occasionally permitted to read a part of the service (two read before Bat Mitzvah, when two gentlemen walked out), or (once or twice a year) to read the *Haftarah*, but as far as religious participation was concerned that was about the limit of their involvement. Some Reform synagogues had already overtaken their leader by allowing women to carry a scroll on *Simchat Torah* – when the suggestion was made at West London, some of their fellow male congregants threw up their hands in horror. Martin Chaplin wrote an article for the *Synagogue Review* bringing the situation to the attention of its readers. 'Do members subscribe to the more orthodox view of virtually second-class citizenship for women in the synagogue?'[14] he asked. He invited his members to reply, stating their sex and age.

Members were not slow to respond. Louis Littman, always to be found when a controversy was threatening, and known for his right-wing views as well as his Jewish scholarship, did not hesitate. 'Judaism,' he began, 'amongst its other features, is indisputably a religion of masculine style.'[15] He went on to suggest that one reason for the separation of the sexes might be to allow them to concentrate on their prayers rather than that 'the House of Prayer might become a House of Fashion, and worse.' He gave a lengthy dissertation on the uprising within the community, Jewish and non-Jewish, of the Women's Liberation Movement, which he deplored, warning his fellow-worshippers not to be tricked by 'trifling arguments or undermined through their own apathy into conceding this or any other un-Jewish demands.' Another letter objected to women reading as 'their voices are not particularly easy on the ear.' This letter, to modern readers now very out-of-date, pointed out that neither the BBC nor ITA (as it was then) employed women to read the news.

It is interesting to note that, apparently unconnected to the stirrings of feminine participants in the West London Synagogue, that same year the RSGB Association of Women's Guilds held a 'teach-in' at Berkeley Street under the title of 'The Role of Women in the Synagogue.' The first lecture, by Rabbi Dr. Katz, dealt with Jewish family life and the changes that had taken place, particularly in traditional Jewish families. 'It is up to the woman to make the choice – whether to take part in the service in the Synagogue, or to look to her duties in the home.'[16] He was followed by Rabbi Dov Marmur who took a different tack, asking the question about a woman's place, 'If she can teach why not preach?' Daring to ask why there should not be women rabbis, he told his audience that there was indeed a woman student at present at the Leo Baeck College. Should she become a Rabbi? If not, why not? The report of the meeting said that 'deep feelings were aroused', and indeed the College did produce a woman rabbi, but it took another three years. Martin Chaplin replied to the furore his original letter had produced, maintaining his stance that women should receive *mitzvot* in the synagogue, and Zena Pettle (wife of Sidney Pettle the *shammas*) agreed in a brief article, asking, are we not all equal in the eyes of the Lord?

The young Minister who had been helping out at Berkeley Street since 1968, Michael Goulston, was hardworking and popular. He had almost been brought up at West London, and had studied at the Leo Baeck College. Then he had finished his rabbinical training at the Hebrew Union College in Cincinnatti and came back to England, first to the Southport Reform Synagogue and then to the Middlesex New Synagogue. It was therefore with particular sadness that the congregation learned of his death, after a short illness, at the early age of forty. In that short time, he had founded and edited the much respected journal *European Judaism*, was Chairman of the Central Education Committee of the RSGB, represented West London on the Board of Deputies, and been appointed a Lecturer at the College. He founded the first teacher training course for progressive students as a joint venture between the College and London University. Trent Park, the north London college affiliated to the university, would not take 'known progressives'. A Memorial Service was held at Berkeley Street, attended by 700 people, at which Rabbi Gryn gave the address, describing Michael as 'one of those rare people who was unafraid of the future, and refused to be paralysed by a romantic notion of the past... a spiritual man who taught by word as well as by example.'[17] His main interests lay in the field of education, and in his memory the Michael Goulston Educational Foundation was set up to further his ideas on Jewish teaching, with particular reference to the use of audio and visual aids. He left a wife and three children.

At the end of 1972 another young Rabbi was inducted as Assistant Minister at Berkeley Street. Thomas Salamon, only twenty-four years old, had trained in Budapest before coming to England, and by coincidence had been born in Czechoslovakia only thirty miles from the birthplace of Rabbi Gryn. In his induction address he said, 'To be a Jew is to know what to do as a Jew and as a human being, to affirm the heritage of our forefathers, to accept the past which should be our light for the future and not something which should be re-lived or followed to the letter.' Rabbi Salamon went on to become co-executive Director of Norwood Homes, then trained as a solicitor and in 1997 went to Westminster Synagogue as leader of that community. He was joined at Berkeley Street later by another graduate of the Leo Baeck College. Rabbi Lionel Blue was no stranger to Berkeley Street, having helped out after Rabbi Reinhart's departure. He, like Rabbi Gryn, had been Director of the World Union, had co-authored the new Prayer Book and was the Convenor of the Reform *Beth Din*.

It was Rabbi Goulston who was instrumental in inspiring the Synagogue to commission the five murals which, until 2012, adorned the Stern Hall. He had seen the work of the artist, Hans Feibusch, exhibited at the Ben Uri Art Gallery, and asked him to lend some of his paintings for Berkeley Street's centenary celebrations. The idea was followed up by Rabbi Gryn who visited the artist in his studio in St. John's Wood and asked him to create some subjects for murals. The Council liked the results and Feibusch set out on five months' work to produce the finished paintings. He explained in an interview that he spent much time on the preliminary studies, with pencil sketches and colour impressions. Then he executed the painting on canvas so that the murals could if necessary be removed from the wall. Feibusch worked on many religious subjects, mostly for Christian places of worship; those at Berkeley Street were believed to be the first murals with figurative subjects to appear on the premises of a synagogue in Britain.

During 1975 the congregation was aware of the devotion and energy of a young woman who had for some time been helping with the education programme at the synagogue. Jackie Acker studied first of all for a teaching diploma and then for the rabbinate at the Leo Baeck College. Before marrying a fellow rabbinical student, Larry Tabick, she went to Australia for a year, and sent back to West London an interesting article on her adventures there as that country's first woman rabbi. She had become interested in Judaism as a small girl, when her father, suffering from multiple sclerosis, was denied entry to his orthodox synagogue in Dublin because he was in a wheelchair. She and her mother came to London after his death and joined the South West Essex Reform Synagogue. It was Rabbi Louis Jacobs, who established the first Masorti Synagogue in this country, who encouraged Jackie to try for the Rabbinate.

In June the RSGB invited Jackie to be the first European woman Rabbi after the German Regina Jonas who was ordained in 1935. Jackie was ordained privately with six others, the ordination taking place after a one-hour study period led by Rabbi Jacobs. There was a public Graduation Service the following day at the Liberal Jewish Synagogue during which Jackie read and translated the *Torah* passage. The address was given by Rabbi Albert Friedlander, Director of Studies at the College, and Rabbi Katz, Rabbi Rayner and Rabbi Gryn all took part. Rabbi Tabick was appointed Education Officer at West London, and known as Mrs. Tabick, later becoming its Assistant Minister. She was responsible for the Synagogue insisting on only kosher food being consumed on the premises. On the High Holydays women were then still sitting upstairs, but to have a woman at the *bimah* who then had to go upstairs for the rest of the service, was patently ridiculous. It was not long before the women were permitted to sit where they liked at all services. With a fine voice Jackie often sung a part of the service. However one gentleman would always put his hands over his ears when she did!

In its increasing attempts to 'modernise' itself the Council put forward a proposition which did not meet the wishes of the whole congregation. It had since its inception kept closely to the seating arrangements that the founding fathers had insisted upon, with the important exception that by this time men and women were sitting together for all services except the High Holydays. On these four services the women were banished to the gallery (at the overflow services men and women sat together). The seat-holders paid a higher subscription; non-seat-holder members could be seated in the overflow service, and non-members could be issued with a Roving Ticket, enabling them to sit anywhere where there was an empty seat. However, they might be 'tapped on the shoulder and asked to move' if the seat was assigned and its owner arrived to claim it. Formerly the seats were graded according to their location, rather like a theatre. For twenty years the 'seat situation', as it came to be known, vexed the Council, but finally it suggested that a) men and women should sit together at all services; b) all existing seat-holders should retain their right to a seat for life (some families had held the same seat for generations); c) that no further seats should be allocated. There would be a pool of vacant seats, growing as time went by. Seats would henceforward be allocated to non-seat-holders alphabetically, so that families could sit together. Not all the suggestions were adopted at the Annual General Meeting. Some felt that the abolition of new seats would reflect badly in the synagogue accounts and it was decided to postpone the full acceptance of the Council's proposals.

✡

Most non-Jews knew very little of the Jewish way of life, even towards the end of the twentieth century. They knew of the Jewish tragedy, of the state of

Israel, and those whose children attended schools in Jewish areas had an idea of the home life of those children's Jewish friends. But rabbis on the whole had something of a bad press. The very word brought pictures of strangely-dressed, bearded gentlemen, with foreign accents who played little part in modern English life. This was much changed by two rabbis of the West London Synagogue who seized on contemporary methods of communication to enlighten their fellow Englishmen, Jewish and non-Jewish. Lionel Blue was invited to speak on the BBC's 'Thought for the Day' programme regularly. The short morning slot gave him an opportunity to tell jokes, much appreciated by the presenters of the programme, to remember his home life and particularly his mother, and even to produce recipes for Jewish meals (Lionel was an excellent cook). He soon commanded a huge audience, and many listeners considered Lionel the only religious radio speaker they ever bothered to tune in to. When asked why he was so popular he replied that he was simply 'ordinary' but that he made day-to-day spirituality accessible

Hugo Gryn's contribution to British broadcasting made him a widely known and loved figure in modern theological debate. He was a regular speaker on *The Moral Maze* programmes, and in 2010 his daughter Naomi edited a collection of his contributions to the 'God slot', with a foreword by Michael Buerck. Called *Three Minutes of Hope* the book recalled some of the contributions, with their gentle humour and unquenchable faith. Buerck wrote, 'He was warm without being soft. He could be angry but never hurtful. He hated only two things – prejudice and bigotry.' [18] There are contributions to the book from Rabbi Lionel Blue, Maureen Lipman, Rabbi Julia Neuberger, Sir Martin Gilbert and several non-Jews. Hugo took part in many other BBC programmes and never failed to interest and intrigue his listeners. Few Rabbis of any section of Anglo-Jewry have had such influence over their non-Jewish fellow countrymen.

CHAPTER XIV

Towards the Millennium

In 1977 an event took place which none of the original members of the West London Synagogue could have foreseen, or if they had would have considered the location unworthy of their English heritage. 800 delegates to the conference of the World Union of Progressive Judaism met in Jerusalem to establish the first Reform Kibbutz in the state of Israel. Referring to the founding fathers of the World Union in 1926, the *Synagogue Review* said, 'They simply could not have imagined that fifty years later the movement's headquarters would be Jerusalem, the capital of a sovereign Jewish State.'[1] Upper Berkeley Street's affiliation with Israel was growing stronger and many young people were by now making their way there, journeys which would never have met with the approval of earlier generations of progressive Jews.

The following year, on the 30th anniversary of the founding of the state of Israel, a group of leaders from Reform synagogues went there, led by Jeffrey Rose, Chairman of the RSGB. They visited Tel Hashomer's new Spinal Rehabilitation Unit (a project of the RSGB), the Leo Baeck School in Haifa and a Reform synagogue in Jerusalem. The Haifa School, thanks to Rabbi Gryn's fund-raising efforts, was the recipient of four beautiful stained glass windows designed and produced by the artist Roman Halter, and installed in its synagogue. The four windows bear the themes *Torah* (learning), *Avodah* (work and prayer), *Gemilut Chassadim* (deeds of compassion), and Tradition, with the school's symbol – The Tree of Life – worked into them all. An RSGB Leadership Group took the heavy windows to Israel as hand-luggage! West London was at last playing its part in the life of Israel, a far cry from the early days of its anti-Zionist stance. It has continued to this day to keep in touch with Reform and other projects in that country, with visits there from its own rabbinical staff and reciprocal arrangements with Israeli religious leaders.

The West London Synagogue by now had a finger in many pies, in this country as well as abroad. When the National Jewish Youth Orchestra was inaugurated in 1979, its first conductor was Sidney Fixman, West London's own choirmaster. Its first three-day course, held at Hillel House, was attended by Rabbi Gryn. There was also a project at this time for a Reform Jewish Day School, which it was hoped would open the following year. To those who feared such a school would 'place a child in a ghetto', Rabbi Dov Marmur, of Alyth Gardens, suggested 'on the contrary there is evidence that a child coming from a warm and homogeneous background may feel less isolated in the non-Jewish world.'[2] The synagogue was also active in raising money for non-Jewish causes through its Charitable Fund: the Vietnamese Boat People, Stoke Mandeville Hospital's Spinal Injuries Unit and the Franklyn D. Roosevelt School for Physically Handicapped Children all benefitted from the generosity of members.

The RSGB was by now one of Anglo-Jewry's leading religious organisations. Like so many Reform groups it had started life in Upper Berkeley Street, but had by the 1980s outgrown its space there, and decided it must find its own premises. It had a number of paid staff and was housing the Reform *Beth Din*. It needed secretarial space, education department facilities and rabbinical offices. Before its eventual move to Manor House in Finchley it found offices in Swiss Cottage. The fact that they were over a uni-sex sauna parlour was a constant source of amusement to all concerned. It was rumoured that committee meetings held at the offices were frequently interrupted by some very strange noises coming from below! It was not the only West London 'squatter' to have expanded beyond the original estimates of its needs. The Leo Baeck College was by now a recognised leader in the field of religious education, growing fast in the community, and offering a wide programme of seminars, lectures and study programmes with all the extra facilities needed to maintain them. Classrooms, a library, tutorial facilities, and staff rooms were crowding themselves out.

The College announced at the beginning of 1981 that it had found premises in Finchley which it proposed, with the help of generous donors, to purchase as the site for the College (to train rabbis and youth leaders), for a Progressive Day School and for housing for the elderly. The site was big enough, after considerable building work, to house the RSGB as well as the College (as it does to this day). The seven acre site of Manor House in East End Road was formerly a convent and a school. Built in 1723 it was a Grade II listed building, for which the College put in an offer of £750,000. It had been told about the site by the New North London Synagogue, the second Masorti synagogue in London, who could not itself use the building. The RSGB was nearly thwarted in its attempt to buy the building by Sir Isaac Wolfson, acting on behalf of the United Synagogue, who was unwilling to let the site go to the Progressive movement. But a higher bid did finally secure the building, though it was a generous member of the Alyth Gardens congregation who was actually responsible for underwriting the cost. The RSGB joined him as a partner and, as the Council of the Association was told, the site 'offered a unique opportunity to create a Centre for Judaism which could not be found anywhere outside the United States.'[3] The lease was signed at the end of the year, and this meant that the long awaited Progressive Day School could open in the autumn of 1981 with little restructuring. The other occupants of the premises might have to wait a little longer for rebuilding and renovation. But at least the project was moving forward and with Rabbi Dr. Albert Friedlander as Director of Studies, the College was already expanding its activities and acquiring a reputation for academic excellence. Berkeley Street agreed to make further contributions to its funds. An ambitious programme of redecoration of the synagogue was already being undertaken, so it is hardly surprising that the Treasurers were becoming anxious for the College to move out.

This was not the only drain on West London's resources. Even if the Reform movement moved out (it was to take space for its offices at Manor House when the building was ready), the buildings on the Seymour Place/Upper Berkeley Street corner needed considerable refurbishment. The houses in Upper Berkeley Street between the synagogue and the corner with Seymour Place were in much need of repair. But the Council was advised that the synagogue should not remain residential landlords any longer. So the Estate Agents, Messrs. Chestertons, were instructed to dispose of the five properties on long-term leases.

✡

Towards the end of 1980 the West London Synagogue had the honour of hosting the BBC's Sunday Night religious programme, *Songs of Praise*. The Synagogue's own choir, under its choirmaster, Sidney Fixman, took part, with the organist, Christopher Bowers-Broadbent, and they were joined by the choir of John Keble Church. The broadcasters turned up with 'an enormous army' of technicians, presenters and producers, five large vans, bank upon bank of arc-lights and the most magnificent and expensive camera equipment ever seen. The synagogue provided head-coverings for non-Jewish participants that would not slide off the head in full view of the cameras, and tried to place its least musical voices in the side seats. Felix Mitchell described how the congregation, in spite of being given song-sheets marked 'Jewish Choir only', and 'Christian voices only', 'sang everything together in a way which none of us had ever heard at Upper Berkeley Street before.'[4] The programme was a great success and much enjoyed by Jewish and non-Jewish viewers across the country.

✡

At the Annual General Meeting of 1982, fears were expressed, not for the first time, about the state of the Synagogue's finances. West London, to its shame, had not paid its annual levy to the Board of Deputies; the move of the Leo Baeck College to Manor House meant that that rental payment had now ceased, and the disposal of the properties in Upper Berkeley Street was delayed. This concern about the Synagogue's income necessitated a rise of 30% in subscriptions, and even then it would be running at a deficit. Nevertheless all the congregation's needs had to be met, with new demands on its purse, such as increased security arrangements, rabbinical cover for Rabbi Jackie Tabick, now on maternity leave, and the departure of Rabbi Danny Smith, who had been with the congregation since 1978, to take up a post at Wimbledon Reform Synagogue. Fortunately a member of the congregation put in an offer to buy a part of the properties owned by the synagogue which would alleviate the pressure to some extent. For the rest an offer was received at a lower figure than had been hoped but, anxious to get matters moving, the Council decided to accept it. Not long afterwards, a higher offer was made. The Council was divided as to whether, as a synagogue, it should take the moral high ground and accept the earlier one, or go for the higher one to obtain the best price possible. As it turned out the difficult decision did not have to be made. The Charity Commissioners, overseeing the negotiations, insisted on the later one being accepted.

In October 1982 The Charitable Fund, its coffers at least partly filled by the income from the Annual Bazaar, hosted a reception at The Manor House. Here the West London Synagogue had its first opportunity to visit the new Centre for Judaism. The beautiful Georgian house had been transformed, redecorated throughout and was already buzzing with activity. Teenagers were attending the *Sha'are Limmud* (Gates of Learning), classes in Hebrew and Bible study were available for older students, the Akiva School classrooms were bright and inviting. The College itself was installed in imposing high-ceilinged rooms with an excellent library, as well a canteen and kitchen. The second floor held the RSGB offices; the extensive grounds, when finance was available, were earmarked for student accommodation, and a Youth Centre. All those attending the Manor House that Sunday morning were impressed with what they found, a far cry from the cramped rooms formerly occupied at Berkeley Street. These rooms, now vacant, could be put to good use and the Council set up the Policy Review Committee to decide how best to deal with the situation. It did find, however – and noted in its Minutes - that it was setting up Committees to oversee other Committees!

There was, in fact, some dissatisfaction in the congregation about the way the lay leadership was running the synagogue. The Council met every two months, but the Executive, responsible for the day to day administration, was unwieldy and inefficient. It was suggested that it should in future be composed of not more than five members, should meet every week, and be composed of the chairman of the Council, one of the treasurers, and three other members of the Council, with the Senior Minister as an ex officio member. This would necessitate constitutional amendment, and in any case it was not certain that enough members could be found who would be prepared to give so much time and energy, even though it was acknowledged that many of the day to day problems that arose did need constant attention. The Council decided to try out these arrangements for a while to see if they worked.

The cooperation of the Reform movement with the Liberals was working well as far as the College was concerned. Students were coming in from both branches of the Progressive Movement, to study as rabbis as well as to participate in the general curriculum. It seemed, therefore, to some of the leaders on both sides that a further measure of association between the two was now possible. It seemed wasteful to duplicate ministers, teachers, even congregations when they had so much in common. On 27th January, 1984 the *Jewish Chronicle* reported that talks were taking place between the Liberal and the Reform movements with a view to a possible merger. 'There are those on both sides,' it said, 'who fear the influence of the other movement on their own entrenched view of Judaism.'[5] Rabbi Hugo Gryn for Reform and Rabbi David Goldberg for the Liberals were in favour. Rabbi Michael Leigh (at Edgware Reform Synagogue) was against. Some envisaged a 'gradual fusion' over three to five years. Most of the leaders of both groups felt they were wasting resources, and that many outside the Progressive movement knew of no difference between the two. The Chairman of the RSGB was Jerome Karet and that of the ULPS Clive Winston. Both sides agreed to go away and discuss the matter of a merger separately and then to present their findings. In early 1985 they presented compromise proposals, which found that 'the creation of a single synagogal organisation, embracing both groupings, is not practicable in the current situation.' And there it was left for the time being – though that was by no means the end of the story. A letter to the *Synagogue Review* from Sir Bernard Drage , an old and valued member of West London, expressed his enthusiasm for the merger. He felt that the two organisations 'would be a much greater force educationally, and their finances and administration could be sounder and more efficient.'[6] He suspected that more lay behind the reluctance to merge – 'a desire to protect vested interests'. He did not explain exactly what these 'vested interests' were, but thirty years after he wrote the letter, the two branches of Progressive Judaism are still going their separate ways.

The West London Synagogue, meanwhile, was again mourning one of its most beloved leaders. Rabbi Werner van der Zyl died in Majorca at the age of 82. He had served two major Reform synagogues in this country, Alyth Gardens and West London. In both he was much loved, 'his popularity matched by the breadth of his scholarship and his eloquence as a preacher. He epitomised the God-fearing decent man whose faith triumphed over the tragedies he witnessed.'[7] When Rabbi van der Zyl retired, an annual van der Zyl Lecture was established in his memory at the Leo Baeck College. Raymond Goldman, Executive Director of the RSGB, who had known him since the time of his own Bar Mitzvah, described him later as 'truly a religious leader; a man of vision; who saw where the future lay, what its needs would be and what must be done to provide it with a stable base for its development.'[8]

✡

At its Annual General Meeting of 1985, the West London Synagogue took a step, perhaps envisaged by the more forward-looking members of the community, but one which would have horrified its Founders and many of those leaders who followed them. The congregation elected a woman warden. Denise Williams took on the onerous job, for the wardenship of such a large and active community, is no sinecure. She needed to have a good knowledge of

Hebrew and of the Berkeley Street Forms of Prayer; she would be committed to attend services twice weekly as well as on the Festivals; and the responsibility of coordinating the administration of the religious side of the synagogue was that of the three wardens, who met there frequently. Perhaps the least of her problems was what to wear! There was no precedent at Berkeley Street for the dress of a woman sitting in the wardens' box, though Westminster Synagogue had had women wardens for some time. The men at Berkeley Street still wore top hats and morning suits, in very sober colours.

At that same A.G.M. the congregation agreed to set up a Committee to consider carrying out a wide-ranging review of the synagogue's present and future activities. It was known as the Bernstein Committee after its Chairman, Ronald Bernstein, Q.C., who had been a member of the Council for some years. The Editor of the *Synagogue Review* had published over the previous few months a series of articles from members expressing their views on what they would like to see in the Synagogue in the future. The Bernstein Committee read them carefully and published its Terms of Reference in the *Review*. These included examining the needs of the members and prospective members, the relationship between the members and the lay management and also that between Berkeley Street and other synagogues, Progressive and Orthodox. They were also to take a look at the Board of Deputies, Israel and the non-Jewish community as regards West London. Then they would consider what changes might be necessary and make recommendations to the Council.

It was a formidable task, excluding matters of finance. In expressing what he and his Committee were setting out to do, Ronald Bernstein reminded the congregation that in 1977 just such a Committee had been charged with a similar task, not very successfully, as its recommendations did not on the whole find favour with the Council. The membership of West London was not increasing and he was determined to find out why. He asked all members to consider the situation and to communicate with him or his fellow Committee members if they wished to make their voices heard.

The following year, the President of the Synagogue, Clifford Barclay, set up a meeting, attended by more than a hundred members, to discuss three of the important subjects before Mr. Bernstein's Committee: Community and Communal Expenditure with special reference to the commitments of the Synagogue to the RSGB, Leo Baeck College and the Board of Deputies; an Endowment Appeal to provide a fund to meet the shortfall in subscriptions; and a comprehensive Community Centre, its establishment and costs. Divided into three groups, those attending the meeting were enthusiastic in their support for the three organisations, for funding those amenities which they believed were precious in the eyes of the congregation and for the establishment of an Endowment Fund to finance the projects. However, not all members were fully in favour of the increased activities at Berkeley Street. One wrote to the *Review* suggesting that the congregation was doing too much, trying to be all things to all men and should go 'minimalist' rather than 'maximalist'. The resulting replies were divided in their answers, but all felt that even bothering to write a letter indicated a degree of interest!

The Leo Baeck College in particular had found itself in dire straits financially, to the point where its very future seemed in doubt. As Rabbi David Hulbert – a former student at the College who went on to head the *Bet Tikva* community at Barking - put it, 'Jews College had plenty of money but no students, while we had more students than ever before, but were facing bankruptcy!'.[9] But the students at the College were more than prepared to help out. They organised a fund-raising Dinner, printed their own New Year cards and calendars, and arranged a 125-mile sponsored walk. They ran quizzes, promoted concerts and ran a mail-order marketing scheme, much encouraged by the new Principal of the College, Rabbi Jonathan Magonet.

The Bernstein Report was welcomed by Clifford Barclay at the 1987 Annual General Meeting, even though it was not yet ready to be sent out to members. However, the President was able to forecast that it would be controversial and stressed the concern of all those involved at the lack of active participation in the Synagogue's affairs by so many members. He estimated that only a quarter of the 3,600 membership did concern themselves actively in what was going on at Berkeley Street, even though it was clear that the Synagogue itself and particularly its services, were very popular. He attributed this in large part to the Rabbis, especially Rabbi Gryn, who did nonetheless need the support of his congregation. He urged the younger members and their families to take a leadership role in the affairs of the community. 'It was', he said, 'too easy to sit back and criticise.' He also regretted the attitudes often encountered by Progressive Jewry from Orthodox leaders. He was not asking for unity, he said, but for greater respect and harmony amongst Anglo-Jewry in general.

The same year West London welcomed a new minister to its ranks, Rabbi Bob Shafritz. He was brought up in America with little Jewish education, but after university went to Iran with the Peace Corps, and then to Strasbourg finally deciding to make his home in England. It was then that he turned to Judaism and enrolled at the Leo Baeck College, where after five years he was awarded *semicha*. He accepted the post of Assistant Rabbi at West London, where he began teaching at the Religious School. Bob Shafritz was much loved at West London, where he spent six years before leaving to become Rabbi of the Wimbledon Reform Synagogue. Jill Leuw spoke of him as 'a true pastoral Rabbi, a sensitive and compassionate man who is there when you need him.'[10] Sadly he died young in 1996 and Berkeley Street marked its appreciation by naming its newly refurbished Library in his memory.

During more than a century of congregational life at Berkeley Street, many rabbis were part of the team who conducted the religious affairs of the large and varied group of Jews. The charismatic memorable ministers, usually in the position of Senior Rabbis, are known to all their flock as well as to many Jews and non-Jews in the outside world. But the Assistant Rabbis, without whom the Synagogue could not have flourished, have not always had 'full coverage'. A list of all the Rabbis who have served at West London over the years would surprise most people. Some came to help out, staying for only for a short time, but others stayed longer and deserve a mention. During the last fifty years, Rabbis Marim Charry, Thomas Salamon, William Wolfe, Dan Cohn-Sherbok, Colin Eimer, Allen Podet, Levi Weiman-Kelman, Larry Tabick, Michael Farbman, Roderick Young, Josh Levy, Malcolm Cohen, Debbie Young-Somers and several others served their apprenticeship here, and even more assisted temporarily. A further number are fortunately still 'on duty' and to all these religious leaders the congregation should pay its respect and thanks.

One reason, perhaps the most important, why the West London Synagogue needed to employ so many rabbinic leaders, was the size of the membership. As had been pointed out countless times since its inception in 1840, a large membership did not mean full participation by those members. All synagogues bemoan the fact that not enough of the congregation pay an active part in the affairs of its community. They do not attend Sabbath services, they do not offer themselves for office, they want only the practical goals of confirmation, marriage and burial. Such had been the complaints of generations of leaders, lay and religious. Nevertheless by the 1990s the West London Synagogue was flourishing as never before. Berkeley Street catered for every age and every interest. Young people could participate in the religious side of synagogue activities, taking part in services, helping to decorate the *Succah* and learning about their religion before and after Bar or Bat Mitzvah. The social possibilities were endless: visits to Israel, group activities for all ages, including an Israel Group, clubs and societies for sport, cultural interests and friendship groups. For the older ones there were lectures and discussions on almost any subject, as well opportunities to meet other people of a similar age; there was even a Job Club to assist those seeking employment. Women's groups, mothers- and babies clubs, a Russian Jewry group, the Waley Club for the visually impaired and the Jewish Deaf Circle, a Parents Association, acting, music, dancing and groups for the elderly. The only problems were how to fit in such a wealth of activities into a building designed only as a House of Prayer. Plans were already being considered for further expansion to Berkeley Street to accommodate them all.

The West London Synagogue was listed by English Heritage in 1989 as a Grade II building for its special architectural and historic interest. Listed buildings, desirable though the listing may be for its cultural interest, have to conform to certain criteria and are usually unable to make any structural alterations without permission. The listing details give a clear description of the building: *West London Synagogue II Gi Synagogue. 1869-70, by Davis and Emanuel. Brick with Portland stone facade; slate roof. Byzantine/Romanesque style. 3-storey facade dominated by pedimented semi-circular arch supported on coupled columns, with richly-carved capitals and set in front of a recessed entrance bay with graduated semi-circular arched windows over 3 doorways framed by semi-circular arched arcade with similar columns; attic storey arcade of 8 round-arched windows with foliate capitals to square piers; similar one-light windows to projecting outer bays; continuous bracketed cornice to parapet surmounted by acroteriae. Interior: panelled entrance hall with beamed coffered ceiling and double-flight staircase with bronze candelabra to newels and rich Byzantine/Romanesque carving to balusters. Very fine synagogue interior: centralised plan with central dome carried on semi-circular arches and quatrefoil-section scagliola piers with foliate Byzantine/Romanesque capitals to decorative balcony fronts and to upper stage crowned by cluster of colonettes with similar capitals; similar grouped colonettes to corbels of barrel-vaulted aisles; apsidal 'sanctuary' separated from main body of synagogue by semi-circular arch over fine domed ark and flanking screens enriched by coloured marble and mosaic, 'Moorish' style screens set in semi-circular arched architraves and richly-carved Byzantine- Romanesque style capitals to arcade piers and colonettes supporting dome; balustraded enclosure oland pulpit in similar style and materials. Fine stained glass to semi-circular arched windows and square-headed 3-light aisle windows with foliate piers. The most important Reform synagogue in Victorian London and, together with Davis and Emanuel's East London Synagogue, ranks as one of the finest Victorian synagogues in London.[11]*

✡

In 1990 West London celebrated the 150th anniversary of its foundation. It was a year of almost constant celebration – parties, lectures, concerts and of course religious services. Talking to the *Jewish Chronicle* Rabbi Gryn said, 'For me the most exciting thing is that 150 years after its foundation, the community is so flexible and youthful in its outlook, although it has kept faith with the intention of its founders. We still have Mocattas and Henriques in our congregation.'[12] The celebrations included a performance of *Gate of Zion,* a play written by Jack Rosenthal (the distinguished playright, husband of Maureen Lipman) and produced and directed by Naomi Gryn. The chairman of the Anniversary Committee was Alan Howard. According to Naomi most of the first meeting about the play was mainly taken up with a discussion of a handsome gift of smoked salmon, whether to offer it free to the audience or to charge for it. The budget was very small, one salami only for the single rehearsal, and there was only one performance. Pamela Howard was the Art Director, Rick Burton did the lighting and the theatrical costumiers Angels (members of the congregation) provided the costumes; as the cast had no time to learn their lines, there was just the one costumed reading. It happened to be a night of heavy snowfall but a good audience loyally turned up and greatly enjoyed the show.

At this time the synagogue's leaders were very much aware of the state of the building; the roof required repairing, new facilities for offices and congregational activities were much needed, and it seemed an appropriate moment to start an ambitious appeal for funds to put these ideas into practice. David Goldstone was appointed head of the Synagogue Development Control Group. It was charged with overseeing the redevelopment of the Goldsmid Hall and the concourse to accommodate the Rabbinate and Administrative Offices and to provide a Youth Centre and a Room of Prayer. Outline planning permission was obtained and the congregation, at a Special General Meeting, gave the go ahead for the plans to proceed.

Another anniversary followed soon after. The Reform Synagogues of Great Britain celebrated its Jubilee in 1992. After its early beginnings during the war years, with only five members, it had grown to a massive organisation, with thirty member synagogues, a fine new building, its own theological College and *Beth Din*. It held an important place not only in Anglo-Jewry but in Jewish circles across the world. A service was held at the West London Synagogue on 29th March 1992, at which many of its Rabbis took part. Rabbi Gryn, as its President, gave the address and Raymond Goldman, Executive Director, read from the Scroll. A young member of Radlett and Bushey Synagogue blew the Shofar and the Rabbinical Blessing at the end was said by Rabbi Cassell, West London's former Rabbi, who having served as minister to Bulawayo's first Progressive Synagogue, had returned to London and still cherished his attachment to Berkeley Street, though a staunch member of Westminster.

In 1993 the Synagogue launched its *L'Dor V'Dor* ('From Generation to Generation') Appeal, whose purpose was to provide further accommodation for all the varied activities which went on at Berkeley Street. It aimed to reach £4,000,000, an enormous sum for such an enterprise. On 11th July, the official opening ceremony of the work took place, when Rabbi Gryn, assisted by Chairman David Leuw, took a screwdriver and lifted the door of the Youth Centre off its hinges, said a blessing on the new enterprise and asked God's blessing on the Synagogue. In his New Year message that year, Rabbi Gryn expected 'noise and dust and dislocation. Familiar routes will be upset', he said, 'and there is a risk that it will all get on our nerves and indeed that we may get on each other's nerves as well.'[13]

The progress of the development at West London was divided into two phases. Phase One included the construction of a new internal concourse, repairs to the roof and the refurbishment of the new rooms downstairs and three floors of offices above. Phase Two dealt with the new building work above the Goldsmid Hall, and members were invited to attend a Development Briefing Meeting to put forward ideas for the new construction and for ways to pay for it. The co-ordinator of the project was Michael Cutter who had played a big part in the administration of West London, and knew as much as anyone about it. The architect was Brian Day of Trench, Farrow and Partners. He was not Jewish but had a great admiration for the Jewish community, and considerable knowledge about how it was run. He worked happily with Michael Cutter and together they made an excellent team. The marketing committee, under the chairmanship of Eva Mitchell, went to work publicising the scheme and produced a video, shown at a fund-raising dinner at the Banqueting Hall in Whitehall. It was decided that the appeal for 'The Vision' should be targeted at the entire community and the congregation was kept informed of the progress of the work as building went ahead, with the plans on permanent exhibition.

The money came in quickly, although those in charge of the project worried about the final outcome, and whether or not the total amount could be met. Work was held up for a time when the first builders to be granted the contract went into liquidation after a few months' work. However another firm was found and the building work restarted. The basement area had to be dug out to reinforce the new structure, but by February 1994 all was going well. A new feature on the ground floor, the Brides' Room, and the area above it, were being refurbished; work was nearly completed on the lift and the Samson Family Concourse was almost finished. The latter was the beautifully designed hall and meeting room that led from the reception area, out to the Goldsmid Hall, just outside the synagogue itself. The Concourse, dedicated by the Samson Family to Heinz Samson's parents and sister, who died in Auschwitz, bears a plaque in the floor, which reads 'May Their Memory Be A Blessing'.

Heinz Samson and his family were generous donors to the synagogue. Heinz said that if nine other sponsors could be found, each to give £100,000, he would bring the amount donated up to one million. He called his fellow donors the 'Minyan Men' and the money was soon collected. Heinz Samson insisted on using his own architects and builders. Later he generously sponsored the refurbishment of the Room of Prayer and the Children's Library, as well as a complete refurbishment of the organ. A Weekend of Rededication was set aside in November, as the building work neared its end. When Geoff Samson was Chairman of the synagogue, a Senate of Elders was set up to invite past Chairmen and Presidents to act in an advisory role (it was later extended to include other senior leaders) so that their knowledge and experience would not be lost to the congregation.

It had been hoped that much of the funding for the redevelopment would come from a large bequest to the synagogue from the estate of Ernest Ascher who lived much of his life in Switzerland. Mr. Ascher died in 1990 but the money would not become available to the congregation until the death of his wife Kate. She did not die until 2003. In 1994 two members of the congregation went to Zurich to try to sort out the problem. Apparently Mr. Ascher's will was incorrectly worded in some minor way and the careful Swiss bankers would not release the funds. It was not until Mrs. Ascher's death that the synagogue was able to benefit. A plaque on the wall of the new offices at Seymour Place is dedicated to Kate and Ernest Ascher, dated Chanucah 5765/ December 2004.

The synagogue leaders were also concerned about plans for the now disused cemetery at Balls Pond Road. They had applied for planning permission to sell at least a part of the ground for redevelopment as a commercial site. Objections were raised by the orthodox community and a question was asked in Parliament. Apart from the ethical constraints of moving the graves (which would be reinterred at Edgwarebury Lane) the proposed Channel Tunnel link was due to run underneath the cemetery, although the construction company handling the link assured the Council that it would run deeper than the graves already in place. It was decided to postpone a decision on the fate of the cemetery for the time being.

A member of Berkeley Street, Alan Bradley, was appointed Lord Mayor of London in 1995 and Rabbi Gryn was made his Chaplain. On 11th July that same year Hugo was the subject of *Desert Island Discs*. He was 'called up' to that great British institution and chose several Jewish songs, some in Yiddish, and revealed something of the tragedy of the Holocaust, in which he had been personally involved. His 'luxury' on the programme was 'a space to park my car'. Sue Lawley replied, 'On a desert island we can give you space to park your car.' The year before Hugo had returned with his daughter Naomi to his home town to film *Chasing Shadows,* the book in which he had recounted the story of his early life. It was broadcast on Channel 4 in 1991. Momentously, the book concluded 'Time is short and the task is urgent'. By the time of the *Desert Island Discs* broadcast he must have already been suffering with the cancer which was to take his life less than two years later.

Hugo Gryn died on 18th August 1996. He was one of those charismatic rabbis almost as well known in the non-Jewish world as in the Jewish community. Never afraid to face controversy or to take up a cause, he put West London on the map. In the article about him written for the *Dictionary of National Biography,* Rabbi Albert Friedlander, an old and valued friend of Hugo and also a concentration camp survivor, said, 'His common sense and practical experience were informed by a rabbinical tradition of knowledge of the text, and an instinctive understanding of human problems ... he was an eloquent spokesman for the religious vision of the twentieth century.' Hugo was active in interfaith work and was to the forefront of the formation of the Interfaith Network, with his friend Brian Pearce. In the collection of some of his broadcasts, edited by his daughter Naomi, he said, 'It seems to me that dialogue is the way towards the commandment (to love thy neighbour as thyself). It may not be everyone's bowl of rice or cup of tea, but how good and pleasant that it did come into being (the Network)'[14] He shared the Chairmanship with Canon Jim Thompson. In 1986 he was the narrator at a performance in Canterbury Cathedral of *Holocaust Requiem – Kaddish for Terezin,* with music composed by Ronald Senator and words by Rabbi Dr.Albert Friedlander. When asked if he could forgive the perpetrators of the Holocaust, Hugo replied that it was not our job to forgive, that was God's job, but we will not forget.

Hugo was mourned by his family, his friends, his congregants and many thousands of Jews and non-Jews across the world. In the edition of the *Synagogue Review* following his death, Rabbi Tabick wrote, 'Hugo taught us that there are no innocent bystanders, we all as individuals bear some responsibility for the state of the world around us, so let each of us do our little bit in the establishment of the greater whole, and so honour the memory of the man we all loved and admired so much.'[15]

The *Jewish Chronicle* obituary said, 'He brought many qualities to his calling: energy, resourcefulness, learning, eloquence, sympathy, patience, insight, but outstanding amongst them was one which can be expressed only in Hebrew – *chasidut* - a lovingkindness and sense of concern which he combined with an understanding of human frailty.'[16] The eulogy in *The Independent* called him the most beloved Rabbi in Great Britain. But it was his effect on his own congregants that was most marked. His extraordinary memory enabled him to recall names and occasions which warmed their hearts. One said, 'He had an ability to make people feel he had all the time in the world, when one was actually with him for only two minutes.'[17]

Always one to welcome controversy, Hugo was followed by it to his grave. For at the Hoop Lane funeral no leader of the orthodox United Synagogue, rabbi or layman, was present. Neither the Chief Rabbi, Sir Jonathan Sacks, nor the previous incumbent, Lord Jakobovits, put in an appearance, though both later called on Jackie Gryn with their wives. The *Jewish Chronicle* made a point of reporting the facts and commenting on them. Chaim Bermant, its distinguished columnist, a member of the United Synagogue, wrote a scathing account, recalling that he had often mentioned in the paper his concern for the progress of that organisation and how best to save it from itself. Now he wondered if it was worth saving. Letters were printed from Rabbi John Rayner, of the Liberal Synagogue, Rabbi Albert Friedlander, Minister of Westminster Synagogue, Sir Sigmund Sternberg, a prominent member of the London Jewish Community, and several others, all asserting their dismay at the attitude of the Chief Rabbi and his followers. The controversy was never to die down, and on many occasions when Lord Sacks was mentioned in connection with the leadership of the Anglo-Jewish community, the story was retold. It sadly coloured much of the fine work he did during his tenure of the Chief Rabbinate.

A Memorial Service for Hugo took place on 8th December 1996. So many people wished to attend that the synagogue couldn't accommodate them all, so it was also relayed to the Liberal Jewish Synagogue. A special Memorial Booklet was printed for the Service 'The Memory of Rabbi Hugo Gryn' and his family established the Hugo Gryn Memorial Trust in his memory. Its objects were to advance education in Jewish history, culture and heritage; to promote the understanding of the Jewish faith in its various forms; and to promote religious and racial tolerance between peoples of all religions, cultures and creeds. Ruth Silver was appointed its director.

Now the West London Synagogue was faced with one of the most difficult decisions it had ever encountered. To appoint a new leader of any organisation is always problematic, but Hugo Gryn, who had died in office, was a remarkably difficult man to replace. His presence was engrained in the whole of Anglo-Jewry and few were prepared to say that no leader is indispensable. Nevertheless the lay leaders of the congregation certainly had a problem to find the right candidate to fill Hugo's shoes.

CHAPTER XV

Into the Future

A Rabbinical Appointments Committee had been appointed in 1995 to consider the future leadership of the synagogue. Addressing it, only a week or two before he died, Hugo had said that 'the congregation needed to have intellectuality, balanced learning, the finest teachers, a centre for learning and complete unanimity of purpose'[1] – a very hard task for any Jewish organisation. Soon after Hugo's death the Committee told the Executive that it believed its remit was to find an immediate successor to Rabbi Gryn but to hold back on any action, allowing time for a review of the current position, bearing in mind the decisions of present rabbinical incumbents.

Meanwhile the synagogue itself, much in need of refurbishment and repair, underwent a systematic programme of work. The Editor of the *Synagogue Review* published an article by Rabbi Tabick describing her feelings of standing in the centre of the Sanctuary, void of pews, while the scaffolding was in place to reach the upper domes and ceilings. The Synagogue had been fortunate to get a grant from the Heritage Fund, which together with other legacies and donations enabled the Council to have new carpeting, colour schemes and some design features. When the old carpet was taken up, a large area of the original marble floor was exposed, which was left as it had originally been, an added feature to the old Victorian structure, now a Grade II listed building. The building work finished on schedule and by the middle of March the congregation was invited to the re-dedication service in the beautifully redecorated sanctuary. The *Torah* scrolls were ceremoniously taken in and replaced in the Ark, and the worshippers heard a special community prayer from Rabbi Tabick. She also gave the sermon reminding her listeners that Rabbi Gryn had called the synagogue 'the powerhouse of the community'. She went on 'Its arches lift our spirits. Its windows, now cleaned and showing such details, allow the wonder of coloured light to fall on the marble. The decorations order our thoughts and the atmosphere is evocative of prayer and spirituality.'[2] His Honour, Judge King-Hamilton, Honorary Life-President of the Congregation and by now 92 years old, read the *Haftarah*.

It was not until the beginning of 1998 that the Rabbinical Appointments Committee finally made up its mind. No candidates from Britain had applied and it was necessary to look abroad for the right person. The choice unanimously fell on Rabbi Mark Winer, the President of the National Council of Synagogues in America, a man experienced in guiding synagogues in his home country and well versed in inter-faith matters. This 'oversized

American' (as he called himself) came to London with his wife Suellen, with the unenviable task of succeeding one of the most loved and most charismatic religious leaders the Jewish community had ever known. His previous synagogue had been in the suburbs with 21 acres of land and all the parking space his congregation needed! A metropolitan synagogue, the largest in Britain, was very different.

Rabbi Winer joined the West London Synagogue under difficult circumstances. No man would find it easy to lead such an organisation, composed of nearly three thousand members of differing opinions and complicated allegiances to religion, family and friendships, most of them articulate and well educated, with individual ideas which they were unafraid to promote. He had visited the West London Synagogue before, first on his honeymoon and later with his children and his wife Suellen. At the Annual General Meeting in 1998, at which Rabbi Winer was confirmed in office, the President, David Leuw, explained the choice of the Selection Committee and put it to the assembled membership. There was an overwhelming vote in favour of Rabbi Winer, with two against and four abstentions, but everyone concerned was determined to smooth his passage and welcome him in.

Rabbi Winer was inducted into office in June, when 900 people crammed into the synagogue. Rabbi Tabick led the service, her last duty before taking a sabbatical, and among the guests – a symbol of Rabbi Winer's inter-faith work - were Sheikh Zaki Badawi who read from the Koran and the Minister of the St. Marylebone Church who read from Paul's Letter to the Corinthians. Rabbi Tony Bayfield, leader of the RSGB, gave the address, reminding the congregation that West London had had only five Senior Ministers in the 158 years of its existence. In his reply Rabbi Winer said that he wanted to launch new programmes, to attract single young Jews and to make adult study a feature of the synagogue's existence. Rabbi Albert Friedlander gave the priestly blessing.

There were still some loose ends to be tied up. It was necessary to find a suitable home for the new rabbi (how to pay for it was even more of a problem as the synagogue was unhappy about taking on a debt). One of Rabbi Winer's particular strengths was his fund-raising abilities, and he was surprised that in Britain it was unusual for a synagogue to raise funds for its own benefit. He was determined that Berkeley Street should stand out as the flagship synagogue in the Reform movement. He was used to an international stage having formed good relationships with the Vatican, with the Muslim leadership and with Jewish communities at home and abroad. On one occasion when Ramadan fell on the Day of Atonement he arranged for members of the congregation to break their fast with some of their Muslim neighbours.

Rabbi Jackie Tabick decided to resign from her ministry at West London at the end of her sabbatical year. She had been a much appreciated member of West London's rabbinical staff, particularly in her pastoral work with the children and the synagogue wished her well for the future. She later served as Chair of the Assembly of Rabbis, of the Council of Reform and Liberal Rabbis and as Vice President of the Movement for Reform Judaism. She joined North West Surrey Synagogue and was later appointed Convenor of the Reform *Beth Din*.

True to his word, Rabbi Winer set in motion an expanded programme at West London. The congregation's student members were visited at university, a youth weekend took place in the Hague, and there were educational trips to Israel and to Budapest. But the Rabbi needed help and a search started for an Assistant Minister. The Rabbinical Appointments Committee reconvened, looking for a Rabbi who specialised in education and pastoral work. They found three suitable candidates who had trained at the Leo Baeck College, their choice settling on Rabbi Helen Freeman, a child of the Reform Movement. Her first career was as a speech therapist, but she was ordained at Leo Baeck in 1990, and after a spell at the Liberal Jewish Synagogue came to Berkeley Street. One of her requests, when offered the post, was that she might continue with her work helping Jewish women prisoners in British jails.

For some time the Synagogue had been working on plans for redeveloping the buildings it owned in Seymour Place. It wanted to include a 'stand alone' residential scheme in the Leo Baeck wing for college students, but this proved so expensive to construct that it was tempted to consider selling off the wing altogether for whatever value it might fetch. In order to obtain planning permission it was necessary to comply with the Fire Officer's requirements, which had to be completed quickly. But financial considerations were uppermost in any decision that might be agreed on.

Meanwhile a new wave of enthusiasm was evident in the congregation. One of these plans to combine religious work with fund-raising activities was the *Torah* Project. The aim was to have a new *Torah* Scroll written with portions of it underwritten by subscribers. The synagogue was particularly anxious to own a lighter scroll which could be easily carried. The project was expected to bring some £220,000 of pledges in the first year, and was warmly welcomed by members. It was an ambitious project which caught the attention of the congregation. Following a community-wide consultation, the first non-orthodox scribe was appointed to oversee the work. Rabbi Ron Berry was a graduate of the Leo Baeck College, and under the supervision of the master scribe, Dr. Eric Ray, he got to work. Many members took part in the writing of the scroll and in the stitching of the parchment sheets, with their special knots, obeying of course all the rules and regulations relating to the writing of a scroll, as had been followed for thousands of years. An exhibition set up in the Goldsmid Hall used the eye-catching slogan 'What will you do today that will last a hundred years?' The congregation felt very much involved in the idea, for they could contribute sums ranging from £1 to many thousands to pay for one letter or a long extract. The synagogue's collection of scrolls was a unique one for they came from many sources, Sephardi and

Ashkenazi, and from countries around the world (see Appendix II). One, shortly to be included, is a scroll from the collection of *Sifrei Torah* rescued from Czechoslovakia in 1964 by Westminster Synagogue.

A new library for children, the Hugo Gryn Library, together with a media centre, was established in a room upstairs, next to the Children's Synagogue, and in Israel the Reform centre at Beth Shmuel opened a Conference Centre in Hugo's memory. A handsome photographic portrait of Hugo was unveiled, now hanging in the Goldsmid Hall. In his address on that occasion Sir Martin Gilbert, CBE, recalled the age-old traditional Sabbath ritual he had enjoyed with the Gryn family, which Hugo invariably turned into a vibrant celebration.

By the Millennium, Jewish life, certainly in progressive circles, was adapting, as indeed it always had, to modern ideas within a religious affiliation. The synagogue was requested from time to time to allow a non-Jewish wife or husband to be buried beside his or her spouse in a Jewish cemetery. The Council agreed to allow two changes to its former ruling: firstly, to permit a spouse to be buried in a synagogue burial ground (or to have ashes interred) even though he or she was not Jewish. Rabbi Winer explained in an article in the *Synagogue Review* that both he and Hugo Gryn had felt this was an appropriate step to take. A cemetery, he wrote, was not a sacred place, as a synagogue was. A grave, containing a body, was sacred. It was a *mitzvah* to show respect to the dead of the non-Jewish community, but he could not agree to any non-Jewish part of the liturgy, nor to any non-Jewish symbolism on memorials.

Another difficult problem, not yet fully resolved, was the situation regarding same-sex partners. In the Liberal community, civil partnerships, after registration, could be blessed in the synagogue, just as marriage between Jew and non-Jew was permitted. But the Reform movement was more cautious. Some synagogues were happy to confirm such partnerships, others were not. Some Rabbis were happy to bless the couple without any 'marriage' being performed. Recently, however, the question of marriage between partners of the same sex has come to the fore. Although at the time of writing nothing has passed into law, the accepted ruling is that in religious communities the minister is not obliged to carry out such marriages, whereas in a civil union, it would be legal for a marriage to take place. But when such marriages do become law West London is likely to be in the lead in carrying them out within the sanctuary. In the Liberal movement, too, Jewish descent through the father's line is considered acceptable. Not all Reform synagogues have yet gone that far. It is likely that in the future either parent's religion will determine whether or not a child is Jewish.

The familiar question of more formal links with the Liberals again came to the fore, though many felt that if a total merger was to take place some constituent members on both sides might secede altogether. The Council was also anxious for a rapprochement with the orthodox community. In fact an independent orthodox rabbi had participated in a wedding at West London and had presented to the couple an orthodox *Ketuba*. But the majority of members were still cautious after what it saw as a snub at the time of the funeral of Rabbi Gryn.

However, towards the non-Jewish community, West London's hand of friendship was warmly outstretched. The BBC recorded a Holocaust Memorial Service at Upper Berkeley Street and a Seder was held for the first time at the House of Lords with the co-operation of Robert Wright, the Speaker's Chaplain and a Canon of Westminster Abbey. Suellen Winer planned the menu for the meal, with a group who tested out each other's recipes and then worked with the House of Lords caterers. The evening was hosted by Lord Parry Mitchell and led by Rabbi Winer, with Chazan Stephen Cotsen. An interfaith *Haggadah* was compiled for the occasion, designed and written by Tina Elliott, with beautiful illustrations. The meal was preceded by a reception in the State Rooms of the Speaker's House, and among those present were members of West London, bishops, imams, MPs and Lords, as well as clergy from other faiths. It was a remarkable occasion in the life of the synagogue.

The committee charged with the proposals for the future of West London was named the 'Plus Five Group'. One of its first decisions concerning the development of the building as a capital or revenue raising project was to conclude that this was not proving to be a viable proposition. The committee suggested that it should instead be used for the Synagogue's own purposes, and among those to which it might be put were an Early Childhood Centre, an Internet Library, a coffee shop, and improvements to the kitchen and the lounges, and a Judaica Shop. Other suggestions included a children's synagogue, a downstairs cloakroom and refurbishment of the synagogue ceiling. The Heritage Lottery Fund was approached for a grant, but this was refused.

The congregation mourned in 1998 one of its most devoted and much loved ministers, Curtis Cassell. Having left West London in 1957 to lead the newly formed Reform congregation in Bulawayo, he returned to participate in the services, and to give sermons, lectures and discussions. His 'English' sense of humour, love of cricket (and puns, all delivered with a German accent), gave him a unique place in the hierarchy of the Reform movement. He had a wide grasp of Anglo-Jewish history, writing articles for the Jewish Historical Society, as well as two unpublished works: *The West London Synagogue: Burton Street, 1840-49* and *David Woolf Marks, the Father of Anglo-Jewish Reform, 1811-1909*. One of his last appearances at Berkeley Street was at the Bar Mitzvah of his grandson Robert. To some extent he had always remained in the shadow of his Senior Minister, Harold Reinhart, but he had an independent turn of mind and was a man of great integrity, kindliness and generosity of spirit.

The Millennium passed peacefully without any of the anticipated breakdown of civilisation so widely foretold by the press, and the West London Synagogue moved into the twenty-first century. All the usual seasonal events were maintained: Bar and Bat Mitzvahs, weddings and funerals but with slight amendments to suit the requirements of modern life. Many of the parents of the young people entering the Bar Mitzvah classes would have preferred to see their children hold centre stage on such important occasions, but so many were the requests for the ceremonies that some doubling-up was essential to squeeze everybody in. Joint ceremonies were arranged, though every young person taking part read from the scroll, gave a *D'var Torah*, and usually read a part of the Service.

One of the congregation's most cherished organisations fell by the wayside. The Women's Guild, a feature of synagogue life for more than forty years, had grown out of the old West London Synagogue Association, when women were playing such an important role in synagogue life. In an account of the Guild on the occasion of its fortieth birthday, Valerie Bello wrote in the Newsletter, 'The Guild from the outset pioneered the increasing participation at all levels of women within the synagogue and in the wider community.' But by now there existed at Seymour Place so many organisations and events that the Guild's functions were subsumed under other heads, though the ladies continued to play a vital part in synagogue affairs. They were largely responsible for the Seymour Group, which met for lunch regularly with an eminent speaker, the Berkeley Group for older members and their friends and many of the other regular and occasional functions which took place in the building.

In 2004 Rabbi Winer's contract was extended for another three years, by mutual consent. His inter-faith activities were an important feature of his rabbinate and he was an excellent fund-raiser. The synagogue's accounts were under great strain at that time. There seemed to be a considerable shortfall in income, and the Treasurers agreed to analyse the situation. They arranged to increase the overdraft and set up a targeted legacy campaign to persuade members to leave money to the synagogue when they died. Over the past few years, in common with other synagogues, and many charities, West London had been feeling the pinch. But the lay leadership, with the support of the community, rabbis and professional staff, had been able to overcome most of these difficulties. At the time of writing, the congregation has come through these troubles with a much stronger balance sheet, enabling it to look ahead to a more viable financial situation, where it could embark on a programme of greater expansion and consolidation.

A Structure Review Group was put in place to improve the efficiency of the whole synagogue, leading to a full discussion by members. The outcome was the division of the organisation into four 'houses': Community, Worship, Education and Finance & Administration. The aim was to make better use of salaried staff and volunteers, a more efficient running of the building, with a more transparent structure for the future.

The situation regarding same-sex relationships was discussed by the Council. Gender neutrality had been a feature of all synagogue affairs for many years, but current legislation concerning civil partnerships was something the leaders of the synagogue needed to deal with very quickly.

They were aware that the feelings of the congregation had to be taken into account, but maintained that the equality of all members was vital to the wellbeing of the congregation; same-sex couples were as welcome in the synagogue as any others. By the end of the year a programme for dealing with such situations was in place, the Council in favour of their rabbis performing religious ceremonies for such situations. Same-sex partnerships were to be celebrated with a *Kiddush* or 'sanctification'. Such celebrants were to be congratulated in the newsletters, and were offered educational dialogue with the Rabbis if they wished it. Private blessings could be arranged where appropriate. As so often before, West London took the lead in such a decision. One of the assistant Rabbis, Roderick Young, who had entered into a marriage in Canada with his long-time partner, wrote an article in the *Jewish Chronicle* in which he expressed his wish that such an arrangement had been possible in this country. 'Civil partnership,' he wrote, 'is a significant milestone on our journey out of the wilderness.'[3]

Other changes were happening in regard to the ritual. A second day festival was included for New Year, though not all the congregation attended. This was the first time that a second day for a Festival had had been celebrated by the West London Synagogue since it had come into being, this being one of the original disagreements that the Founding Fathers had with the orthodox establishment. Some Reform synagogues had brought this about many years earlier. Under Rabbi Marmur Alyth Gardens had celebrated a second day on certain Festivals, and there were murmurings in the community that West London was 'turning to the right'. Another such 'turn' was the proposal for the institution of *tashlich* on *Rosh Hashanah,* the old custom of casting sins into the water, when the *shofar* was blown and stones thrown into the river (in this case, the Serpentine). The *Jewish Chronicle* reported these innovations and quoted Rabbi Winer as saying, 'One of the joys of having a large congregation is that it offers many opportunities for people to grow Jewishly.'[4]

As it had always done in the past, West London accepted changes in the outside world, particularly in London. New buildings were going up around the synagogue, Edgware Road had become a centre of the Arab community, the congestion charge came to stay. Orthodox London Rabbis within the congestion charge area went to court to fight the charge, but for Berkeley Street , Rabbi Winer felt, in his most optimistic Texan way, it was 'no big deal'. It did not apply at weekends and it would surely not be beyond the realms of possibility for those visiting the synagogue during weekdays to park outside the zone and walk a few hundred yards.

In 2004 the *Jewish Chronicle* published a 'Community Profile' on West London. It gave a potted history of the synagogue and its rabbis, with an account of its activities. Its congregational profile said, 'The congregation is diverse with members from every background and many countries. Dress is smart and some women cover their heads.'[5] The building was described as 'a piece of Victorian splendour in which rich colours set off the ornate wood, elaborate metalwork and stained glass. The synagogue has as its focus a beautiful and intricate ark The atmosphere is warm with choice of traditional or alternative service.' The report failed to say whether the congregation could choose which they preferred.

The plans for improvements to the synagogue building, long discussed and frequently changing; were now becoming very urgent. The organ needed to be rebuilt, the heating and air-conditioning were inadequate, the seats were worn and the whole interior of the sanctuary needed a fresh look. As far as the organ was concerned, a complete overhaul necessitated sending the pipes to Strasbourg where they could be rebuilt and then returned. One which had been hired for temporary use, was replaced by a secondhand one which could be sold when the original was back in place. One development regarding the music was that the synagogue considered employing a *chazan*, once the organ was back, to work with Sidney Fixman, but this was not accepted. Sidney was the congregation's much respected Director of Music, who was due to retire in a year or two. He was a professional, highly-gifted musician, with a university degree in music, and a specialist in Jewish music, an expert in putting together both participating and non-participating musicians. After his retirement an advertisement in the *Jewish Chronicle* enabled the congregation, after a long and heated debate, worthy of their forebears, to appoint Ela Zingerevich as its next Director of Music, later to be succeeded by Christopher Bowers-Broadbent, for some time the synagogue's much cherished organist.

In 2010 Rabbi Mark Winer decided it was time to return to America. Although he had informed the Council earlier in the year, it was not until the autumn that final arrangements were made for his departure. He had served the synagogue for twelve years, coming at a difficult time for West London which had lost its much-loved Rabbi, Hugo Gryn. The post of Senior Minister had never been an easy one to fill. The Council was very concerned about the financial state of the synagogue and the AGM for that year was delayed while their deliberations continued. It was felt by some members - a difficult meeting by any standards - that the congregation had no right to appoint a new Rabbi until its own house was put in order. The team of assistant Rabbis was an excellent, hardworking one and might indeed cope with the onerous task of running the synagogue on its own. But the argument that the leading Reform congregation, with a membership of nearly 4,000 souls, could hardly operate without a strong leader, won the day. Indeed, the advertisement in the *Jewish Chronicle* seemed to indicate that someone in the order of a Jewish saint – or perhaps a Chief Executive Officer - was needed to fill the post. The applicant, who could be male or female, 'should be an experienced and motivated leader, with exceptional interpersonal and organisational skills, and be able to engage with, motivate and guide all elements of the community.'[6]

Some twelve applicants replied, and interviews for several were soon put in place. At the beginning of the following year the Council decided to offer the post of Senior Minister to Baroness Julia Neuberger, DBE. Rabbi Julia was the daughter of long-time members of Upper Berkeley Street, Walter and Alice Schwab. Walter's brother, S.G. Schwab (Siggy) had also played an important part in the leadership of the congregation, and Julia was brought up there. She went to South Hampstead School and then to Newnham College, Cambridge, where she studied Archaeology. She took as her subjects Assyrian and Hebrew. She was awarded *semicha* at the Leo Baeck College, where she was taught by Louis Jacobs, whom she later described as 'the greatest scholar that Anglo-Jewry has ever had.' She was the first woman Rabbi to have her own congregation. She married Professor Anthony Neuberger, one of a distinguished family of lawyers, physicians and academics (her brother-in-law, Lord Neuberger of Abbotsbury, is President of the Supreme Court). She has a son and a daughter.

Rabbi Julia's list of honours is a long one: she was Rabbi of the South London Liberal Synagogue, Chancellor of the University of Ulster, Visiting Fellow at Harvard Medical School and Chief Executive of the King's Fund, sitting on the Liberal Democrat benches of the House of Lords as the Baroness Neuberger, DBE, of Primrose Hill. When the 'call' came to serve at Upper Berkeley Street Rabbi Julia decided that what she really wanted was to return to pastoral care, to sit on the cross-benches, be known simply as Rabbi Julia, and come back to her childhood sweetheart, the West London Synagogue. She was voted in unanimously.

By the spring of 2011, the secret was out. The *Jewish Chronicle* called it first of all a rumour, but soon spoke of the appointment as a matter of fact. Julia had agreed to work part-time until September, so that she could get her various affairs in order, taking up the post full time in the autumn. Those who were concerned that her Liberal roots (she was after all at one time the President of the Liberal Jewish Movement) might betray West London's position as the principal synagogue of the Reform movement, soon found that her beliefs and ideas coincided to a large extent with their own. It became clear that she followed in the tradition of the strong and affectionate leadership enjoyed by all Berkeley Street's Senior Ministers. Rabbi Julia spoke on the radio and at public meetings, unafraid to face politicians on all sides, as well as her own congregants when she felt she had something to say to them. At one Limmud meeting she told them to 'up their game' and look nearer to home when helping the community.

When Rabbi Neuberger first came to West London she was shocked by several things, among them the state of the building and the quality of the sound system in the sanctuary, both of which are now being remedied. She wanted to see more participation in the services by lay readers and by young people. She also felt that much more could be done in the field of social service, such as for asylum seekers and the old. She was determined to see improvements in all that West London could do, and her hands-on leadership is surely just what the synagogue needs.

✡

Now that nearly 175 years have passed since that first meeting at the Bedford Hotel when the founding fathers saw a vision of the future for the Jewish community of this country, the changes have been vast. How could they have envisaged a woman rabbi as their leader, strong links with Israel or a congregation of nearly 3,000 souls? West London, incidentally, is no longer the most numerous congregation in Britain. That honour lies at the moment with the Edgware and District Reform Synagogue. But that tiny spark lit in such prosaic surroundings all those years ago, has been fanned into a warm flame. Community groups for the young and old, musical events, visits abroad, and families already proudly acknowledging some seven generations of descendants still worshipping as they did then; all this is the outcome of that first inspiration. And what lies ahead? Rabbi Gryn said in 1970, addressing the RSGB Conference, 'The paramount ideological function of the synagogue should be to help the Jew find his identity and provide purpose and direction for his life.' That is as true now as it was in 1840. If we should dare to anticipate the future for Berkeley Street, some things are certain to remain. As long as there is need for a metropolitan Reform synagogue, Berkeley Street must take a leading place. It seems likely at some time that the two branches of Progressive Judaism will come together as one body, perhaps with a woman at the head. An alternative Chief Rabbi perhaps.

Gender differences will seem less important in the community, with marriage possible for any couples, men or women. Or perhaps Reform services may become more right-wing, even forming a link with, say, the Masorti movement. The orthodox community must surely soften its stance towards the Progressives, though it seems unlikely that any close rapprochement will happen soon. A new Chief Rabbi may look more kindly on the 'renegades'. Perhaps the Jewish community as a whole will refrain from in-fighting and quarrelling amongst itself. Who would dare to forecast the future of the stiff-necked ones? All we can say for certain is that Jews in London will survive and that the West London Synagogue will be among the first to lead them, growing in size and influence as it does so.

NOTES

PROLOGUE – Before the Beginning

1. Philipson, David, *The Reform Movement in Judaism*, Ktav Publishing House, 1967, p.30
2. Anon, *A Peep Into the Synagogue*, n.d.
3. *Ibid.*, p.8
4. *Ibid.*, p.10
5. Gaster, Moses, *History of the Ancient Synagogue of the Spanish and Portuguese Jews*, Privately Printed, 1901, p.154
6. Montefiore, Sir Moses and Lady, *Diaries*, ed. L. Loewe, Griffith Farran Okeden and Welsh, 1890, p.69
7. Gaster, *Ibid.*, p.188
8. See Picciotto, James, *Sketches of Anglo-Jewish History*, Soncino Press, 1956, p. 287-293
9. Bermant, Chaim, *The Cousinhood*, Eyre and Spottiswood, 1971, p.3
10. Philipson, *ibid.*, p.3
11. *Ibid.*, p.3
12. Meyer, Michael, *Response to Modernity*, Oxford University Press, 1988, p.173
13. Quoted in Cecil Roth, *The History of the Jews in England*, Oxford University Press, 1942, p.250

CHAPTER I – Burton Street

1. He had refused to be called if he had to swear on the Christian Bible, but an Old Testament was brought and he was duly sworn.
2. WLS Minutes, 24.10.40
3. Ibid.
4. Ibid.
5. Wolf, Lucien, *Essays in Jewish History*, Jewish Historical Society of England, 1934, p.319
6. For a detailed account of the Damascus affair, see Picciotto, James, *Sketches of Anglo-Jewish History*, The Soncino Press, 1956, p.340
7. *Jewish Chronicle*, 11.12.1863
8. See Barnett, Arthur, *The Western Synagogue Through Two Centuries*, Vallentine Mitchell, 1967
9. Alderman, Geoffrey, *Modern British Jewry*, Clarendon Press, Oxford, 1992, p.22
10. WLS Minutes, 18.5.40
11. *Ibid.*, 13.7.40
12. *Ibid.*, 21.9.40
13. Information from Hyamson, Albert M., *The London Board for Shechita 1808-95*, London Board for Shechita, 1954
14. For an account of this, see Kershen, Anne J., and Romain, Jonathan A., *Tradition and Change, A History of Reform Judaism in Britain, 1840-1995*, Vallentine Mitchell, 1995, p. 16
15. Quoted in Montefiore, Leonard, Reminiscences of Upper Berkeley Street, *Synagogue Review*, Vol. 34, 10, June 1960
16. Theodores, Tobias, *The Rabbinical Law of Excommunication considered in its bearing on the case of the Margaret Street Synagogue of British Jews*, Charles Simms, Manchester, 1854

17. Quoted in Hyamson, Albert H., *The Sephardim of England*, Methuen & Co., 1951, p.291
18. Information from the London Weather Bureau
19. Marks, David, *Sermon on the occasion of the Consecration of the West London Synagogue*, 1842
20. *Ibid.*
21. *Ibid.*
22. *Ibid.*
23. *The Times*, 1.2.1842
24. Quoted in the *Synagogue Review*, October, 1952

CHAPTER II – Margaret Street

1. WLS Minutes, 2.2.1842
2. For information on the West Metropolitan Jewish School, see Curtis Cassell, *The West Metropolitan Jewish School*, in Transactions of the Jewish Historical Society of England, No. 19, 1955-59, p.115
3. Rubenstein, Hilary, *Oxford Dictionary of National Biography*
4. *Jewish Chronicle*, 29.6.1849
5. *Ibid.*
6. *Ibid.*
7. *Ibid.*
8. Quoted in Lipman, V.D., *A Survey of Anglo-Jewry in 1851*, in Transactions of the Jewish Historical Society of England, 1951/2, p.177
9. Anglo-Jewish Archives, Southampton University
10. Langham, Raphael, *250 Years of Convention and Contention – A History of the Board of Deputies, 1760-2010*, Vallentine, Mitchell, 2010. p. 30
11. WLS Minutes, 24.11.1858
12. *Ibid.*,12.9.1859
13. *Ibid.*
14. Diamond, A.S., *The Building of a Synagogue*, West London Synagogue, p.5
15. Salaman, Charles, *The Music Used in the Services of the West London Synagogue of British Jews*, Novello and Co., (n.d.), title page.
16. Hillsman, William, *Organs and Organ Music in Victorian Synagogues*, in Christianity and Judaism, Ecclesiastic History Society, 1992, p.422
17. *Jewish Chronicle*, 5.10.1860
18. *Ibid.*, 12.10.1869

CHAPTER III – Upper Berkeley Street

1. WLS Minutes, 18.1.1862
2. *Ibid.*, 11.5.1862
3. Anglo-Jewish Archive, 17.10.1864
4. WLS Minutes, 4.2.1866
5. *Ibid.*, 28.2.1869
6. *The Builder*, 3.8.1869
7. *Jewish Chronicle*, 20.5.1870
8. *Ibid.*, 23.9.1870

9.   *Ibid.*
10. *Ibid.*
11. WLS Minutes, 21.10.1871
12. *Jewish Chronicle,* 23.12.1870
13. WLS Minutes, 17.3.1872
14. *Jewish Chronicle,* 14.7.1871
15. *Ibid.*
16. *Ibid.*
17. *Ibid,* 1960
18. *Ibid.*

CHAPTER IV – Fifty Years Young

1.   The scandalous case in Italy of a young boy, Edgardo Mortara, who was taken from his Jewish parents, and brought up as a Catholic, in spite of remonstrations by Sir Moses Montefiore and others. For further information see Kertzer, David, *The Kidnapping of Edgardo Mortara,* Random House, 1997.
2.   Langham, *op. cit.,*p.77
3.   *Ibid.,* p.33
4.   WLS Minutes, 29.4.1883
5.   Anglo-Jewish Archive, Southampton University, MS140, AJ59, 3/13
6.   *Jewish Chronicle,* 10.5.1888
7.   Anglo-Jewish Archive, MS140, AJ59, 7/24
8.   *Ibid.*
9.   WLS Minutes, 14.4.1888
10. *Jewish Chronicle,* 22.1.1886
11. WLS Minutes, 14.4.1888
12. *Ibid.,* 11.5.1888

CHAPTER V – Into a New Century

1.   *Jewish Chronicle,* 29.1.1892
2.   *Ibid.*
3.   *Ibid.*
4.   *Ibid.*
5.   Dictionary of National Biography
6.   WLS Minutes, 30.4.1893
7.   *Jewish Chronicle,* 5.2.1892
8.   *Ibid.,* 20.5.1892
9.   *Ibid.,* 28.10.1892
10. *Ibid.,* 15.9.1893
11. *Ibid.,*10.1.1896
12. Military Records, South Lancashire Museum
13. WLS Minutes, 3.11.1901
14. Ibid.

15. Montefiore, Claude, *Liberal Judaism – An Essay*, Macmillan & Co., 1903, p.1
16. *Ibid.*, p.65
17. *Ibid.*, p.144

CHAPTER VI – War and Revolution

1. Joseph, Morris, *Judaism as Creed and Life,* Routledge & Kegan Paul Ltd., 1958 (Fourth Edition), p.vii
2. *Ibid.*, p.408
3. *Ibid.*, p.290
4. *Ibid.*, p.xv
5. WLS Minutes, 15.6.1906
6. *Ibid.*
7. *Ibid.*, 20.5.1909
8. *Jewish Chronicle*, 7.5.1909
9. *Ibid.*
10. Lipman, V.D., *Social History of the Jews in England, 1850-1950,* Watts and Co., 1954, p.142
11. Illustrated in Cohen, Stuart A., *English Zionists and British Jews,* Princeton University Press, New Jersey, 1982, p.32
12. Elon, Amos, *Herzl,* Holt, Rinehart and Winston, 1975, p.207
13. Joseph, *Ibid.*, p.170
14. *Jewish Chronicle*, 16.7.1897
15. *Ibid.*, 9.4.1909
16. Elon, *Ibid.*,p.174
17. Quoted in Loewe, L.L., *Basil Henriques – A Portrait,* Routledge Kegan Paul, 1976, p.13
18. WLS Minutes, 15.6.1906
19. Ibid.
20. Ibid., 20.5.1909
21. Ibid.
22. Ibid., 25.1.1917
23. *Jewish Chronicle*, 23.1.14
24. *Ibid.*, 31.7.1914
25. *Ibid.*, 25.6.1915
26. *Ibid.*, 7.8.14
27. Anglo-Jewish Archives, Southampton
28. *Jewish Chronicle*, 23.3.1917
29. Text of the Declaration

CHAPTER VII – The Twenties

1. WLS Minutes, 1.7.26
2. *Ibid.*, 21.12.21
3. *Jewish Chronicle*, 25.4.1930
4. *Ibid*, 13.3.25
5. Quoted in the *Jewish Chronicle*, 28.10.1927
6. WLS Minutes, 11.7.26

7. Ibid.
8. *Jewish Chronicle*, 1.1.1926
9. *Ibid.*, 22.1.1926
10. *Ibid.*, 20.7.1928
11. Anglo-Jewish Archive, Southampton, Reinhart Papers
12. Quoted in Evelyn Waley, *International Relations,* Privately Printed, 1999, p.55
13. *Jewish Chronicle*, 2.4.1926
14. Anglo-Jewish Archive, Southampton, Reinhart Papers
15. Ibid.
16. Ibid.
17. Ibid.
18. Ibid.
19. *West London Synagogue Magazine,* April 1930
20. *Ibid..*

CHAPTER VIII – 'A Sense of Growing Darkness'

1. *West London Synagogue Magazine,* May, 1931
2. *Ibid.,* July, 1931
3. *Ibid.,* March 1933
4. WLS Minutes, 14.5.34
5. Langham, *op. cit.,*p.137

CHAPTER IX – Berkeley Street At War

1. *Jewish Chronicle*, 1.6.1934
2. *Ibid.*
3. WLS Minutes, 6.3.35
4. Ibid.
5. Ibid., 14.10.36
6. *Synagogue Review,* December 1937
7. *Ibid.*
8. Endelman, Todd M., *The Jews of Britain, 1656-2000,* University of California Press, 2002, p.202
9. Anglo-Jewish Archive, Southampton University, Reinhart Papers
10. *Synagogue Review,* October 1939
11. *Ibid.,* May 1940
12. *Ibid.,* Junior Supplement, October 1940
13. *Ibid.*
14. *Ibid.,.* January 1941
15. *Ibid.,* October 1941
16. *Ibid.,* February, 1942

CHAPTER X – A Hard-Fought Peace

1. WLS Minutes, 22.5.44
2. 'Focus' in *Synagogue Review,* September 1943
3. Minutes of Special General Meeting, 28.10.45

4. Kerchen and Romain, *op. cit.*, p.198
5. Curtis, Michael, 'The Beth Din of the Reform Synagogues of Great Britain', in Dov Marmur, (ed.), *Reform Judaism*, Reform Synagogues of Great Britain, 1973, p.131
6. Endelman, *op.cit.*, p.233
7. Quoted in Langham, *op.cit.*, p.179
8. WLS Minutes, 15.1.47
9. Ibid., 1.11.49
10. Ibid.
11. *Synagogue Review*, October 1952
12. *Ibid.*
13. *Ibid.*, September 1954
14. *Ibid.*, August 1955
15. *Ibid.*, March 1954

CHAPTER XI – The Second Schism

1. Littman, Ellen, 'The First Ten Years of the Leo Baeck College', in Dov Marmur, (ed.), *Reform Judaism*, Reform Synagogues of Great Britain, 1973
2. *Synagogue Review*, October 1956
3. Bermant, *op.cit.*, p.325
4. WLS Minutes, 7.2.56
5. Ibid.
6. Ibid.
7. Ibid., 21.3.56
8. *Dictionary of National Biography*
9. WLS Minutes 10.5.56
10. *Synagogue Review*, August 1956
11. Golden, Lewis and Jacqueline, *Harold Reinhart 1891 - 1968, A Memorial Volume*, Westminster Synagogue, 1980, p.11
12. WLS Minutes, 28.5.56
13. *Jewish Chronicle*, 24.5.56
14. *Synagogue Review*, July 1957
15. WLS Minutes, 28.5.57
16. *Jewish Chronicle*, 14, 21.7.57
17. Anglo-Jewish Archive, Reinhart Papers
18. Ibid.
19. Ibid.
20. *Synagogue Review*, August 1957

CHAPTER XII – A Change of Leadership

1. Kershen and Romain, *op.cit.*
2. Anglo-Jewish Archive, van der Zyl Papers
3. *Synagogue Review*, September, 1957
4. *Ibid.*
5. WLS Minutes, 22.7.57

6. *Synagogue Review, August, 1958*
7. Quoted in *Werner van der Zyl, Master Builder,* The Reform Synagogues of Great Britain, 1994
8. *Synagogue Review,* September, 1958
9. *Ibid.*
10. *Jewish Chronicle,* 25.3.60
11. *Synagogue Review,* December 1959
12. *Ibid.*
13. *Ibid.,* September 1959
14. *Ibid.,* October 1959
15. *Jewish Chronicle,* 2.10.1964

CHAPTER XIII – The Synagogue in the Seventies

1. *Synagogue Review,* January 1964
2. Van der Zyl, Werner, Unpublished paper on the progress of the College, undated
3. *Jewish Chronicle,* 19.4.68
4. *Synagogue Review,* October, 1968
5. *Jewish Chronicle,* 20.4.84
6. *Synagogue Review,* June, 1984.
7. *Ibid.,* July/August, 1970
8. *Ibid.*
9. *Ibid.*
10. *Jewish Chronicle,* 23.10.70
11. *Ibid.,* 27.11.70
12. *Synagogue Review,* December, 1970
13. *Ibid.,* January, 1971
14. *Ibid.,* January, 1972
15. *Ibid.,* February, 1972
16. *Ibid.,* October, 1972
17. *Ibid.,* January, 1973
18. Gryn, Naomi (ed.), *Three Minutes of Hope,* Continuum International Publishing Group, 2010, p.xvi

CHAPTER XIV – Towards the Millennium

1. *Synagogue Review,* January, 1977
2. *Ibid.,* March, 1979
3. Kershen and Romain, *Ibid.,* p.289
4. *Synagogue Review,* June, 1980
5. *Jewish Chronicle,* 27.1.1984
6. *Synagogue Review,* July, 1984
7. *Ibid.,* April, 1984
8. Goldman, Raymond, *A Personal Appreciation on the Occasion of his Tenth Yahrzeit.*
9. *Synagogue Review,* June, 1986
10. *Ibid.,* October, 1990

11. English Heritage Listed Buildings
12. *Jewish Chronicle,* 30.3.1990
13. *Synagogue Review,* September, 1993
14. Gryn, ibid., p.166
15. *Synagogue Review,* September, 1996
16. *Jewish Chronicle,* 30.8.1996
17. Personal conversation

CHAPTER XV – Into the Future
1. WLS Minutes, 29.7.1996
2. *Synagogue Review,* January 1998
3. *Jewish Chronicle,* 2.12.2005
4. *Ibid.,* 16.6.2000
5. *Ibid.,* 26.3.2004
6. *Ibid.,* 12.11.2010

APPENDIX I

PRESIDENTS AND CHAIRMEN OF THE COUNCIL

Presidents

1977	His Honour Judge M.A.B. King-Hamilton, Q.C.
1983	Clifford Barclay
1988	David Walsh
1991	Sir Peter Millett
1995	G. David Leuw
2000	Graham Zellick
2006	Morris Bentata

Chairmen of the Council

1840	Daniel Mocatta
1866	Sir Francis Goldsmid
1878	David Mocatta
1882	Jacob Q. Henriques
1890	Sir Julian Goldsmid
1896	Frederick D. Mocatta
1904	Sir Philip Magnus
1911	B. Elkin Mocatta
1914	Herbert G. Lousada
1918	H.S.Q. Henriques
1925	Philip S. Waley
1937	Julian G. Lousada
1940	Harry Cecil Marks
1945	Owen E. Mocatta
1957	A.S. Diamond
1965	His Honour Judge M.A.B. King-Hamilton, Q.C.
1972	Edward E. Mocatta
1977	Maxwell Simon
1981	David Walsh
1985	Martin Chaplin
1987	Anne Silverman
1991	G. David Leuw
1995	Geoffrey Samson
1998	Morris Bentata
2002	Stephen Moss, O.B.E.
2005	Robert Shrager
2008	Jonathan Lass

On 1st June 1977 the Offices of President and Chairman of the Council were separated

APPENDIX II

THE SCROLLS OF THE WEST LONDON SYNAGOGUE

LITTLE RED

Together with all its silver, this scroll was purchased in Israel. It was found and checked for the synagogue by Rabbi Hugo Gryn, and the purchase was made through the generosity of the Women's Guild about 1984/5 when Denise Williams was elected as the first Lady Warden.

SAMSON

One of the heaviest scrolls, this was made for Heinz Samson, together with the breastplate and *yud*, in Israel; the *Rimmonim* were made in London by a member of the congregation, Neil Lasher. It was presented by Heinz Samson in 1986/7 in memory of his family.

ROBINS

This is on permanent loan from the Robins family, given on *Simchas Torah* by Charles Robins' father.

COLLESANTI

This was given Stephanie Collesanti in memory of her parents. It was not a new scroll but was made of the good parts of a few scrolls. It came from Israel and was checked by Rabbi Michael Marmur. The silver was also donated by Stephanie and was purchased in London.

CALLMAN

On permanent loan from His Hon. Clive Callman and his family, this scroll, including its silver, survived Kristallnacht (9th November 1938). It was found after the war by the caretaker of the Synagogue which had owned it, wrapped up in the rubble. After much searching there was found on the roller the name Dr. Kurt Callman. Clive Callman was traced to London, where the scroll was kept at his home. When his son Jeremy was Bar Mitzvah, Rabbi Gryn asked him to read from this scroll and it was then given on loan to the synagogue. In 1999 it was restored and made Kosher, and is now always used on the Sabbath of Remembrance because of its special connection to the Holocaust.

HIGH SCROLL

This is the scroll which was created for the *Torah* Project.

Of the silver on the scrolls, donated by members on family occasions, the most famous *Rimmonim* are the D'Olivera set made for West London by the first Jew to be given his own set of hallmarks, as quoted in some of the Goldsmith and Silversmith literature. There are two sets of copies of these bells.

GLOSSARY

Beth Din Rabbinic or Ecclesiastic Court of Law

Bimah Reading Desk

Chazan Cantor, who sings in the Synagogue service

Cherem Order of excommunication

Chuppah The canopy under which a wedding ceremony takes place and, by extension, the ceremony itself

Dvar Torah Explanation of the reading from the *Torah*

Etrog a citron held, with the *lulav,* on the Festival of Succot

Had Gadya A song sung at the Passover meal

Haftarah Reading from the Prophets

Haggadah Prayer Book used for the Passover Service

Haham the leader of the Spanish and Portuguese community

Kaddish Prayers for the dead

Ketuba Marriage Certificate

Kiddush Prayers over the bread and wine on Shabbat

Kol Nidre The synagogue service on the eve of *Yom Kippur*

Lulav the palm sheaf shaken in the synagogue during the Succot service

Mishna The Oral Law, codified by Jewish tradition

Mizmor l'david Psalm of David

Mitzva literally a commandment, but often used to mean an honour or good deed

Mohel The rabbi or doctor who carries out circumcision

Ner Tamid the everlasting light which hangs above the Ark

Sefer (plural *Sifrei*) *Torah* Scroll of the Law

Semicha Rabbinical diploma

Shechita The ritual killing of animals according to Jewish law

Shiva (Usually) seven evenings of mourning prayers

Shochet One who oversees the ritual slaughter

Shulchan Aruch The authoritative rabbinic code of the Law for orthodox Jewry

Tallit Prayer shawl

Tefillin Phylacteries – small cases bound around the forearms and forehead of Orthodox Jews which contain verses from the Bible

A SELECT BIBLIOGRAPHY

Alderman, Geoffrey, *Modern British Jewry*, Clarendon Press, Oxford, 1992

Anon., *A Peep Into the Synagogue, n.d.*

Barnett, Arthur, *The Western Synagogue through Two Centuries*, Vallentine Mitchell, 1967

Barnett, R., *The Bevis Marks Synagogue*, Society of Heshaim, 1970

Bermant, Chaim, *The Cousinhood*, Eyre and Spottiswood, 1971

— *Troubled Eden*, Vallentine Mitchell, 1969

Black, Gerry, *Jewish London*, Breedon Books, 2007

Brooks, Stephen, *The Club – The Jews of Modern Britain*, Pan Books, 1990

Cassell, Curtis E., *The West Metropolitan Jewish School*, Transactions of the Jewish Historical Society of England, No. 19, 1955-59

— *The West London Synagogue of British Jews, Burton Street, 1840-1849*, Privately published, 1988

Cesarani. David, *The Jewish Chronicle and Anglo-Jewry*, Cambridge University Press, 1994

Cohen, Stuart, *English Zionists and British Jews*, Princeton University Press, New Jersey, 1982

Cowen, Anne and Roger, *Victorian Jewry through British Eyes*, The Littman Library, 1986

Curtis, Michael, *The Beth Din of the Reform Synagogues of Great Britain*, in Dov Marmur (ed.), *Reform Judaism*, Reform Synagogues of Great Britain, 1973

Diamond, A.S., *The Building of a Synagogue – A Brief History*, West London Synagogue, 1970

D'Israeli, Isaac, *The Genius of Judaism*, Moxon, 1833

Elon, Amos, *Herzl*, Holt, Rinehart and Winston, 1975

Emden, Paul, *The Jews of Britain*, Sampson Low, 1944

Endelman, Todd, *The Jews of Georgian England, 1714-1830*, Jewish Publication Society of America, 1979

— *Radical Assimilation*, in English Jewish History 1656-1945, Indiana University Press, 1990

— *The Jews of Britain, 1656-2000*, University of California Press, 2002

Finestein, Israel, *Scenes and Personalities in Anglo-Jewry, 1800-2000*, Vallentine Mitchell, 2002

— *Studies and Profiles in Anglo-Jewish History: From Picciott to Bermant*, Vallentine Mitchell, 2008

— *Jewish Society in Victorian England*, Vallentine Mitchell, 1993

— *The Anglo-Jewish Revolt of 1853*, Jewish Quarterly 26, 1978-9

Fletcher-Jones, Pamela, *The Jews of Britain*, Windrush Press, 1990

Friedlander, Albert H., *Leo Baeck: Teacher of Theresienstadt*, Routledge & Kegan Paul, 1973

Gaster, Moses, *The History of the Ancient Synagogue of the Spanish and Portuguese Jews*, Privately Printed, 1901

Gilbert, Martin, *The Boys*, Weidenfeld & Nicolson, 1996

— *Exile and Return*, Orion Publishing Group, 1978

Golden, Lewis and Jacqueline, *Harold Reinhart, 1891-1968, A Memorial Volume*, Westminster Synagogue, 1980

Gryn, Hugo, with Gryn, Naomi, *Chasing Shadows*, Penguin Books, 2001

— Naomi (ed.), *Three Minutes of Hope – Hugo Gryn on The God Spot*, Continuum International Publishing, 2010

Heilbron, Michael, *The Origins of the West London Synagogue,* PhD Thesis, 1971

Hillsman, William, *Organs and Organ Music in Victorian Synagogues,* in Christianity and Judaism, Ecclesiastic History Society, 1992

Hyamson, Albert M., *The History of the Jews in England,* Methuen & Co., 1928

— *The Sephardim of England,* Methuen & Co., 1951

— *The History of Jews College,* Jews College, 1955

— *The London Board for Shechita, 1808-95,* London Board for Shechita, 1954

Jenkinson, H., *Jewish History and Archives,* Jewish Historical Society, 1954

Joseph, Morris, *Judaism as Creed and Life,* Routledge & Kegan Paul, 1958

Kadish, Sharman, *Bolsheviks and British Jews,* Frank Cass, 1992

Katz, David, *The Jews in the History of England, 1485-1850,* Clarendon Press, 1994

Levin, *A Century of Anglo-Jewish Life, 1870-1970,* United Synagogue, 1973

Levy, Amy, *Reuben Sachs,* MacMillan & Co., 1889

Lipman, V. D., *Three Centuries of Anglo-Jewish History,* Transactions of J.H.S.E., 1961

— *The History of the Jews in Britain Since 1858,* Leicester University Press, 1990

— *A Survey of Anglo-Jewry in 1851,* Transactions of J.H.S.E., 1951/2

— *The Social History of the Jews in England, 1850-1950,* Watts & Co., 1954

Littman, Ellen, *The First Ten Years of the Leo Baeck College,* in Dov Marmur (ed.), *Reform Judaism,* Reform Synagogues of Great Britain, 1973

Loewe, L. (ed.) *The Diaries of Sir Moses and Lady Montefiore,* Griffith Farran Okeden and Welsh, 1890

— *Basil Henriques, A Portrait,* Routledge, Kegan Paul, 1976

Margoliouth, Moses, *The History of the Jews in Great Britain,* Bentley, 1851

Marks, David Woolf, *Sermon on the Occasion of the Consecration of the West London Synagogue, 1842,* West London Synagogue, 1850

Marks, David Woolf and Lowy, Albert, *Memoirs of Sir Francis Goldsmid,* Kegan, Paul, Trench, 1882

Marmur, D. (ed.), *Reform Judaism,* Reform Synagogues of Great Britain, 1973

Meyer, Michael, *Response to Modernity,* Oxford University Press, 1942

Montefiore, Claude, *Liberal Judaism: An Essay,* MacMillan & Co., 1903

Montefiore, Leonard, *Reminiscences of Upper Berkeley Street,* in The Synagogue Review, 1960

Persoff, Meir, *Faith Against Reason,* Vallentine Mitchell, 2008

Philipson, David, *The Reform Movement in Judaism,* Ktav Publishing House, 1967

Picciotto, James, *Sketches of Anglo-Jewish History,* Soncino Press, 1956

Raphael, Chaim, *Memoirs of a Special Case,* Rossel Books, 1985

Romain, Jonathan (ed.), *Great Reform Lives – Rabbis who Dared to Differ,* Movement for Reform Judaism, 2010

— *The Jews of England* (first published as *Anglo-Jewry in Evidence),* Michael Goulston Educational Foundation,1988

— *Faith and Practice,* Reform Synagogues in Great Britain, 1993

Roth, Cecil, *The History of the Jews in England,* Oxford University Press, 1988

— *Anglo-Jewish Letters,* Soncino Press, 1938

— *Essays and Portraits in Anglo-Jewish History,* Jewish Publication Society of America, 1961

— *The Great Synagogue of London, 1690-1940,* Edward Goldston, 1950

Salaman, Charles Kensington, *Jews As They Are*, Simkin Marshall, 1885

Sebag-Montefiore, Ruth, *A Family Patchwork*, Weidenfeld & Nicolson, 1985

Shaftesley, John M. (ed.) *Remember the Days, Essays on Anglo-Jewish History presented to Cecil Roth*, Jewish Historical Society of England, 1966

Simmons, Vivian, *Reform in Judaism*, North Western Reform Synagogue, 1942

Simon, Maurice, *Jewish Religious Conflicts*, Hutchinson University Library, 1950

Sugarman, Martin, *Fighting Back*, Vallentine Mitchell, 2010

Theodores, Tobias, *The Rabbinical Law of Excommunication considered in its bearing on the case of the Margaret Street Synagogue of British Jews*, Charles Simms, Manchester, 1854

The Jewish Chronicle: 1841-1941, The Jewish Chronicle, 1949

Waley, Evelyn, *International Relations*, privately published, 1996 (updated by Joyce Morton, 1999)

Werner van der Zyl: Master Builder, Reform Synagogues of Great Britain, 1994

Wolf, Lucien, *Essays in Jewish History*, Jewish Historical Society of England, 1934

INDEX